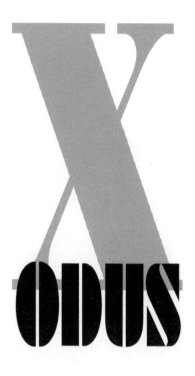

X
ODUS

An African American Male Journey

Garth Kasimu Baker-Fletcher

FORTRESS PRESS, MINNEAPOLIS

XODUS
An African American Male Journey

Cover graphic: Slave factory at Goree Island, Dakar Harbor, copyright © Chester
  Higgins, Jr. and used by permission. All rights reserved.
Cover and text design: Lois Stanfield, LightSource Images.
Author photo: Sioux Bailly.

Library of Congress Cataloging-in-Publication Data
Baker-Fletcher, Garth, 1955–
    Xodus : an African American male journey / Garth Kasimu Baker
  -Fletcher.
      p.   cm.
    Includes bibliographical references (p.).
    ISBN 0-8006-2918-3 (pbk.)
      1. Afro-American men. 2. Afro-Americans—Race identity.
  3. Afrocentrism.   I. Title
  E185.86.B26   1996
  305.38'896073—dc20   95-39271
                                                                       CIP

The paper used in this publication meets the minimum requirements of American National Standard for Information Sciences—Permanence of Paper for Printed Library Materials, ANSI Z329.4-1984.

Manufactured in the U.S.A.   AF 1-2918
00   99   98   97   96   1   2   3   4   5   6   7   8   9   10

Dedicated to my children, especially my beloved son Kenneth Taylor "Ikenna" Baker-Fletcher, that he might grow into a strong, loving, compassionate Souljah; and my bright-eyed daughters, Kristen Joelle "Adwin," and Desiree Aisha Dawn, that they will continue to blossom in intelligence, prophecy, and beauty. My prayer is that they will all be living examples of partnership.

CONTENTS

PREFACE

oday's TV news reports are filled with scenes of African American males as criminals: arms handcuffed behind their backs, faces pushed down on top of cars or against walls, held under the power of an officer of the law. Such scenes have become so commonplace that they pass for normal occurrences. But things are not "normal" for African American males — unless you consider being prejudged as a criminal, brutalized by the enforcers of what is touted as law, and being continually portrayed to others and to yourself as "guilty because you're alive" a normal state of affairs! It is time for African Americans, male and female, to stand up and demand a change of course, a new direction. It is time to "cry aloud and spare not." It is time for all the Black community, from the most highly educated and "successful" to the poorest and most disadvantaged, to begin to shake up the comfortable status quo that is destroying the fiber of self-esteem and self-respect of so many young African Americans, males in particular.

My voice arises from the experience of being raised in a mixed-class, multinational family. My mother had completed graduate school in an Ivy League institution and was an educator, while my father was a factory worker. She was an eighth-generation African American, while he was a Jamaican immigrant. The genetic material of many nations flowed in our multicolored bodies, from the darkest earth tones of Africa to the red hair and green eyes of the Scotch-Irish. We lived in a middle-class neighborhood, while most of my family lived in working-class neighborhoods that other folks called "the ghetto" back in the 1960s and '70s. Everybody worked hard. All my uncles and aunts taught all of us sons, daughters, nieces, and nephews about the importance of education, hard work, and personal sacrifice in order to attain one's life-goals. All of my cousins finished high school. Most of us completed college, and the ones who did not are not unemployed even today.

My mother, although "middle-class," worked most of her career in the inner-city Black "ghetto" of Cleveland, Ohio — Hough, at Addison Junior High School. Her heart, will, and determined intellect were focused on educating these poorest of poor African Americans. Single-handedly she provided dozens of students the opportunity to escape the "iron cage of oppression" by helping them write A Better Chance (ABC) Grant proposals. Once accepted by the government as promising leaders of the future, recipients of these ABC Grants received full tuition, room and board, books, clothing, and spending money. Through ABC Grants young women and men raised in the most disadvantaged environments were able to attend prestigious private schools for the rest of their secondary education, and went from there to prestigious colleges and universities. I shall never forget meeting one of my mother's favorite students, Abraham Parker, on a plane going to Boston where I was then studying at the New England Conservatory of Music. Abraham had just completed his MBA at Harvard Business School and had a job at a prestigious corporation. I was raised to believe that one person can make all the difference in the world, especially if that person really believes in helping others. My mother was a strong adherent of this belief, valuing what in the early part of our century used to be called "racial uplift."

Today I debate with myself and others continuously about the efficacy of programs such as ABC, the so-called "failed liberal agenda" of the 1960s. Was it a house of cards that collapsed under the onslaught of Euro-American backlash in the Reagan Revolution of the '80s? Or was it the best that could be done for that time? Was it a continuation of the progressivist ideal of evolving racial uplift toward ever higher and better horizons? Or was it the pitiful continuation of an elitist DuBoisian "Talented Tenth" policy bound to create the kind of intracommunal fury and disillusionment for African Americans that has helped to fill the ranks of gangs and jails?

In my particular case, being pan-African in the truest sense, my Jamaican ancestry continues to subvert and challenge the questionable claims of race propagated on North American soil. In Jamaica all ancestral claims — whether they be Chinese, German, English, African, or Indian — are superseded by the embrace of citizenship. To be Jamaican signifies much more cultural information than to claim one's Africanness, or Europeanness. Yet even with the positive claims of inclusive citizenship rights for persons of all races and backgrounds in Jamaica, there still are rigid (albeit suppressed) codes of acceptability and propriety based on Europeanized values of beauty and rightness. As a Jamaican American, I am increasingly aware of how even institutionalized inclusion, such as has been the civic assumption of all Jamaicans, cannot mask the barely concealed fangs of European-originated domination. So is there a place or a Space in which brown and black-skinned persons can be free?

I am still not completely sure of the answers to my questions, but the fervor and passion that I bring to the topic of social justice for African American males arise from that racial uplift social philosophy I saw practiced by my mother, our church, and our family.

This book has been in the making for several years, evolving through the several stages of growth, devolution, and revolution that have characterized my own personal journey. My growth as a Christian, a scholar, and writer-activist has paralleled the evolving shift in social mood in the United States of America from the late 1980s into the mid-'90s. I have lived through the high water of the Reagan-Bush Republican conservative era, moving from the status of student to professor during that time. Each event, from the Persian Gulf War of 1991, to the Los Angeles Rebellion of April 1992, to the first free elections for Black South Africans in April 1994, to the Republican tidal wave that swept the U.S. Congress in November 1994, has shaped the mood, attitude, and content of the following pages. Further, as I have made the journey, I have undergone several personal transformations, each one reaching back into my historic-cultural heritage to increase the breadth and scope of this project. Originally I thought of this project as relating only to African Americans, but as I began to see how my pan-Africanness manifested itself in the cadence and passion of a Jamaican, I realized that the journey inscribed here reaches much further than that of a North American "Black."

Many persons have accompanied me on the journey that created this book. I am grateful to all of my ancestors — my grandparents Annie B. and Henry Christ Parham, Barham and Winnifred Fletcher, and my parents Superia B. and Kenneth B. Fletcher, who gave me life, love, and security. All of them have passed over to the land of ancestors. I write in loving memory to a Spirit-filled aunt, Minnie Ruth, who was a spiritual mother to all of us cousins, and her sisters Audrey and Pauline, whom I love very much. My Fletcher aunts and uncles: Roy, Lunney, Bonnie, Winston, Herbie, Haldor, Enid, Woody, Joyce, and Rawlin — all helped to teach me what family really means as I was growing up. I send family-love and thanks to my cousins: Ruane, Sheila Lynn, Mona, Faye, Charmaine, Shane, Lyndon, and his wife Heidi.

The immediate ones who have helped me in writing this text include several colleagues and ministers. Professors Dwight Hopkins, Karen Jo Torjesen, Emilie Townes, Rev. John Henry Scott, and attorney Dawn Scott have all read many different versions of this text before the final product you are reading. I bless their supportive friendship.

The ideas for chapter 2, "New Males?" were refined and argued in the course "The Ethics of Male and Female Reformation" I taught at the Christian Theological Seminary (CTS) in the Spring of 1992. All of those who participated in that course helped me to shape ideas. My colleagues at CTS also made helpful comments: Rufus Burrow, Ursula Pfafflin, Bernie Lyons, Clark Williamson, Newell Williams, and Joe Jones in particular. Their continual prodding at me to deepen my christological and theological underpinnings remains with me even as I have moved on to a teaching ministry at the School of Theology at Claremont (STC).

I am grateful to my STC colleagues for their support, especially Lori Anne Ferrell, who spent a good deal of time with me discussing "The Council of Ancestors," and Cornish Rogers for his critical insights and comments. I thank Dean Marjorie Suchocki and President Bob Edgar for their ongoing support and dynamism in advocating for creative projects such as this book.

Most of all I thank my family, especially my closest companion who teaches with me, loves me, and has stood by me through the good and bad — Karen Baker-Fletcher. Her wit, intelligence, careful attention to detail, and powerful mind have made an indelible mark on the creation of this text. Standing with her has been and always will be the very best thing I have ever done with my life. Our children. Kristen Joelle, Kenneth Taylor, and Desiree Aisha Dawn, are living reminders of the future for which we work to make Xodus Space a reality.

INTRODUCTION

I n an era of increasing racial misunderstanding and conflict, and after seasons of urban unrest, it is time for African American Christians and Black churches to respond seriously to the crisis of opportunity and self-image Black males are facing in the dawn of a high-tech, multicultural world. *Xodus: An African American Male Journey* is one African American's excursion into postmodernity, taking seriously the voices of womanist theologians, "new male" literature, rap activists or "raptivists," and the resurgent interest in the teachings of Malcolm X, Martin Luther King, Jr., and Howard Thurman. All these disparate voices are treated as dialogue partners in the creation of a new constructive theological ethic — an Xodus discourse.

As womanists have seriously reconstrued their idea of Black womanhood, drawing their sources from African and biblical-mythic narratives, so *Xodus* reexamines Black maleness in light of folk and mythic narratives. Applying a critical liberative norm and dissonant voice, *Xodus* proposes that African American men need a radical reconstruction of self that values the criticism and partnership of women, critically appropriates the visions of Martin and Malcolm for our historical moment, and moves toward Howard Thurman's interfaith eschatological goal of "Common Ground" by understanding the dire warnings of violence proclaimed by raptivists as a possible destructive apocalypse. Such an apocalypse would not be the long-expected Second Coming, but the dramatic end of a Black future. Therefore *Xodus* creates a particular kind of theology and ethic out of these many disparate voices, at once subversive and postmodern. It is time to propose community liberation as our appropriate telos. The goal of community liberation uplifts the ethical norms of inclusiveness and solidarity espoused by womanists, Black male theologians, and many radical European social theorists.

The purpose of chapter 1 is to provide the autobiographical and theoretical grounds justifying the need for creating an African American postmodern text known as *Xodus*. It is not enough to acknowledge the crisis facing young African American males. Daring to piece together the fragments of provocative ideas (*bricolage* in French) into an adequate theo-ethical discourse is the challenge faced in this chapter. Such a response to the African American crisis of faith and identity is a particular Space within the generalized emergence of what has become known to many as postmodernity. Further, it is written in a Black voice to Black folks, but ought to be seen also as part of the transgressive naughtiness that challenges all persons to partake of its particularity as a way of looking at their own cultural, religious, and racial particularities. In the traditions of Cornel West and Jeffrey Stout, the introductory "Awakenings" of *Xodus* weave a diverse *bricolage* of critical voices into a new something that is deep enough to touch the souls of African American males, and broad enough to resonate with the struggles of all freedom-loving persons. This chapter invites the reader to drink of Blackwater[1] in order to appreciate and utilize the wellsprings of creativity and Spirit lying neglected and untapped in your own cultures and traditions.

Chapter 2 presents an alternative to recent so-called "new male" literature that is not interested in including African American males and that erases or steals our cultural contributions (such as drums, storytelling, and vision quests). The self-conscious construction of an inclusive, nonsexist, and vibrant maleness is my goal. Setting a critical tone toward current configurations of "new maleness," this chapter attempts to undermine the atmosphere of loss and primal calls for a reinvigorated "deep" maleness while embracing the larger, positive aims of "new male" advocates. Summarizing and reviewing the various types of stances "new males" advocate — from Jungian psychological perspectives to feminist-appreciative, this chapter presents the relatively unknown work of Africentric psychologists such as Na'im Akbar, Amos Wilson, and Richard King as representative of where *Xodus* maleness is heading. As first conversational partner, the "new male" movement provides an important emergent structure for us to contact. The fragility and promise, the peril and the unexamined power of maleness require an African American *deconstruction* in order to be reconstructed into a finer future.

Chapter 3, "Taking Sisters Seriously," completes Part One of *Xodus*, entitled "Conversations, Deconstructions, Reconstructions." In order to "hear ourselves into being" (an evocative phrase of feminist liberationist Rebecca Chopp), we need to take the criticism, experiences, and challenges of

African American women as an important first step toward moving into Xodus Space. This chapter draws together the voices of womanists such as Katie Cannon, Frances Wood, Renee Hill, Karen Baker-Fletcher, and Delores Williams. It seriously considers womanist calls for a communitywide vision of liberation, an inclusive norm that values and honors the unique experiences of Black women as well as Black men, and the challenges to African American males to work on our sexism as strenuously as we have worked to eradicate racism. After looking into the complex ethical analyses of various womanists, this chapter reviews how Black males have already responded to womanism with an appreciative and critical eye. Finally, the twin concepts of liberatory body-selfhood and liberatory partnership between African American females and males, encouraging men to develop critical listening skills and participatory praxis, are introduced here. Like the "new male" movement, womanism is an emergent discourse with which the quest for an Xodus Space needs to be in ongoing contact.

Part Two of *Xodus* is named "The Gathering of the Elders" because it brings together the historical voices and contributions of the past as an essential task of *Xodus* construction. Chapter 4, "Council of Ancestors," analyzes the positive and negative valences of Black male myths — Sambo, John Henry, High John de Conquer, and Nat Turner. The comic figure Sambo is examined in his historic trajectory; we see how African Americans have used this mythic figure positively and negatively. "John Henry" is more than a folk ballad for Black folks — he was an actual figure in West Virginia history. He is the embodiment of a certain kind of Black manliness, that of superhuman physical strength. An interesting combination of a Christ figure and West African trickster is High John de Conquer. Using the accounts of High John as told to Zora Neale Hurston, I analyze the theological and ethical valences of High John for Xodus manhood. I also examine the historic figure Nat Turner as the consummate Black rebel archetype in African American history. Nat Turner has become more than a concrete historical figure, he is a hero. These mythic voices ground Xodus creativity in both concrete history and equally important myth and symbol. Such a regrounding of manhood subverts the patriarchal Euro-dominated imagery of manhood, turning African American males away from desiring the things of domination. Such regrounding turns us back to our historic self, a self that fought Euro-domination the best way it could, working within very limited parameters of choice. Further, this council of mythic heroes demonstrates that *Xodus* annunciates maleness as a theological project.

Chapter 5, "Malcolm's X," is a theological and ethical evaluation of the "X" as the formative symbol of Xodus. Young people today idolize Malcolm X without knowing the content of his thought. He symbolizes for them rebellious, defiant Black maleness. In a time when teenaged Black males are four times more likely to die from homicides at the hands of another young Black male than from all other causes of death, and when there are more Black males in prison than in college (some 657,000 in prison versus 438,000 in college),[2] Malcolm X represents hope for a better future. In his autobiography he creates an important myth, the rise. The rise is how a convicted felon can uplift himself through the aid of a committed spiritual community (in Malcolm's case, the Nation of Islam), educate himself, and eventually attain national and international prominence as a liberator of the oppressed. Yet Malcolm X was not a god, nor was he perfect. Unpacking the mythos from the man, this chapter begins with an ethical interpretation of what the "X" might symbolize for contemporary African American male construction. Malcolm's "X" symbolizes defiant, outspoken, unrelenting, face-to-face criticism of racism. Such a stance is the embodiment, the praxis, of a subversive discourse — the Xodus journey.

Theologically, the "X" is a symbol meaningful to adherents of the Nation of Islam, suggesting that the Xodus reconfiguration of Black maleness ought to be interreligious in its outreach. A pertinent and oft-neglected fact about the letter "X" is that it was the ancient secret sign for *Christos* that early Christians drew on the ground in greeting each other, arising in a time of martyrdom and betrayal. Thus, the invocation of the "X" suggests that we are living in a time of a new messianic secret, the secret of eternal Blackness accessible to those who have been initiated into its transformative ways. This secret is part of the Xodus inner circle, a Space that is inclusive, but not open for the pillaging, stealing, and overly grasping minds of Euro-domination. Notions of conversion — losing a former self, dying and rising again, and claiming a new self — are all ingredients of both Christian conversion and the submission of the will to Allah by Muslims. The Xodus recasting of such ritual transformations also makes concrete how such conversions may be incorporated into recent renewed interest in rites of passage within African American communities. The creation of Xodus Space is an invitation to serious ethical, interreligious God-talk as Afrikan peoples struggle to find ways to reclaim Black prisoners and build a Space of flourishing for both women and men.

"Martin's Dream," chapter 6, reveals that although Martin Luther King's "Dream" was only a part of a militant Christian visionary's sociotheological program, the "Dream" speech uplifts King's understanding of affirming both Black struggle for freedom here in the United States and the possibility for a dramatic Beloved Community where all peoples are welcomed. Popular caricatures of the "Dream" misrepresent it as being the quintessential statement of Martin's primary goal, which is then stated as "integration." Martin's

Dream was much more than a de-fanged, whitewashed, and tokenized version of nonthreatening integration. The Dream symbolizes the telos (or moral goal) of a multicultural community in which particularities are acknowledged and not washed away in the pseudo-melting pot of "color-blind" policies — as called for by the most extreme elements of the political Right. The Dream proclaimed a radical norm of inclusion where all are welcomed because of the justice-making power of agape. Agape is a central theological and ethical concept in King's thought whose multivalence or many-sidedness moves beyond the confines of status quo justifications. Agape moves us toward the telos of creating just policies and institutional structures in society because it affirms that every human being is a child of God. Such an interpretation of agape refocuses our attention on the social justice results of a theological concept, rather than quibbling about whether or not Black folks need to be nonviolent. In King's mind agape enabled persons struggling for justice to claim a new sense of dignity, a sense of *Somebodyness* that I have already treated in the book *Somebodyness: Martin Luther King and the Theory of Dignity* (Fortress Press, 1993). As we learn to incarnate agape we are required to develop skills in organizational planning, leadership development, and clearly stated goals in order to bring our plurality of Afrikanness into positive relationship. The Dream is essential in affirming the agapic energies necessary for Xodus travelers to hope in a better future. Agape is radical and militant, but it is hopeful as well. It does not condemn any people by demonizing their essence, or giving up on their capacity for transformation. Agape preserves the prophetic edge of historic Black preaching within the framework of Xodus Space.

The last chapter of Part Two is "Common Ground." Howard Thurman's *In Search of Common Ground* affirms an ecological symbol which suggests that all creatures (human and otherwise) have a common heritage emerging from the "dust" of the earth. In West African cultures the earth is spoken of as both divine and revelational. The earth is a living thing. The living ground underneath us occasionally quakes, the air above us sometimes becomes a frenzied tornado blowing fiercely. The soil teems with countless microorganisms, from single-celled amoebas to the most complex forms of life. Thurman's usage of Common Ground ties Xodus creativity both to contemporary ecological concerns and to a neglected African heritage that valued the earth more highly than Western cultures have traditionally done.

Common Ground has important symbolic value to Xodus maleness because it suggests that one cannot be a "man" without affirming one's biological solidarity with the earth and all creatures. Such a simple theological insight has important symbolic ramifications for ways that Afrikan males can begin to discuss our bodies outside of the commodifying discourse that has constrained our thoughts. To value our bodies as aspects of a greater whole — the earth, the cosmos — is to see ourselves in a continuum of creatures. In this way the Xodus journey becomes a mystic communion with the earth, again transforming our values and goal orientation away from the "making it" mental death of mental slaves. Reconstruing our body-selves as part of an ongoing continuum, an ever-changing process, surely resonates with aspects of process theology — creating another region of Common Ground.

Part Three of *Xodus* is entitled "Xodus Space: Afrikan Ecclesiology." It brings together the voices of raptivists, the affluent Black middle class, and African American churches. Chapter 8, "Rap's Angry Children," engages rap artists such as Sister Souljah, X-Clan, Arrested Development, and Public Enemy. These rappers provide a nascent critique, unsystematic and even crude in form but highly relevant toward making the connections between racism and economic disempowerment of Black persons, sexism and violence both on the streets and in homes, and oppressive police presence with Black male criminalization. While romanticized by some literary critics, such as John Wideman and Henry Louis Gates, Jr., as a form of cultural expression or as the "breaking forth of angry ancestors," rap is a transgressive art form that is morally ambiguous. The violent misogyny of rappers such as 2-Live Crew and Snoop Doggy Dogg cannot be seen as anything other than promoting a disregard and disrespect for African American women. Xodus males must join forces with any and all who stand against such demonic art. A genuine proposal for an Xodus manhood must analyze the ambiguities of various rappers and find ways to incorporate their voices in order for the Xodus to be meaningful for young Black males. For example, Xodus conceptuality ought to develop Sister Souljah's notion of community activists as "Souljahs in the struggle." Another area for analysis is in relating the inversionary rhetoric of rap (where "ruff" can also mean "smooth and elegant") to insurrectionary potential. Such strengths are balanced by a debunking of many rappers who defend random violence as "art" in their lyrics. In fact, by emphasizing the strengths of the positive symbolizations, we might provide a more credible way of reaching into the hard core of the hip-hop generation's heart, in a way that is persuasively transformative.

One important aspect of analyzing rap's "angry children" will be the development of a positive sexual ethic within the Xodus framework. Issues of purported Black male sexual prowess must be balanced by the cost paid to women's self-esteem, self-respect, and bodily harm. Issues of homophobia within rap lyrics must be interpreted in light of how an Xodus ethic would incarnate the goal of welcoming all members of the Afrikan community.

"Rage, Privilege, and Perseverance: The Middle Class," chapter 9, reveals how Ellis Cose's bestseller *The Rage of a Privileged Class* brings to light the whole complex business of being Black and middle class in the late twentieth century. Cose demonstrates how, having gained educational excellence, material gains, and a modicum of "success," the Black middle class is still being held back by lowered peer expectations, poor advancement prospects, and a growing sense of rage at the invisible yet tangible racism still prevalent in Euro-American-dominated corporations. Such things cripple the Black middle class. While such problems do not seem to have the immediacy or intensity of the crisis facing young and poor Black males and females in the city, it is part of the dilemma that trying to "make it" in the U.S.A. entails for African Americans. Is the Xodus for the middle class too?

The ways in which the African American middle class can develop a contributive ethic are detailed in this chapter as an appropriate way of participating in the Xodus. Having educational and financial resources ought to enable African American middle-class persons (and others in solidarity with us) to move beyond traditional redistributive measures to a richer understanding of how we can "give back" to the 'hood. The "give-back" ethic arises from the popular Black folk expression, "Remember where you came from, and remember those who helped you out." Such an expression forms the heart and soul of an African American contributive ethic: Those who have education provide educational opportunities, those in politics open political doors, those in business create jobs, and those who can organize bring us together. Theologically it is an African American praxis analogous to the Pauline "body of Christ" symbol where all members claim and use their spiritual gifts for the uplifting of the common good.

The aim of chapter 9 is to move beyond rage as the only emotion African Americans are perceived as capable of producing. "Perseverance" is a more organic term to describe the Black middle class's dogged determination despite setbacks, and the historic will-to-struggle we have learned from our ancestors. Unlike the self-limiting idea of rage as a comprehensive term for Black male experience, perseverance highlights aspects of African American manhood hidden by the sound and fury of inflammatory rhetoric. Perseverance is an important ethical virtue that an African American contributive ethic can offer toward the construction of an Xodus Space.

Xodus concludes in chapter 10 with "Souljahs in Partnership." Here the previous themes will be summarized into a constructive proposal for affirming one's self, listening to the sisters, and joining a journey forward into the future. An Xodus future recognizes the contributions of "The Council of Elders" in our history, embracing the rage and the realism of Rap's "angry children," and the perseverance and contributive ethic of the African

American middle class by building a Space for the reinvention of Afrikan self. Such a Space insists on the goal of liberatory partnership with African American women, the poor, and young people.

The institution most suited for the Xodus reinvigoration of Afrikan maleness and femaleness is the Black church. It is our oldest communitywide institution, our Ark of Zion. The Black church is the fount, the holy space where Black folks have come for generations in the U.S.A. to find refreshment, release, and revival. With some remarkable exceptions, at this stage in its history this sterling institution is not answering the needs of those who most need its strengths — the poor, women, and young people. It has become irrelevant, increasingly unresponsive, and unwilling to engage in the kind of radical newness that Xodus requires. But African American churches (a more specific and accurate way of addressing the symbolic term "Black church") must step in and take a leadership role in recovering Black women and men from prison together with our Muslim brothers and sisters, finding creative ways to attract young people away from the drug culture, and helping to form partnerships with business leaders to provide satisfying careers for grossly unemployed sectors of various African American communities. African American churches are the places where the contributive ethic of inclusion and partnership can find institutional support. I will mention examples of such liberating partnerships between the community and a few churches in the Los Angeles area. Such partnership is a goal worthy of African American churches, of our best prophetic traditions, and our finest moments in the arduous history of African people here in the U.S.A. The message of apocalypse, genocide, and self-destruction that many raptivists issue can be averted by the Spirit-filled efforts of an Xodus African American church, holding hands with mosques, synagogues, and anyone else willing and able to meet the impending chaos with hope.

Notes

1. The evocative title of Manning Marable's sociological treatise, *Blackwater* (Niwot, Colo.: University Press of Colorado, 1993).
2. 1990 U.S. Census Bureau Statistics.

PART I

Conversations. deconstructions, REconstructions

CHAPTER 1

Awakenings

I am much more than rage, so much more. This book is written out of an experience of being Black, Christian, and male in the United States that goes beyond the stereotypical description of "rage." The word *rage* has adorned the headlines of *Time, Newsweek,* and many other magazines in their attempt to exploit the fears of the Euro-American masses. Louis Farrakhan was described as carrying on a "Ministry of Rage," and the Black middle class was unflatteringly portrayed through the staring scowl of a well-dressed African American businessman in an issue entitled "The Rage of a Privileged Class" (an extended review of Ellis Cose's book of the same title).

So many words symbolize aspects of the mood, the sense, and the feeling of being a Black man in an environment dominated by values, mores, and customs inimical to healthy self-affirmation of that Blackness. Frustration and disillusionment are aspects of the kind of disappointment I experience daily. Another is a sense of apathy, or turning away from engaging persons from the dominant race, for fear that they too may turn out as disappointing, as embedded in the secret chasms of "white racial narcissism" (Delores Williams's delightfully accurate phrase[1]) as so many of the Euro-American persons I have befriended before. What English word could express at once a sense of disappointment, frustration, rage, disenchantment, disillusionment, and determination? I can find none. What group of words can adequately describe an experience not meant to be captured in this language?

The urgency of such questions is heightened for me as I re-member and reincorporate the brownness and blackness that are ambiguously affirmed and denied in Jamaican culture. Living on the boundary between African Americans and Jamaican Americans, I have come to see that the polysemic and multivalent qualities of being "Black" are flattened out into a torpid pool of sameness in the racialized pseudo-consciousness of color dominating North America. In the self-enclosed miasma of "race," all peoples whose skin tones range from ebony to dark brown, reddish brown to café au lait, almost-yellow-brown to hardly-can-tell brown are stigmatized. Such a range of colors includes many peoples: Amerindians, Latino/Latinas, several Caribbean nations, as well as African Americans. This quest for a sufficient word, therefore, is both pan-African and pan-American in scope. It is forged and tempered in the same historical march of domination that created the creolized mixture of Blackness that so many "New World" pan-African peoples have experienced.

This book is an extended attempt at stretching the English language beyond its native capacity for expressing Anglo-defined categories of thought. Beyond a doubt, African experience is devalued linguistically in English. "Black" and "dark" are adjectives that portray negative, evil, and woeful characteristics for English-speaking peoples. There is no space in this language for my experiences to breathe; no room for my self or a larger, pluriform Afrikan self[2] to come to expression in the fullness of all that it could be. There is no philosophical music sonorous enough within English to sound forth all the power, pathos, and complex passions of what it means to be a Black man in the 1990s in the United States of America. There is barely enough rhythm and movement in the language to articulate the explosive power of Afrikanness, but there is enough malleability, fluidity, and life in English for us to wring Afrikan meaning out of it. Somehow our Journey toward manhood must be written in the language that ninety-nine percent of us use every day, every hour, every minute. So I write, filled with all of that raging, frustrated, disillusioned, determined passion that English can barely hold. I might be so bold as to create a newword to describe this multiple feeling, this *disillragedeterminassion*.

In response to our *disillragedeterminassion* African American males are beginning to undertake a psychic-spiritual and cultural Journey. It is a Journey within the confines of an English-speaking, linguistically negated world. Indeed, the Journey of African American males is not even officially welcomed as an aspect of the "new male" movement sweeping the social landscape. Unrecognized and invisible to others, we still sing, pray, and are organizing ourselves. This Journey takes place in churches, auditoriums, and school gymnasiums, as well as in the privacy of our own homes with family. It is a move of the Spirit — not quite a movement. At present it is more diffuse and less articulate than a genuine revolution, but it is real.

Since every movement ought to have a name, I have deigned to name this new sense of African American masculinity *Xodus* in honor of one of the reigning "saints" of Black folks throughout the world, Malcolm X. The "X" in his name signified the unknown, the lost, the "dis-remembered" past (to use Toni Morrison's wonderfully appropriate newword, which Karen Baker-Fletcher has fleshed out theologically[3]) that may finally be claimed as an essential aspect of one's self. Malcolm's journey through the "X" toward becoming El Hajj Malik El-Shabazz carried him through the Nation of Islam's tutelage, demonology of whites, uplift of African heritage, and Moslem faith. Such a faith journey is a part of this new Journey (capitalized because it represents the newness of this particular symbolic and mythic-narrative event), but is broader and more inclusive than that of the Nation of Islam. Many of the most prominent proponents of the African American male Journey are local pastors and preachers in Christian churches, as well as Africentrists not interested in Christianity at all, but in reviving traditional African religions or the ancient faiths of Egypt. So the Xodus Journey includes a broad conglomeration of various faiths and mythic narratives. The aim of Xodus Journeying is not a matter of religious dogma or of building a new religion, but of psychospiritual liberation. Such a Journey participates in a kind of remythifying of pan-African cultures, aiding all Black peoples in a process of intentionally building narrative meanings outside of the pervasive European and American-centered myth of "modernity." Such remythification[4] boldly asserts the right of Afrikans (another word for all pan-African peoples) to create and propagate new myths to re-member within our psyches and our cultures what has been dis-remembered for too long. Xodus is an event of the mind and the spirit, embracing both the mental/cultural realm and those secret places of the human spirit in communion with the divine.

Since no one can say or be all things, the particular voice I speak in is that of an ethicist and theologian. Although *Xodus* is a multidisciplinary undertaking, the academic lens I look through is that of theology and ethics. I take this limitation to be liberating because our Journey must be evaluated along the lines of how it deals with issues of right and wrong, how values are decided, how the Ultimate is viewed, and how human beings relate to the realm of the divine. Furthermore, since Xodus is both something that *is* and *is yet to be*, it could easily evade the more empirical observations of the scientist. Yet as theologians describe the reign of God as Here and Not Yet, so I discern the presence of a new humanity arising from the ashes of oppressed history, a living and liberating New Being named Xodus.

An important aspect of that liberating Xodus New Being is inscribed into my writing, in its symbolism and usage of metaphor. As noted earlier, there is not enough linguistic "space" in the English language to capture, express, and metamorphosize African American experiences (let alone African American *male* experiences). Our manyness, our plurality, our diversity require the repetition of phrases that English syntax normally labels as redundant. Our verbosity and loquacity must imagine itself into a new discourse, a new English that goes beyond the confines of "good English." I will capitalize "Black" instead of following the Eurocentric *Chicago Manual of Style* because I fundamentally disagree that "black" is an adequate description of my culture, religion, style, and Space. I will CAPITALIZE and *italicize* freely, all with the visual purpose of *demonstrating the inadequacy of English in its "standard" form*. When one scans this text, one ought to be visually enticed and arrested by the repetition of "***XODUS SPACE***." Such linguistic boldness is part and parcel of the ***XODUS*** calling, the prophetic summons to leave the sinful Space of Euro-domination, and to *wake up!* In fact, the very first step of Xodus liberation is to wake up. This moment of awakening is the shedding of Euro-domination in one's desires, values, and attitudes. Awakening is the enlightening moment when one announces to the world that the Afrikan self within will no longer be denied, ignored, and suppressed. Such a moment has tremendous psychospiritual significance. It is the moment when the Afrikan self proclaims its Sepia-centricity and refuses to accept heteronomous (meaning "authority coming from outside of oneself," the opposite of "autonomous") Eurocentricity as its final authority. Coming out is Sepia-centric for Xodus seekers who find ourselves in the process of moving from Euro-Space to Us-Space — a Space named, defined, owned, and maintained by the bold and persistent creativity of Afrikan self.

Xodus: An African American Male Journey is my contribution to the much larger Xodus, the greater exodus of many peoples from the yoke of Eurocentricity. All around the globe various cultures are grappling with the effects of colonization of their minds, devaluing of native cultures, and the disruption of meaning instilled by several centuries of Euro-domination. The greater exodus is inclusive enough to embrace the unusual and occasional European desiring to escape the clutching myopia of that heritage. Such European seekers may be found in the call for a postmodernity to subvert and overthrow a failed modernity. The greater exodus is postmodern, because it seeks to overthrow the negative cultural imprisonment and imperialism of Europe and America while retaining (and this is often not noted) the positive aspects of democracy, personal autonomy, and technological advancement. As a postmodern discourse, those on the Xodus Journey join other members of the greater exodus in seeking to discover new ways to be human in a world that values plurality rather than unity, diverse cultural contributions rather than focusing on the singular cultural contributions of Europeans, and ecological development of human technology rather than crass capitalist exploitation of the earth and all of its creatures.

To share such a postmodern, fundamentally subversive discourse with all peoples, including those happily submerged and subsumed in Euro-domination, is a strange but necessary exercise. Xodus writing and thinking must move beyond the parameters of tolerance devised by the architects of the so-called Enlightenment era. The Founding Fathers of the United States and other influential European thinkers like John Locke and Jean-Jacques Rousseau desired to end the vicious religious wars that had decimated the populations and the spirit of many European nations. These fine European minds created the notion of tolerance as a means of negotiating religious differences, as their first step into the cosmos we now name pluralism. Xodus and greater exodus thinkers must take a step beyond tolerance in order to address the wreckage of humanity that the "tolerant" Euro-American imperialists have created. While Europeans and Euro-Americans practiced "tolerance" with each other (and *that* barely!), they brought an imperialistic and tyrannical version of Christianity in league with an expansionist economic agenda to the shores of virtually every other continent. Democracy, love of neighbor and enemy, and individual conscience — the positive ideas of the Enlightenment — arrived for the rest of the world wrapped in garments of deceit, hypocrisy, and cruelty. The sword and the cross intermingled in a bloody genocidal display of Euro-domination. So we must move beyond the sham of "tolerance" as practiced in the history of Euro-domination toward a new notion large enough to confront the new historical moment. Our moment requires a combination of several different ideals:

1. *Genuine interest* in the cultures, religions, and differences that comprise the globe, rather than the grasping and assimilative "curiosity" of Euro-dominators;

2. *Genuine nonvolatile confrontation,* where differences between cultures and groups cannot be overlooked, dismissed, or trivialized; and

3. *Genuine perseverance* in maintaining respect, dialogue, and communication even after significant differences have been noted and addressed.

To maintain genuine interest, nonvolatile confrontation, and perseverance is a difficult thing, but not beyond the scope of our imaginations. Tolerance was practiced too selectively; genuine interest/nonvolatile confrontation/perseverance must be inclusive of all peoples. It ought to be practiced both between different cultural and religious groups and among the various subgroups within a larger grouping. Xodus offers genuine interest/nonvolatile confrontation/perseverance as a trinity, a three-in-one ethical norm. This book attempts to exercise such a norm, practicing what it preaches. As such, no one can be excluded from Xodus Space, even those Euro-dominators who might try to join. A warning is in order, however, because if one remains fixated on categories of thought that negate and erase Sepia-ness, then the going might get rough!

The "**X**" of Xodus is not immediately coterminous with the phenomenon known as Generation X,[5] although members of the so-called "twentysomething" crowd (of all cultures and colors) may find places of resonance within it. I am thirty-eight years old, having thankfully survived my twenties without an arrest, jail sentence, or any skirmish with the occupying force known as the police past a few scary moments when Euro-American officers attempted to provoke me into saying or doing something to them which they could use to justify beating me. I am grateful to God to be alive and well and "thirtysomething." I do not fit easily into that older crowd known as the baby-boomers, although I have vivid memories of JFK, MLK, RFK, and Vietnam in a way that most "twentysomething" persons may not possess. Nevertheless, I believe that the kind of psychospiritual Space and cultural awakening that Xodus symbolizes may resonate with some members of the so-called Generation X. It is my hope that the theological, philosophical, and ethical musings here may give members of that "X" a particular voice from which their own progressive and conflictual sense of identity and meaning may flourish. Most African Americans of that age category eschew naming themselves as "Generation X." Rapper Dr. Dre may have summed up a popular sentiment among young African Americans in his quote, "I haven't heard anyone in my 'hood talking about it . . . the only X I know is Malcolm X."[6] I cannot help but notice that all of this attention to the so-called Generation X arose *after* African Americans, particularly young African American males, began idolizing Malcolm X as a model of defiant Black manhood. Generation X came into being alongside Spike Lee's commercial drive to prime audiences for *Malcolm X,* his biographical epic movie about Malcolm X. Is the Generation X hype yet another rip-off of Black culture? Is it like swing, cool jazz, bebop, rock and roll, soul, and hip-hop music — only ours until the white public has assimilated and appropriated it? In other words, have Euro-American dominators stolen even our "X"? Perhaps, and if so, then it is vitally important to begin an extensive communitywide discussion of what the "X" means for us.

Social Metaphysics

The awakening that is Xodus arises as an affirmation of certain social metaphysics that can be summarized in seven points.

1. *There is no amoral Space anywhere or anytime.* To be human at all is to be moral — to have some sense of how and why one is choosing to do *this* act instead of *that.* As long as human beings are living, moving, they are choosing and making decisions — even when their choices, actions, and decision-making are extremely confined by poverty, racial discrimination, or a lack of gender justice. Choice, therefore, is not restricted to the rational creatures of Immanuel Kant's *Metaphysics of Morals* but represents the hard data of concrete humanity from an ethical viewpoint. Underlying the claim that there is no amoral Space is the corollary ethical truth that to be human is be moral in some fashion.[7] So the responsibility of an ethicist is to seek to articulate why someone has chosen, why a choice was immoral. Immoral choices can be understood as those decisions and actions inimical to the flourishing and welfare of life, human and otherwise.

2. *There is no apolitical Space.* Politics is not what professional image-projectors "handle" in public in order to get elected, but it is the associated fashion in which people's values and norms embody themselves toward a common good in society.[8] Politics is an intensified arena of power relations as well. Africentric psychologist and author Amos N. Wilson has noted that Afrikans (or pan-African people) need to become more conscious of how we must resist the subtle social lie that the fields of science and economics are purportedly neutral and objective. We must be aware of how "apolitical" economics taught at prestigious universities across the country trains young African American minds to desire to become members of Euro-dominated institutions rather than giving them the kind of liberating economic information that would encourage them to start their own businesses. Wilson says this quite crisply:

We thus produce a bunch of educated people . . . who, the more degrees they get in business administration the fewer businesses they have to administer; who, as they go into the colleges and the Wharton Schools of Finance and the Harvard Business School, etc. find their communities being inundated by Asians and other groups. Apparently their degrees are not designed for them to control their own economic situations and circumstances. But because the information in the courses in economics is seen as "neutral" and "non-political," the student is more radically politicized than in any other way.[9]

Being sensitive to the ways in which power relations are embedded in the warp and woof of our lives does not mean that we have to be pessimistic about the inescapability of power dynamics. The great

French philosopher Michel Foucault advocated the primacy of power relations so forcefully that he appeared to be promoting a kind of power-relations determinism in which personal agency and individuality are absorbed into an imperialist web of discourses, regimes of truth, and viciously subtle constructs of power/knowledge. I thank Foucault (yes, it is possible to be Africentric *and* use concepts from a European philosopher . . . on occasion!) for helping late-twentieth-century social theorists to consider the ramifications of power relations with wide-open eyes.[10] His strong emphasis on power relations demystifies power — it clarifies and unlocks the interweaving and contradictory meanings that have become hidden behind a fog of meaning.[11] Xodus theory must build itself on a demystified view of politics which affirms that all Space is political — in other words, deal with it, don't hide from it!

3. *Every particular reality is a sociocultural construction.* Peter Berger's oft-noted *The Social Construction of Reality* makes it clear that we view our world through an interpretive lens fashioned by human minds over a period of time. African Americans have a different take on reality than do our Caribbean brothers and sisters, or Brazilians, or various tribal peoples in the mother continent of Africa. Each of these peoples has a distinctive claim to being considered African, all being members of the pan-African diaspora, yet each has a different understanding of reality. Xodus Space is pan-African Space in its inclusive spirit, and thereby it is Afrikan in the broadest sense of the term. Xodus cannot be defined or confined by any one particular African people, especially African Americans, as we seek to establish a self-inscribed and self-described identity. Thus I take the writing of this book to be a contribution toward the creation of Xodus Space, from my own sociocultural niche in the global Afrikan diaspora. This book reflects one African American/Jamaican American's construct of reality in the hope of encouraging conversation to envision yet another reality more comprehensive and vast than my puny experience could offer. *Xodus* offers a particular construct in the creation of something that might have universal significance.

4. *Space is made sacred by conscious psychospiritual naming and ritual acts.* Afrikans, spread across the far-flung frontiers of the globe, are in desperate need of a Space of our own. Such a Space necessarily must be more than a romanticized ideological projection, or a fervent wish articulated in saccharine impotence. It must be something tangible and palpably meaningful for the minds, spirits, and emotions of Afrikans. Xodus Space has the potential of being such a Space for Afrikans, but

only if we understand it to be sacred in Mircea Eliade's sense of the term. That is to say, Xodus Space must be a Space that is demarcated, set apart from everyday "profane" space.[12] Further, such a Space is made sacred by the ritual acts of Afrikan peoples, in all their diversity.

I would not arrogate myself to prescribe what kinds of rituals would make Xodus Space sacred, but the sacred ought to be understood to be an actual physical as well as psychospiritual reality. I perform certain acts as prayer and meditation to resacralize myself. They are part of the way that I announce to others that they are entering my Space, Xodus Space. By the playing of African music (gospel, reggae, and jazz are personal favorites) and burning of distinctively Afrikan fragrances (Amber and Kush), an atmosphere of Xodus is ritually created. This atmosphere of Xodus can be ritualized in lectures, sermons, and in private counseling sessions. It is in the Sepia mood, the dusky meditation, that this kind of ritual activity summons Afrikan sacrality into reality. For many who are cut off from the sensuality of the sacred — the sounds of music, the smells of incense, and the rhythms of drums — the kind of ritual activity I bear witness to may be too much. For them a more cerebral meditation might be more meaningful. What is most important at this point is for Xodus Space to be generated and named by Afrikans, in whatever creative way we desire.

5. *Most people are mentally asleep.* In the United States of America this mental sleep manifests itself in an unyielding ahistoricism that blinds itself to anything unpleasant in the past on the one hand, and on the other hand fuels itself on an uncritical progressivism where all history is viewed as part of the great "march toward democracy and freedom." For African Americans this mental sleep has led to mental slavery far more troublesome than physical servitude because it is a "sleep unto death" for us. While our young men are killing each other, mentally asleep Black folks seem to be waiting for the government, the church, the rich folks, or anybody else to rescue us! Xodus is a summons to wake up and rescue ourselves, with God's help and the solidarity of others.

6. *To awaken from mental sleep requires an adequate notion of history.* The creation of Xodus Space requires not only a firm theoretical grasp of ethics, politics, and culture, but also a concept of history. History is not a singular movement, neither an unremitting devolution from civilization to chaos, nor a steady march toward greater and higher forms of civilization from the primeval slime. Rather, history is a series of integrations and disintegrations, of cyclical movements of great social ferment and decline. History is not linear, nor is it a monotonous

circle of rise and fall, but it moves along in abrupt jumps, starts, smoothness, and roughness, like riding a skittish horse or boating on a fast and unpredictable river.

History itself must be differentiated from written history, which is often the ideological by-product (waste product?) of the "winners." Written history is a grand narrative of how "my" people overcame all of "them." It serves as an ideological tool of justification, so that one can "educate" one's children to not feel guilty about exterminating, maiming, raping, and eliminating whole peoples and entire civilizations from existence. Written history, at least as it is conventionally taught and understood, serves as a dangerous tool for continuing to oppress the oppressed, enforce oppressors, and keep all asleep. History as I would like to see it ought to be an arena or field of contentious narratives, reconstructions, and conscientization. History must become a place where African-centered historical reconstructions are heard with the same seriousness as European-centered histories are heard. It must emerge as a genuinely global discipline, and not merely the arcane preserve of Euro-American professors. In such an approach to history we examine the positive and negative effects of history as propaganda, myth, and ideology[13] with a view toward changing conditions for people who have no education. History must become sensitive to the meanings of graffiti on walls, piles of garbage in alleys, and the stench of pollution that chokes the poorest primarily.

The mental sleep that affects Afrikan peoples is caused by the drug of Euro-domination. It is a centuries-long sleep for those of us here in the United States, but it appears to be spreading to many of the newly liberated countries of Africa. It is the narcotized sleep of technological "progress," of the "advance of civilization," of materialist values that devalue human life in favor of an impoverished economic bottom-line of profit, and of the inevitability of technological might-makes-right militarism. We must wake up, come to a new awareness of the place and potential of Afrikan consciousness in this particular time in world history. I insist that there are profound spiritual, cultural, moral, and philosophical contributions that only Afrikans can make in order to save our generation. The self-conscious creation of Xodus Space may be our last opportunity to assert ourselves before some cataclysmic plague, nuclear accident, or ecological event occurs. Our wisdom may help prevent a grievous end for the world, but we must wake up, stand up, and proclaim the wisdom of the Ancestors now.

7. *Stripping away scapegoating strategies and hatred is a profoundly difficult but necessary social task.* Laying the blame for racism, patriarchalism, militarism, and other forms of systemized abusiveness requires an eye for details and attention toward limiting sweeping gestures. While "Euro-domination" is an oft-repeated phrase in this text, I am not making a carte blanche indictment of all Europeans and Americans. Nor am I saying "all whites are devils." Avoiding such demonization is important in actually getting at the power relation of domination that "Euro-domination" names. The term refers to a particular kind of dominating power relation that arose from certain elite monarchs and bourgeoisie living in Europe, from the time of Columbus until now. Euro-domination may be traced by a historical-critical strategy of uncovering how certain thoughts arose and became social practices named "genealogy." Cornel West provides an excellent genealogy of racism in his first book, *Prophesy Deliverance!* (1982). West notes that racism emerged from a "modern discourse" that was "the creative fusion of scientific investigation, Cartesian philosophy, Greek ocular metaphors, and classical aesthetic and cultural ideals."[14] West cites particular individuals who gave "scientific" justification to racism: the classificational strategies of Francois Biernier in 1684 and Carolus Linnaeus in his *Natural System* of 1735. These classificational schemes divided humanity into distinctive "races" to which were attributed certain essential qualities. West points out that while these classifications were purported to be value-free, one can readily detect value judgments of inferiority and superiority:

European. White, Sanguine, Brawny. Hair abundantly flowing. Eyes blue. *Gentle, acute, inventive. Covered with close vestments. Governed by customs.*

African. Black, Phlegmatic, Relaxed. Hair black, frizzled. Skin silky. Nose flat. Lips tumid. Women's bosom a matter of modesty. Breasts give milk abundantly. *Crafty, indolent. Negligent. Anoints himself with grease. Governed by caprice.*[15]

What Xodus construction takes from West's genealogical analysis of the West is that it is important to name both representative and influential individuals who contributed to the formation of a discourse and to the systemic regime of ideas that oppress. In such analysis there is little room for the negative energies of hatred.

Many radical Africentrists have focused much recent attention on the so-called "Jewish Conspiracy" to control the world in general and Black folks in particular. While it is apparent that these particular African Americans (Tony Martin and Khallid Muhammad, to name two) are in profound conflict with Jews, it is not apparent that there is a major rift between Jews as a group and African Americans as a group. Yet the conflict has been presented by the media as a major breakdown into vicious hatred between our two groups. I criticize any person, African or Jewish, who is incapable of reasoning from the facts. The facts are clear: Some Jews have oppressed some African Americans, no doubt about it. Some African Americans are making highly anti-Semitic remarks publicly, without apology or caution. We must learn to name the individuals and their particular sins clearly without obscuring the matter behind a wall of generalizations that inflame hatred.[16] It is a shameful but true fact of history that many Africans and African Americans grew rich and prosperous from the slave trade, and that some Jews did as well.[17] In Xodus historical reconstruction we ought to spend more time examining the economic system of oppression that compromised so many rather than blaming whole groups. Xodus Space demands attention to these kinds of particular details, carefully delineating its generalizing metaphors.

Now that the basepoints for Xodus travel have been enumerated, it is time to begin the Journey . . .

Notes

1. Found in *Sisters in the Wilderness* (Maryknoll, N.Y.: Orbis, 1993).
2. "Afrikan self" is a newword I have created based on current Africentric/nationalist practices that tie all peoples of African descent together in the word "Afrikan."
3. Toni Morrison uses the term *dis-remembered* in *Beloved* (New York: Alfred A. Knopf, 1987). Karen Baker-Fletcher develops the word as a way of revalorizing neglected and historically devalued African female mythological figures such as the Egyptian Maat, the Tar Lady whom Morrison elevates, and perhaps even the Medusa. See Karen Baker-Fletcher, *A Singing Something: Anna J. Cooper and the Foundations of Womanist Theology* (New York: Crossroad, 1993), 198–201.
4. My usage of this term arises from a series of conversations I held with a strongly Africentric African man, the Rev. Dr. Okechukwu Ogbonayya, in March and April of 1994.
5. There is great contention about whether the diverse racial, cultural, and class groupings of "twentysomethings" ought to be classified as one. The struggles these young people are having in meeting the unique challenges of our contemporary era are well documented in Jeff Giles, "Generalizations X," *Newsweek*, 6 June 1994, 62–72.
6. Ibid., 64.
7. Charles Kammer makes this as his fundamental anthropological claim in *Ethics and Liberation* (Maryknoll, N.Y.: Orbis, 1986).
8. This is my definition as influenced by Aristotle's in *Politics*, Bk. 1, in *A New Aristotle Reader,* ed. J. L. Ackrill (Princeton: Princeton University Press, 1987), 507.

9. Amos N. Wilson, *The Falsification of Afrikan Consciousness: Eurocentric History, Psychiatry and the Politics of White Supremacy* (New York: Afrikan World InfoSystems, 1993), 17.

10. Michel Foucault, *Power/Knowledge: Selected Interviews and Other Writings 1972–1977*, edited by Colin Gordon (New York: Pantheon, 1980), 78–133.

11. My definition of "demystification" owes much to Cornel West in his recent *Keeping Faith* (New York: Routledge, 1993).

12. The following definition of "sacred" owes much to that outlined in Mircea Eliade, *The Sacred and the Profane*, trans. Willard R. Trask (New York: Harcourt, Brace, 1959).

13. Wilson, *Falsification of African Consciousness,* 15–20.

14. Cornel West, *Prophesy Deliverance! An Afro-American Revolutionary Christianity* (Philadelphia: Westminster, 1982), 53.

15. Ibid., 56, quoting Winthrop Jordan, *White over Black: American Attitudes toward the Negro, 1550–1812* (New York: W. W. Norton, 1968), 3–98.

16. The work of carefully outlining the particular Jews and Blacks who have practiced racist hatred toward each other is not the mission of this text. I intend to give the problematic of Black-Jewish conflict more attention in a future text.

17. The complicity of African Americans in the slave trade is one of the most painful research areas for Afrikans to excavate. Some work was presented on this topic at the Society for the Study of Black Religion in Atlanta, Spring 1994.

New Males?
Same Ole Same Ole

For African American men desiring a transformation of consciousness, the models provided by Euro-American males, no matter how "new" the predominantly white "men's movement" portrays them, are not new enough. Where can we find a place to call our own, where our concerns, issues, crises, and values may be explored without an abusive use of dominating power? Among many quarters of the national African American community, a resurgent Black Consciousness movement is under way: Africentrism. A renaming of the popular Afrocentrism movement based on the commonsense idea that we have attained our cultural heritage from a continent known as Africa and not Afroca,[1] Africentrism has taken hold of the imaginations, hearts, and souls of many African American persons, particularly those living in poor, urban neighborhoods. The appeal of Africentrism is that it places Africa and Africans as *subjects* of history and culture, and describes us as more than the mere *objects* of European history.[2]

Is Africentrism a fancy, intellectual name for reverse racism? Simply answered, no. Is Africentrism an anti-white movement? Again the answer is no. What makes Africentrism so compelling to African Americans is that it places us in the center of things, as movers and shakers, shapers of our own destinies, and names those of African descent as influencers of culture (writ large) — global culture. Such a naming is an important aspect for African American males as we seek to find a place to stand that is not dependent on Euro-definitions of what is true, authoritative, and right. To put it another way, Africentrism provides a Space of our own. Africentric scholars have been working avidly to redefine the parameters of manhood and masculinity. One particularly instructive example is Muslim Africentric psychologist, Na'im Akbar. Africentric authors like Dr. Akbar are revising definitions of masculinity to fit the subtle harshness and everyday cruelties of being Sepia in a Euro-colored world.

Na'im Akbar's *The Community of the Self* presents a very different picture of the inner world of the mind than do Sam Keen, Robert Moore, and Douglass Gillette of the "new male" movement. Hearkening back to the common African notion of community being primary, Akbar portrays the human self as an internal community of psychic "citizens." This community is a hierarchy that moves from the more primal drives to the ruling will. Notice that Akbar arranges the Community of Self into an interacting circular image (at right). Drives are the "motors of the self," moving persons in a twofold direction either toward pleasure or away from pain.[3] The senses are channels of communication connecting the self to the outer world. The ego functions as that inner citizen who speaks up for the rights of the individual, using emotion as its voice.[4] Memory serves as the library and archives of the inner community, preserving experiences and providing continuity. Reason organizes and brings order to the information brought to it by the senses, classifies and interprets our experiences, and provides meaning for the inner community.[5] Conscience is the moral arbiter, the bringer of justice to the community, that citizen which Akbar reminds us is called "the self-accusing spirit" in the Qu'ran (the Holy Book of Islam) which determines the goodness or evil of our thoughts and actions.[6] Finally, the "Khalifah" or ruler of the community is the will, the only inner citizen with the power to draw on all parts of the community and "pull the mind and flesh in the direction of Truth."[7] Each inner citizen must do its unique and particular part as member of the Community of Self, because whenever one of the citizens deigns

WILL

CONSCIENCE

DRIVE

REASON

SENSES

MEMORY

EGO

to exalt itself as ruler, it usurps the proper role of the will, which Akbar sees as the "Divine representative within the person when working with the higher parts of conscience and guided by proper direction."[8]

The aim of *The Community of the Self* is to provide both a theoretical and practical guide for African Americans to gain access to their inner citizens, from whence will arise both individual and corporate power. Akbar spends most of the text providing practical suggestions, such as: (1) learning to listen to our inner "powers," (2) restraining outside "noises" such as TV and certain kinds of distracting music styles, (3) developing self-control as we "hear" what our inner voices are telling us, and (4) gaining control over outside influences, or developing an independent voice of our own that is not authorized or controlled by Euro-Americans.[9] Akbar, like most Africentrists, spends a good deal of space enjoining African Americans to "Know thyself," learning the rich and neglected histories of African cultures.

The fundamental premise of *The Community of the Self* is an Africentric and communal presentation of those governing, ordering, motivating, and restraining psychological energies that I call The Elders. These Elders are the community of voices responsible for bringing us into a rich and complete personhood. Unlike the anachronistic and morally outdated Jungian archetype—the King—popular in the new male movement, The Elders operate in a nonhierarchical, cooperative relationality. Working together they integrate the self. Their coordinated choices balance the urges of individuation, or autonomy, and embeddedness, or group conformity. Like Akbar's inner citizens, as The Elders cooperatively relate with each other they create the kind of communal, inner psychic Space necessary for the emergence of an Afrikan self. This emergence is an awakening, the first step of Xodus Journeying.

I am not the only African American who senses the need to leave Euro-dominated Space. Akbar calls for an "Exodus" into manhood in his *Visions for Black Men* (1991). In *Visions* Akbar deepens his Egyptian and Africentric research and imagery, which can aid us in building a variety of liberating new images and new archetypes. For example, Akbar insists on reclaiming for pan-African males the historical "truth" that we are the fathers of civilization,[10] the original symbolic Adam and Abraham, human beings who were capable of both envisioning and building great cultures. (I would supplement Akbar's contention with the claim that we fathers/Adams/Abrahams envisioned and created cultures and civilizations side by side with the great women/mothers/Eves/Sarahs of our peoples.) As Adam, Akbar insists that our role is that of being keeper of the garden, tending to the "garden" of our communities — the women and children — as well as to the attendant processes of nature.

of these images of maleness, what I am calling new images, are guided by will, which Akbar describes as possessing character and the ability to direct one's own life.[11] Further, all of these metaphorical characters follow the Kemetic (ancient word for "Egyptian") practice of seeking to attain the status of *geru maat* — the one who has mastered the self and is thereby considered an exemplar of Maat. Most Western and Christian theological or philosophical discourse does not appeal to ancient Kemet as a discursive authority, but Akbar and I do. What are the substantive Kemetic philosophical and ethical assumptions that underlie both Akbar's work and my own?

The primary moral assumptions of ancient Kemet were based on an elaboration of the concept of Maat. Maat is the sevenfold cardinal virtue of ancient Kemet, whose multivalent meaning included justice, truth/order, balance, harmony, levelness, righteousness, and self-control. The ancient texts of Kemet extolled Maat as that for which every person ought to aim — or, in the language of the ethicist, Maat is the *summum bonum* or highest good. Maat is the telos or end toward which we ought to aim our entire lives. In the cosmologies of the great city of Memphis, at the end of one's life the goal was to declare in the underworld that one had lived a life of Maat — welcoming strangers, feeding the hungry, clothing the naked, and visiting the sick.[12] Such injunctions sound familiar to Christians who are acquainted with the social justice imperatives of Matthew 25. Some Kemetic scholars like Maulana Karenga insist that Christianity (and Judaism before it) learned these things from the great Maatic priests of Kemet. My point is not to debate origins as much as to make it clear to Christians that the ancient value system of Kemet has moral resonance with the kind of contemporary liberating forms of Christianity that an Xodus Journeyer seeks to embody.[13] It must be affirmed that when we call for Maat to be embodied in our lives, we are calling for a restoration of moral balance, justice, and truth by holding to the high moral standard of Maat:

> The balancing of the land lies in Maat — truth, justice, and righteousness. Do not speak falsely for you are great; do not act lightly for you have weight; be not untrue for you are the balance and do not swerve for you are the standard. You are on the level with the balance. If it tilts, then, you will lean too. Do not drift, rather steer. . . .[14]

The power of this excerpt for those beginning their Xodus Journey is that it exudes an air of personal responsibility and a high sense of moral accountability. Such moral qualities are sorely needed in our contemporary society, by both oppressors and the oppressed. For the Xodus Journeyer such an injunction calls forth a noble ideal, something all Afrikan peoples may aspire toward even while we fight multiple forms of oppression: from within our communities (sexism, patriarchalism, classism, colorism) and without (racism, militarism, environmental destruction, nuclearism).

A further Kemetic assumption not specified by Akbar ought to be included as well: the psychospiritual value of Blackness. Africentric psychologist Richard King, M.D., challenges us to understand that the kind of psychic and spiritual "Space" that I am constructing (Xodus) may be understood as the mythical "Eye of Horus" — the pineal gland, or "third eye" of ancient Kemetic religion.[15] Excavating the secret mystery cult symbolism of the Kemetic priesthood (only those who were initiated could understand the language of the so-called hieroglyphs that the priests called Senzar), King writes of blackness as representative of the collective unconscious of the entire human race, which the Kemetic priests called *Amenta,* the under-world.[16] The "Black Dot" or third eye has both a physical seat in the pineal gland and a psychic location as the "hidden doorway" to the "temple of the human mind/body." King notes that the ancient Kemetic people adorned their temples, obelisks, and pyramids with black obsidian stones that represented this symbolic blackness.[17] This blackness serves as both a Space to enter into and a psychic door to pass through — part of the manyness of meaning inherent in a rich and spiritually charged symbol. Blackness, therefore, can have a divine meaning for all peoples today, but especially for Afrikan peoples. Blackness in ancient Kemet and for us is a profoundly positive spiritual symbol that connects blackness of color to something spiritually valuable, necessary, and wholesome rather than the kind of negative colorism associated with "black" in the Western context.

Is such a tremendous historical leap (some three thousand to four thousand years) necessary for contemporary Afrikan peoples? No and yes. No, we are not compelled to dig up ancient myths to prove to ourselves and others that we are beautiful, meaningful, and morally valuable. It is possible for us to take a Kierkegaardian leap of faith, imagining ourselves into an utterly new Xodus Space that has no historical precedents. Yet to do such a thing would ignore a tremendously complex and intriguing heritage, maybe even wasting precious time and energy since Blackness has already been affirmed for us, albeit a very long time ago. Yes, we ought to use the myths and symbolism of Kemet and other myths from around the world to overturn the Manichaean divide that forever places "black" on the negative side of the dyad connoting "less than," "evil," or "not good enough" in contrast to the purported positive attributes of "white."

Blackness might be a challenging word for us to use to reform Carl Jung's Shadow. Instead of owning our negative, violent, and repressed aspects of self, we could embrace our Blackness in all of its spiritual energy. We have indeed been shadows of our former Black selves, incomplete, alienated, and kept from owning our complete histories. Perhaps if we expand the psychospiritual Space of Blackness within our minds we might begin to find the words to describe our *disilluragedeterminassion*. If radical Africentric psychologists like Richard King are correct in affirming that the core of all human beings is in the melanin-suffused *loecus coerulus* (the primal brain stem), then getting in touch with our fundamental Blackness is more than an Afrikan task — it is a global responsibility.[18] While such a totalizing view of Afrikanness could easily corrupt itself into a form of racism, there is no doubt that Blackness is a Space that is yet the undiscovered country of spiritual wisdom.

New Males, or Same Ole Same Ole?

I contend that the fate of the "new male" movement championed by Robert Bly, Robert Moore, Douglass Gillette, Sam Keen, and others rests in its willingness to include as many diverse and powerless voices as possible. It will never be able to construct a "new male" without the creative voices of excluded men and women as part of that constructive conversation. The genuine "new male" will need to be shaped by the perspectives, criticisms, pain, and joy that African American, Asian, Hispanic, Native American, and poor Euro-American men and women can contribute. "New males" will not be new at all if they merely absorb, steal, or ignore the message of Africentric Xodus Journeyers, because we have something profound to add to the conversation. When the powerful separate themselves in order to regroup and recoup what they believe has been stolen from them, the powerless have good reason to shudder or laugh in derision. Why should we believe that what is created will not be a warmed-over version of the "same ole same ole" (as my ancestors used to call it)?

Why is such a concern so pressing? It is vitally important toward gaining a new and more communal understanding of power — a power that incorporates the wisdom of Blackness and the new images. The traditional understanding of power practiced by the upper- to middle-class Euro-American male establishment has been confined to a coercive force that only a privileged and dominating minority can hoard, accumulate, and use to preserve its own self-interests. Such power is interwoven into the interstices of society, manifesting itself in the institutional practices of churches, academic institutions, businesses, and political structures of the modern West.[19] Such an understanding of power controls the attitude, tone of voice, and level of dialogue that passes between those who possess it and those who do not. The powerless are compelled to demand a fair share of something that is constructed to never be distributed in an egalitarian manner. Thus, even the highest ideals of Western democracy, such as equality, are subverted by actual practices and ideology of coercive power that confronts the pow less. A new understanding of power must necessarily undermine this fundamentally elitist definition of power as false. Power is not something that can be possessed and hoarded by the few, whoever that few may be. Such an assumption must be named as a delusion and as an example of weakness, not strength.[20] Coercion or elitist grasping is not power, for power is persuasive and increases through shared interaction. The inner model of such persuasive shared power may be located in the interaction of the Elders within the inner community.

A transformed understanding of power names intimate communal interaction as genuine and creative power. A man's "intimate connections"[21] with God, neighbors, natural environment, and family would become the determining factors of power. The traditional glorification of the autonomous man who disconnects from community in order to attain dominating power over the community will be transformed by this intimate understanding of power. Power, so named, is intimate. Intimacy becomes the necessary close interaction of human beings for the benefit of all. Intimacy is a journey of maturation that involves many persons working together, not the heroic trial of the one. Intimacy has often been targeted as that aspect of maleness that is the least developed and needs the most work.[22] I agree wholeheartedly. To yoke intimacy with a revised understanding of power is the next step men should take.

When a communal, cooperative, and interactive understanding of power becomes the cultural norm, then every American will understand the wisdom of the African American poet Haki Madhubuti's belief that power is life-giving and life-saving: "I define power in terms of the ability to make life-giving and life-saving decisions as well as the ability (knowledge, resources and desire) to deliver on the decisions made."[23]

After naming false power, we must find ways to cooperatively work together to search for new ways of redefining power. Those who are considered powerful need to share what they have been ideologically conditioned to grasp and not let go. Sharing what has been hoarded and possessed will never occur unless a new understanding of power is embraced by all parties.[24] Such a new understanding will facilitate the release of resources — economic, political, and educational — in order for the genuine power attained by sharing to be born.

This new power, Xodus power, will be forged in the sharing of personal testimonies about the power of community. My personal testimony includes the stories of pain, exclusion, and resistance I have heard from my parents, feminists, womanists, and radical men of all races. My Xodus Journey toward a new understanding of maleness was motivated by the stories of unfair exclusion of my mother, Superia Fletcher; the stories and analysis of abuse by Black women like Audre Lorde and Katie Cannon; as well as the critical insights of Euro-American feminists such as Sharon Welch, Carol Christ, and Margaret Miles. I cannot journey toward a new maleness without including the thought of both James Cone *and* Katie Cannon,[25] raising their intellectual voices together for the uplift of the community.

An important biblical resource of the communal experience of power may be found in the Pentecost story (Acts 2). In that experience, the disciples were given divine power to speak in new tongues to all nations. This divine empowerment manifested itself first in the creation of a new community that shared "all things in common" (Acts 2:44). The conversion of the disciples was accompanied by a spiritually empowered willingness to change their attitude toward possessions. Such a change enabled them to have the power to create and sustain a new community.

Power needs to be distributed multiculturally in units of care. Care is not abstract, but manifests itself by the conscious providing of economic opportunities for the powerless to develop both their own communities and more meaningful concrete ties with the dominant community. Dignity, self-esteem, and self-worth in the United States are measured in units of economic power, so it is the single most important aspect of power to be restructured in a just fashion. I am not asking for government handouts, or currying favor with any current political party line. Rather, I am speaking of the economic crisis that is crippling the African American community in general, and Black males in particular, as one of the most important areas in which new men and a new vision of power can effect a positive change. The economic uplift and empowerment of all poor persons is also part and parcel of my concern.

Such power would transform the importance of listening away from listening in order to effectively silence criticism to listening in order to grow together. The first kind of listening envisions a combative activity in which one's intellectual guard is always on the defensive. The second kind of listening is open to instruction, correction, criticism, and praise because its intent is to upbuild community. Further, the listening would include women as well as men, deliberately avoiding the kind of devaluing of women's perspectives still present in the men's movement. These ideas will be developed more fully in chapter 3.

As I move toward constructing a new understanding of African American maleness, a genuinely new definition of power is fundamental. Such a new definition of power suggests an Xodus definition of masculinity that incorporates the Elders, Adam (the Keeper of the Garden), and Abraham as

Africentric new images. Xodus males are not afraid to operate out of their Blackness or to go through the Eye of Horus to embrace the spiritual energy of their Blackness. An Xodus man is one who courageously contributes educational, spiritual, and material resources to the community. He values the outer community he lives in because he is so attuned to the inner Community of Self. As a person who values the community first, he is powerful because he is intimate, willing to listen, imbued with spiritual power, and able to "hear" the inner citizens as well as the women with whom he journeys. Taking himself, his Afrikan self, and his Blackness seriously, he is able to take the concerns, criticisms and pain of the sisters seriously also. It is to this particular form of "hearing" that we turn in chapter 3.

Notes

1. This definition arises from my association with Rev. D. C. Nosakhere Thomas, founder of Southern California's Toward Black Manhood, Inc. He is currently developing his own pastoral counseling model in an Africentric voice.
2. This is the classic definition given by Molefi Kete Asante in several of his texts: *The Afrocentric Idea* (Philadelphia: Temple University Press, 1987); *Afrocentricity* (Trenton, N.J.: Africa World Press, 1988); and most recently restated in *Malcolm X as Cultural Hero* (Trenton, N.J.: Africa World Press, 1994).
3. Na'im Akbar, *The Community of the Self* (Jersey City, N.J.: New Mind Productions, 1985), 2.
4. Ibid., 4–5.
5. Ibid., 7–8.
6. Ibid., 9–10.
7. Ibid., 11–12.
8. Ibid., 12.
9. Ibid., 15–24.
10. Na'im Akbar, *Visions for Black Men* (Nashville: Winston-Derek, 1991), 7.
11. Ibid., 52.
12. See Ron Maulana Karenga, *Selections from the Husia: Sacred Wisdom of Ancient Egypt* (University of Sankore Press, 1989), 58–60 in "The Book of Amenomope," and 109–11 in "The Book of Coming Forth by Day."
13. See Karenga, *Selections from the Husia,* as well as *The Kawaida: Introduction to Black Studies* (Los Angeles: University of Sankore, 1979), for further elaboration of the connections between Kemetic ethics and Western religions.
14. Karenga, *Husia,* p. 32 in "The Book of Khun-Anup."
15. Richard King, M.D., *African Origin of Biological Psychiatry* (Germantown, Tenn.: Seymour-Smith, 1990).
16. Ibid., 23.
17. Ibid., 28.
18. It is intriguing to me that King insists that this melanin core has an anthropological meaning such that "Humanity may differ in outer appearance, with

variations of colors but internally they are all black, all African at the core."
Ibid., 24.

19. This understanding of power owes much to the work of Sharon Welch.
20. Based on a revelatory conversation with Prof. Clark Williamson on the nature of power (Christian Theological Seminary, Indianapolis, 20 August 1991).
21. To build on the insightfully phrased title of *The Intimate Connection: Male Sexuality, Masculine Spirituality* (Philadelphia: Westminster, 1988), an important work on intimacy by James Nelson.
22. Sam Keen deals with this issue in *Fire in the Belly: On Being a Man* (New York: Bantam, 1991); cf. all previous titles cited in this chapter, plus James E. Kilgore, *The Intimate Man: Intimacy and Masculinity in the '80s* (Nashville: Abingdon Press, 1984), and John Lee, *The Flying Boy: Healing the Wounded Man* (Deerfield Beach, Fla.: Health Communications, 1987). Robert Moore and Douglass Gillette explore themes of power and intimacy in their volume *King, Warrior, Magician, Lover* (San Francisco: HarperCollins, 1990). Cf. also Aaron R. Kipnis, *Knights without Armor* (New York: Jeremy Tarcher/Pedigree Books, 1991).
23. Haki Madhubuti, *Black Men: Obsolete, Single, Dangerous?* (Chicago: Third World Press, 1990), 68.
24. I agree with Reinhold Niebuhr that the powerful will not voluntarily release their power. Cf. *Moral Man and Immoral Society* (New York: Scribners, 1932).
25. Cf. Katie G. Cannon's thoughts in *God's Fierce Whimsy: Christian Feminists and Theological Education,* edited by Katie G. Cannon, Carter Heyward, Beverly Harrison, Ada María Isasi-Díaz, Bess B. Johnson, Mary D. Pellauer, and Nancy D. Richardson [The Mudflower Collective] (New York: Pilgrim, 1985); and *Black Womanist Ethics* (Atlanta: Scholars Press, 1988).

CHAPTER 3

Taking Sisters Seriously

A t a time when most talk about the relation between male and female is cast metaphorically as "the battle of the sexes," it is good to affirm a love and respect for one's maleness as we learn to take sisters seriously. I love being an Africentric Christian male whose bright dashiki clothing incarnates a warmly embroidered heart, whose extroverted gestures are expressive of a fullness of personality, and whose creativity and love of the folk are passionate and enduring. This ode of self-respect and self-regard comes at a time when being "Black" and "male" could be considered a dangerously toxic combination, but some of us do *not* have prison records! Yet I cannot boast of not having a prison record while so many brothers languish in prison. Out of this chastened celebratory African-centered maleness must emerge a celebration of Black women too. The history and culture of woman-degradation that devalues the minds, hearts, bodies, and spirits of womenfolk cries for recognition by Black males if there is to be a liberating future. Of course, to posit the phrase "liberating future" is to express a hope for a future in which social, political, spiritual, and economic fortunes of both women and men are brighter than they are now. A major threat to a bright African American future is the crisis of relationship between African American females and males.

In light of this crisis, it is time to examine the most striking fundamental moral imperative of womanist theological ethics: the challenge to African American males to rid ourselves of sexism. It is but one aspect of the tri-dimensional reality of oppression (race/sex/class) that affects Black women's existence. The challenge of addressing sexism, however, is most salient to this particular analysis. Beginning with the thought of Jacquelyn Grant,[1] Katie Cannon, and Delores Williams, various womanist views condemning sexism can be understood as inseparably tied to aspirations of community liberation and racial solidarity. Liberation is the telos and ultimate value womanists have used to encourage African American males, especially those who benefit from positions of authority in the hierarchy of Black churches, to end discriminatory practices based on gender within Black churches. Womanists have asked, "How can a community be liberated without full participation by all of its members?" So the task of this analysis is: (1) to lift up the critical moral imperative of attacking sexism in light of womanist multidimensional analyses,[2] particularly in Black churches and in the writings of Black male theologians as voiced by Delores Williams, Jacquelyn Grant, Frances Wood, Karen Baker-Fletcher, and Katie Cannon; (2) to affirm the work of James Cone and Dwight Hopkins in attacking Black male sexism and incorporating womanist theology as essential to a constructive Black theology; and finally, (3) to begin building the twin concepts of liberatory body-selfhood and liberatory partnership between African American females and males that encourage men to develop critical listening skills and participatory praxis.

Black Women's Experience: Window of Theo-Creativity

Delores Williams's *Sisters in the Wilderness* and Katie Geneva Cannon's *Black Womanist Ethics* proclaim the call for Black women's theological reflection to begin with a positive valuation of Black women's experience. While Cannon emphasizes that Black women's experience of the tridimensional reality of race, gender, and class oppression can be explored most fruitfully in the writings of Black women such as Zora Neale Hurston, she also makes it clear that Hurston's stories describe Black male sexist behavior as inextricably bound up in the daily experiences of Black women.[3]

Cannon has a particular interest in highlighting the power of Black male sexism within the church to relegate Black women's energies, skills, and talents.[4] As a theological ethicist, Cannon insists that Black men understand that this kind of relegation jeopardizes Black women's agency and compromises Black male liberative rhetoric at the same time. She sees the task of womanist ethical reflection as that of "revealing the hidden power relations inherent in the present social structures,"[5] both inside African American communities and outside them. Another way of understanding Cannon's project is to see it, to use her own words, as the demystification of "large and obscure ideological relations."[6] I would restate Cannon's challenge for Xodus creativity as follows: How can Black men loudly proclaim the denial of agency effected by the pervasive institutionalized presence of racism, while at the same time participating in an equally oppressive denial of Black women's agency? Such a restatement sharpens one's attention to the fact that those "large and obscure ideological relations" operate inside African American communities and institutions as well as outside. In fact, the very call to demystify ideologies of oppression must come to grips with the ways in which African American males contribute to female-relegating, sexist enclaves of exclusion.

By valuing the concrete daily institutional experiences of Black women, Cannon insists that her ethical work must direct "critical attention not only to scholarship in the fields of study but also to its concrete effects on women in the pews."[7] She insists that Black men understand the kind of "objectification, degradation, and subjection of the female" that takes place in Black preaching.[8] This is a particularly irksome thing for Cannon; she notes that a great deal of harmful mental content lies hidden in seemingly innocuous jokes, stories, and inferences. My cousin, Ruanne Jeter, calls this kind of lethal yet seemingly innocuous speech "mental mal-practice" or MMP. Combining Ruanne's phrase with Katie Cannon's, we can say that Black male preachers are too often guilty of MMP in regard to women's dignity, wrapped up in jokes about length of dresses or necklines. African American churches cannot reach the end-goal of an inclusive ethic until such MMP is faced squarely and honestly.

Williams also focuses specifically on Black male sexism in her ecclesiology, reminding us that even though Africentrism is becoming a positive force of cultural renewal in African American denominational churches, Black women must always stand against any ideological perspective that does not "take seriously Black women's experience as a source."[9] For Williams and for Cannon, Black women's experience, which Williams elaborates to mean "African American women's oppression and their intellectual, social, and spiritual history,"[10] is the fundamental place to begin taking Black women seriously. I interpret this statement to mean that one cannot truly claim allegiance to the African American community's liberation or to Black churches unless one takes the entire history of Black women's experience as seriously as that of Black males. To stand *for* African Americans is to stand *with* Black women, their tridimensional experience of oppression, their intellectual, economic, political, literary, and artistic achievements and disappointments. Taking Black women's experience as a source means to stand in solidarity with Black women. Such solidarity is the first step toward divesting ourselves of sexism because it moves beyond nodding and reluctant recognition to an appreciative willingness to let the whole story of Black people be told, by all members of the community.

Working Together: Solidarity

Karen Baker-Fletcher interprets solidarity as the incarnation of an operative norm, Black men working together with Black women. This working together is not a mere toleration of each other's presence, forgiving occasional sexist slights, gestures, and attitudes, but involves a second operative norm. In order to genuinely work together in solidarity, Black men need to be willing to remain open to ongoing challenges concerning our sexism.[11] African American male solidarity cannot be understood to be a static achievement, a settled state of affairs, but it is an ongoing process toward a just and loving manhood and womanhood. Solidarity is a becoming, a happening, an event that involves long-term commitment. Solidarity is a processive act of the will.

Toinette Eugene notes that Black women have often placed their own agenda and concerns secondary to what they considered to be the more inclusive concern for addressing racism. She attaches the moral values of care, compassion, and concern to the moral agenda of Black women from the antebellum Black church to the present.[12] Eugene rejoices in what she perceives as a kind of sexual equality in the domestic life of slave quarters, quoting approvingly from Angela Davis's work on this topic in her classic text *Women, Race and Class*. Citing egalitarian images of Black slave women as "strong, self-reliant, proud of their roots and of their ability to survive,"[13] Eugene holds up Harriet Tubman as an exemplary figure representing what innumerable other Black women did during those troubled times. For Eugene, Black women have always been ready to be in solidarity with Black men on the key issues of the day, from the suffrage movement of the late nineteenth and early twentieth century to contemporary attitudes toward feminism. In fact, Eugene provides an extended quote of the 1977 Black lesbian Combahee River Collective that calls for solidarity with Black men in fighting racism while at the same time fighting with Black men about their sexism.[14] For Eugene solidarity and survival are inseparable propositions, wedded throughout the historical trajectory of Black folk in the United States.

Marcia Riggs calls the African American community to address its classism as a way of advancing solidarity. In her thorough excavation of the almost-forgotten and surely neglected Black clubwomen's movement, Riggs notes that contemporary African Americans must retrieve the collective uplifting consciousness of Black clubwomen in order to exorcise demons of "false Black consciousness." Riggs names the contemporary Black struggle as an entrapment to false Black consciousness, "lacking awareness or understanding of what the relationship between individual autonomy and communal autonomy should be for Black persons and Black people as a community."[15] This entrapment is particularly apparent, for Riggs, in the upwardly mobile Black upper and middle classes. She names their moral crisis as that of buying into an ethos of "competitive individualism" in contradistinction to the Black clubwomen's ethic of "collective solidarity and intragroup social responsibility."[16] While retaining aspects of Black folk solidarity, Riggs faults Black affluent classes for their lack of vital connection and empathy with the lower classes of Black folk. She presents a comprehensive critique of the ways in which the lack of vital connection, participation, and empathy for lower classes of African Americans leads to problems of isolation and alienation. The point Riggs is driving home is that such isolation and alienation create "disunity where *functional* unity is essential for liberative struggle."[17] She sounds the almost forgotten clarion call of the Black clubwomen, "Awake! Arise! Act!" as three moral imperatives the African American community must act on in order to move into a liberating future.

Riggs provides Xodus reflection with a detailed description of the way in which class analysis must begin to be incorporated into a genuinely multidimensional cultural analysis. Class analysis ought to be an essential part of our critical reconstructive reinvention. As African American womanists challenge each other to become cognizant of ways that different class backgrounds, opportunities, and education skew understandings of the problems of Black people, so Xodus seekers must learn to listen to the various classes of African American women and men. There is not *one* story, or one way of looking at how we can come to a bigger and better future, but the folk have many stories, many problems, and many differing ways of telling "how they got over."

From Silencing to Metanoia-Mutuality

Solidarity is impeded by a vicious kind of silencing and dismissal of women's experience, according to Frances Wood.[18] Naming the locus of sexist behaviors as practiced in Black churches, as did Williams, Wood provides a scathing indictment of Black male silencing of women's voice, experiences, and suffering. Wood notes that Black men provide female churchgoers with a choice of two impossible roles, either as madonna — pure and undefiled, asexual — or the sexually promiscuous whore. Condemning both alternatives, and the absence of adequate prophetic fervor concerning gender justice, Wood's solutions call for Black men to change their attitudes dramatically — a metanoia.[19]

Wood is convinced that the unwritten "eleventh commandment — thou shalt not criticize male behavior," can be transformed into an Ethic of Mutuality wherein Black men will join Black women in "seeking justice, loving kindness, and humbly walking with God" more than seeking a patriarchal form of manhood.[20] Such an ethic deliberately extracts sexism from Black male attitudes, behaviors, and socialization.[21] The Ethic of Mutuality insists that part of the liberation task of Black churches is that issues of gender justice join the platform alongside issues of racial justice. Wood's Ethic of Mutuality holds that racial solidarity must become more important than being "real men." The kind of metanoia required of Black males calls for a kind of inward turn that details ways in which African American males have: (1) internalized misogyny; (2) been in collusion with degrading images of women; and (3) left male gender-privilege unchallenged.[22] Such a challenge goes to the heart of the kind of concrete "hard internal work" African American men are being called to do if Xodus Space is to become real.

Traditional arguments of what Cornel West has aptly named "liberal structuralists," which emphasized a kind of "environmental determinism" that condemned Black males to a life trajectory from poor educational opportunities to unemployability and criminal behaviors,[23] cannot aid African American males in this endeavor. Indeed, such ideas have often been used by apologists for the Black community as a means of describing certain pathologies without taking responsibility for them. In this way, and only in this certain sense, Xodus Space agrees with various conservative "New Black Vanguard" thinkers (Glenn Loury and Shelby Steele) who decry such Black apologetics as irresponsible, while proclaiming the importance of moral formation to a better Black future. The kind of intragroup and collective social responsibility that Black clubwomen extolled resonates with the intra-African community orientation that Xodus imparts. So the rapprochement with the conservative crowd disappears rather quickly when tested by womanist norms of collective responsibility.

Brothers Respond . . .

Responding to the earliest challenges of Jacquelyn Grant and Katie Cannon, James Cone's "Black Theology, Black Churches, and Black Women" chapter in *For My People* contains a detailed denunciation of Black male sexist behavior in Black churches. Cone takes a critical view of the exclusionary practices of African American males in a historical summary, offers support and openness to the project of womanist theology, and presents the following six points as a prophetic denunciation of Black male sexism:

1. Black male ministers must take responsibility for the ways in which women's humanity, women's service, and women's potential are developed in their churches.
2. Black men need to recognize that women's liberation is viable, to be treated with serious respect, and not as an object of derision.
3. Black men ought to learn the "art of listening" to women's stories and experiences.
4. In order to understand what we are listening to, Black men need to educate ourselves about women's history and issues by reading as much of the literature available as possible.
5. Male ministers must insist on affirmative action for Black women with a view toward greater access to leadership responsibilities in the churches.
6. Black male ministers ought to support the historical research Black women are doing, searching for female role models.[24]

The previous six points are the most comprehensive and direct critique of Black male sexism by an African American male theologian. Cone's critique does not push beyond the confines of the church walls to address Black male sexism generally, however. Cone's most recent monograph, *Martin & Malcolm & America*, reveals the ways in which prominent leaders such as Malcolm X and Martin Luther King, Jr., were bound by the sexist ideologies of their day. He strongly encourages African American males to self-consciously move beyond traditional female-exclusionary modes of thought and practice as a necessary aspect of a contemporary Black liberatory praxis.[25]

Cornel West suggests the possibility of widening the discourse, making complementary references to the womanist prophetic tradition in *Prophetic Fragments*,[26] but he does not develop a consistent or coherent criticism of Black male sexism. We must look elsewhere to find Black males speaking out against sexism. For example, Michael Eric Dyson takes on the issue of sexism in his excellent cultural critique, *Reflecting Black*.[27] Haki Madhubuti's radical Africentric cultural critique weaves the issue of Black male sexism throughout his two recent books, *Black Men: Obsolete, Single, Dangerous?*[28] and *Why L.A. Happened*.[29]

It is time to lift up the fact that no Black male theologian has chosen to dedicate an entire book to the matter of self-conscious African American maleness from a theological and ethical perspective. Sexism must be confronted both in the churches and in the streets. More urgently, it is the moral responsibility of African American males to name sexism wherever it arises

— in churches, mosques, community meetings, and the street corners. It is a moral imperative to actively fight the internal cultural construction and external manifestations of sexism, and to encourage each other in the struggle to exorcise sexism's grip over the colonized desires of all males. In conversation with womanists, Black male theologians and ethicists must go about the task of reinventing African American maleness by recolonizing male desire in such a way that dismissing and silencing women is considered a moral evil.

Second-generation Black theologian Dwight Hopkins has chosen a different way of addressing womanism. His *Shoes That Fit Our Feet* includes womanist theological reflection and ethical norms as necessary aspects of a contemporary constructive Black theology. Dubbing Toni Morrison's wonderful novels *Song of Solomon, The Bluest Eye,* and *Beloved* "womanist" texts, Hopkins presents Black women's folk religiosity as representative of a "spirituality of funk."[30] In agreement with Cone, Hopkins takes on the "male chauvinism" of both Martin Luther King and Malcolm X, suggesting ways in which Black women's role in the freedom movement can be better appreciated.[31] No other Black male theologian has included as detailed an analysis of a Black woman's writings as Hopkins, indicative of a serious intent to meaningfully incorporate Black women's thought into the constructive project of second-generation Black theologians. Hopkins's chapter on Black women's thought, however, according to womanist theologian Karen Baker-Fletcher, does not reveal a true conversation or dialogue with womanist theologians and ethicists. Instead, Hopkins extrapolates from the writings of Morrison an interesting religious interpretation that he calls womanist. It is an open question whether Hopkins's womanism is the same as that of Baker-Fletcher, Cannon, Grant, Williams, and others. So, while I will not condemn a brother Black theologian for a noble attempt at practicing the norm of inclusion of women's voices, and while it is clear he takes Morrison's voice seriously, concrete conversation with womanists is missing.

I propose that African American males cannot rid ourselves of sexist thought and practice without a general cultural critique that deconstructs sexist behaviors, attitudes, and beliefs; that names how Black sexism is interwoven with the pervasive presence of a patriarchy that reproduces itself in the behaviors of both men and women; and that moves toward reconstruction and reinvention of male selfhood, valorizing an inclusive, nonsexist, and communal ethos. Such a generalized cultural critique of sexism in Black men must become part of the current Africentric movement that I refer to as our Xodus. We are reinventing ourselves in light of our lost-found African heritages, intentionally moving outside of European-American intellectual and cultural hegemony. Xodus is our rediscovery of and recentering in a past as ancient as the pyramids, as rich as the oil under the Sahara, as vast as the Kalahari, as mysterious as the great Zimbabwe, and as relevant as our everyday struggles to live a dignified life within the walls of Euro-domination. It is "X"-odus because we are still a people "in search of" our identity, our ancestry, and our disrupted, "dis-remembered"[32] tribal names — as Malcolm X and Elijah Muhammad's teachings persistently reminded us in the 1960s. Such a communitywide reinvention cannot be a liberating rein-vention if it is not the self-conscious Journey of both Black women and Black men. Further, such a reinvention cannot be complete unless it includes a comprehensive debunking of the ways in which Black males have bought into patriarchal ideals of masculinity.

Loved-Filled Listening as Shared Power

A thoroughgoing masculine reinvention involves cultural critique. Cultural critique cannot be credible without developing ongoing critical listening skills and dialogue. Such listening requires a new valuing of the importance of women's voices, thoughts, opinions, and criticism based on the funda-mental theological dictum that we are all created in the image of God/dess. It means that we must listen to *all* of the sisters, including lesbians.

Renee Hill insists that acknowledging the active and committed presence of lesbians (and gays) in Black churches is an important listening issue. Such deep listening, a listening that compels heterosexist feelings and intuitions to surface, is a justice issue in Hill's view.[33] Hill claims that the issue of sex-uality is rooted in our perception of human nature because "sexuality is a part of human nature, the human nature that God created and called good." As a Christian lesbian, Hill demands that African American churches begin to widen the boundaries of what it means by "sexuality" beyond the sexual "act (genital sexual contact)" to viewing sexuality as an integral "part of liv-ing, an aspect of understanding one's self, and as a way of being in rela-tionship with other people."[34]

Having been raised in a traditional community, I admit that I have strug-gled at times with ways in which we can affirm homosexuals and yet be obedient to the biblical injunctions concerning homosexuality. Many Christians within the African American community believe sincerely that we cannot affirm both homosexuals and the Bible. I have heard many a ser-mon and teaching where homosexuals were summarily dismissed to "burn-ing in hell." The other strategy often employed by many Black churches is akin to President Bill Clinton's policy on gays in the military — "Don't Ask, Don't Tell!" Such a policy encourages avoidance and denial, and does not grapple with the flesh-and-blood reality of those brilliant and ordinary, tal-ented homosexuals who preach, play the organ, and sing glorious songs of praise to God in our churches. Both condemnation and avoidance fail to listen to the pain, the promise, and the hopes of flesh-and-blood lesbians and gay men.

Am I saying that we ought to affirm homosexuals and ignore God's Word? I am saying that if we believe in a God whose message of salvation, healing, deliverance, and redemption is for *all* people, then some of those "all people" are homosexual. The gospel's message has an indescribable effect, transforming gangsters into teachers, prostitutes into preachers. If we do not present the gospel to gays and lesbians in a manner that listens to their flesh-and-blood sexuality, we have failed the gospel because we have prevented souls from being saved and lives from being transformed. Am I saying that homosexuals need to be transformed? Yes, just as much as heterosexuals, but the transformation God renders should not be predicated on whether a person changes his or her sexual orientation.

In a recent workshop two questions were asked of the participants: (1) Write down the first things that come to your mind when you think about your spirituality; and (2) write down the first things that come to mind when you think about your sexuality. We were all amazed to find out that the lists compiled for both questions were remarkably similar. Both questions elicited feelings of ecstasy, compassion, passion, pure love, warmth, and power. For flesh-and-blood human beings our spiritual connection to God is intimately related to how we experience ourselves as sexual beings. This is not scandalous. It is part of what God apparently intended. Such a divine intent ought to be extended to homosexuals, even if we heterosexuals do not "understand" them, or feel uncomfortable around them. We become God's people, in the fullness of what that phrase means, when we can sustain our community and nurture all of its members, no matter what their sexual orientation. We are living through a pivotal chapter in the history of Christianity where questions about sexuality and gender roles are in a state of transformation and flux. We must hold on to each other and to God's "Unchanging Hand" until we "understand it better, by and by."

It is important that Xodus Space pry open all forms of oppressive behaviors that degrade, defile, and negate life energies, especially (though not exclusively) within the global African community. Black men must find ways to listen to women who love women (in every way), because they are our mothers, daughters, sisters, aunts, cousins, and nieces too. Xodus cannot afford to shut out anyone in this freedom struggle, even though such "out of the closet" theologizing and ethical reflection has usually been ignored by Black Christians. The debate, discussion, and contention about this issue must begin for Xodus men around the issue of listening.

Listening takes seriously the words, gestures, tears, anguish, and joy of Black women because listening is a profound expression of love. Such love-filled listening takes Black women's soulful interpretation of who they are, what they have been through, and why they are continuing to trust in God — their experience — with tender seriousness.

The kind of deep, love-filled listening I speak of is also a form of shared power. Emilie Townes deconstructs traditional patriarchal construals of power as being based on the obedience model of dominance-submission. Power, so construed, becomes a property of discrete and separate entities that identifies some as possessing dominance and others as submissive.[35] Instead, Townes calls on a new form of shared power that "requires openness, vulnerability, and readiness to change." Townes provides a transforming view of power. In her view, shared power includes the following attributes:

1. dynamic
2. responsible to moral agents for personal and social transformation
3. active in cooperation and mutual respect
4. a process happening through us
5. a summons to develop nurturing capacities
6. a summons to develop empathy
7. a summons to develop capacities of interconnectedness
8. a justice project [36]

Even more radically, if Black men believe that listening honors the image of God/dess in women, and that part of listening is to be open to the challenging critique of our sexism, then we ought to honor the developing consciousness of our own image of God/dess. When I listen to my spouse criticizing sexist attitudes and behaviors, and I receive her challenge as an expression of her love and not as an emasculating polemic, I grow in spiritual and moral perfection. By "perfection" I refer to that act of continuing ongoing moral and spiritual renewal and transformation that Wesley called sanctification, and the old saints in my home church called "running the race." Such listening becomes a way of becoming our best self — a self that is internally and externally connected to one's thoughts, emotions, and actions. This connected self is, I think, more aptly described as our Becoming Bodyself. It is a self-in-the-making, open to reform, challenge, criticism, hugs, embraces, fire, and rain. The Becoming Bodyself cannot emerge unless we value listening.

The Becoming Bodyself

The Becoming Bodyself of African American Xodus masculinity ought to embrace all efforts taken by Black women to value all necessary skills: survival, "setting things aright" (Toinette Eugene),[37] and liberation. Too often, according to womanists, Black males have focused solely on what "white folks" are doing to "us," instead of looking at the resources, skills, and talents within the community. This is not to say that constant challenge and resistance of racism is unnecessary, but to correct the distortion of Black male thought that race is the sole issue affecting our people. As Becoming Bodyselves learn to rejoice in the things we have achieved — Black women and men working together — we can learn to value the amazing physical and bodily struggle that continues to unfold for many Black women.

For instance, the dangerously high incarceration rates that criminalize or make ineligible (for marriage or lifelong commitments) over 50 percent of young Black males (18–34 years of age) have a profoundly negative effect on Black women as well. The problem is not just what happens to young Black boys; the crisis is crippling Black girls too. The crisis is threatening all aspects of African American life — from the affluent middle class who "remembers who and whose they are" to the most unemployable person living by the quickness of his trigger finger and luck. Learning to value our male Becoming Bodyselves, we ought to urge others to value the Becoming Bodyselves of sisters.

Such is not an easy value to impart, particularly in light of the currently fashionable norm proclaimed in many Black churches that emphasizes building up Black men first before Black women's concerns. Such a view purports and supports the "headship" of the male in family and society based on a sexist biblical hermeneutic. In order to overturn the momentum of the popular "Guys First" sexist mentality, it is a moral imperative that African American male theologians and ethicists speak out against sexist biblical hermeneutics. We ought to encourage African American churchgoers to become familiar with the kind of sexually inclusive biblical scholarship exemplified in the writings of Cain Hope Felder, Clarice Martin, Renita Weems, Thomas Hoyt, Vincent Wimbush, and other African American biblical scholars. We ought to encourage parishioners to read *Troubling Biblical Waters* (Felder), *Stony the Road We Trod* (edited by Felder), and *Just a Sister Away* (Weems). Conquering sexist biblical interpretations of "headship" ideals and so-called biblical nuclear families with balanced liberating biblical interpretation may stop the oppressive harangue black Christians have recently been seduced to believe is true.

Overturning sexist biblical hermeneutics that constrict the roles of women to the private sphere of domestic concerns is not a way of disrespecting motherhood or the family. Motherhood and family will not be affirmed in Xodus Space without an equally strong affirmation of fatherhood, but not patriarchal fatherhood. To affirm a nonpatriarchal, nonsexist fatherhood is a full-time Xodus project because we are living at the edge of a new era of parenting. This new era is uncomfortable for all people because it has released women from a self-understanding that confined their aspirations to the raising of children, flooding the public sphere with highly motivated and educated women competing with males for positions that used to be held only by men. At the same time that women have been liberated from a constricted private sphere, men have not been challenged to discover new roles, responsibilities, and obligations in the private sphere. Men, including those millions of Afrikan males who are employed, still aspire to enter the public sphere of workplace, public duty, and leadership in their communities. Men still believe that the home is the sphere of family, warmth, and womanhood that a man retires to after dealing with "the Man" all day. Unfortunately, such a view is not in step with the reality that women are working too. Who is there to raise the children? Who is present and willing to take care of the bruised egos, hurt feelings, and exhaustion that daily labor in the public sphere always creates? No one. Nobody is willing to recognize the ways in which we require women to be superwomen, especially Black women. Black women are expected to be competent, hard-driving, professional workers all day long, and then shift hats and become sexually alluring, child-rearing, family cooks at night. Where is the Space for Afrikan women to take care of themselves unless Afrikan males find ways to create that Space together with Afrikan women? The challenge of our age is to discover new ways to be male and female. Xodus listening insists that we ought to discover these new ways in solidarity.

Xodus men recognize that men must learn to be competent in the private sphere of cooking, cleaning, sewing, and washing. Such a public declaration of the importance of male competence in the private sphere of family, hearth, and home is a revolutionary declaration of war against patriarchal fatherhood. We must utterly deconstruct and destroy all the firm foundations of privilege that sexist fatherhood practices rely on, because being a father is a state of mind first. Xodus men therefore need to learn how to cook (if we don't already know how), how to sew, how to take care of a home in order to be fully competent men, not overly dependent on women's domestic skills in order to be comfortable.

I was blessed to have a Jamaican father who enjoyed cooking and was good at it. His savory seasoning is ingrained in my home memories just as much as my mother's. My father vacuumed the carpets while my mother washed the floors, every Saturday morning. I was taught how to keep house by both of my parents. The beautiful thing about such memories is that those times of "keeping house" were important for bonding as a family. It was a Saturday morning ritual in the Fletcher home to put on "the music" while we worked. That music was played on the then-revolutionary breakthrough in audio equipment, the "stereophonic hi-fi." The music was a combination of Jamaican calypso, Harry Belafonte, South African Miriam Makeba, European classics like Rimski-Korsakov's "Scheherazade" and Tchaikovsky's "Nutcracker Suite." As I became a teenager, my parents and I danced-mopped to the sounds of Diana Ross and the Supremes, the Temptations, Marvin Gaye, and even an occasional Beatles hit. We laughed, talked, and shared weekly stories during that time of "keeping house." One of my most vivid memories of those Saturday mornings was how particular my father was about getting things "right," which meant getting the floors, carpets, clothes, and whatever else spotlessly clean. He took as much pride in having the house being a place of sparkling brightness and good smells as did my mother. From my parents I first learned the importance of women and men creating a liberating Space at home together. My mother and father were liberatory partners.

My father remains my primary example of what an Xodus male ought to be. An Xodus man is free enough to liberate himself from overdependence on women to perform domestic duties while affirming women's independence and need for male interdependence. To affirm this is to imply that any male who rests easily in patriarchal roles of maleness and fatherhood is not really a fully mature human being because he is too dependent and not willing to gain competence in the private sphere of fatherhood . . . Xodus fatherhood.

Xodus males must join womanists and all Afrikan women in a liberatory partnership so that together we might create Xodus Space within our churches and community. We need Xodus Space in Black churches, where the praxis of liberation is led and supported by both women and men. While the task of developing what Xodus Space within Black churches could be will be more fully elaborated in the last chapter, we can begin here. Xodus Space ought to join Emilie Townes in calling for Black churches to affirm a "New Covenant" that moves us beyond "a ritualized, a sterilized, a codified, and a magnificently vacuous faith to one that comes from the heart, soul, and intellect."[38] Such strong rhetoric is not meant to "diss" (rap language for "disrespect") Black churches, but to challenge them to move beyond the dramatic cultural "form-and-fashion" faith (that is exciting without being necessarily transformative) to a dramatic New Covenant faith that incarnates a dynamically inclusive ethic. A New Covenant faith for African American churches will radically transform traditional patriarchal practices in Black churches, reviving "dead bones" into living bodies.

African American churches need to be the site where Black women and men can hear each other's pain, insecurities, sufferings, and longings without reproach, fear, or intimidation. But liberatory partnership cannot be achieved until Black men help make churches safe places for women to be fully human. The onus of responsibility is on African American males. We must make it clear to men and women who have internalized self-hatred that sexist attitudes and expressions are morally unacceptable, spiritually bankrupt, and bereft of prophetic power. There is power in standing up as liberating partners, female and male. It is a power that our children will sit up and watch, and with God's help, eventually incarnate as part of what it means to be a mature adult.

Being liberatory partners means aiding each other in the ongoing self-critical process that creates healthy Becoming Bodyselves. It means trusting that we will come through our lives from youth to old age enfolded in each other's respect, sharing all things. Such acts are not romanticized or utopian, but necessary for envisioning a healthy Black future. Liberatory partners are not afraid of envisioning because they know that through the sharing of our dreams and hopes we put ourselves into the right spiritual Space to be blessed by the divine. The "Godforce" Williams honors as the invisible "Black Church" — something she adamantly distinguishes from "African American denominational churches" because of the latter's insidious sexism[39] — operates in the Holy Xodus Space that liberatory partners create. The Godforce allows for times to be separate and times to be together, because in that healing Space black women and men have enough room to flourish. For now, such an Xodus Space is real only in visionary proclamation and on the written page. It *is* coming, just as surely as we can envision it. It is coming, just as soon as we will to make it.

In the last three chapters we have set forth a philosophical, theological, and ethical justification for the creation of Xodus Space. We have set forth the importance of revaluing and embracing Blackness as a positive spiritual force for reinvigorating Afrikan life. In the next part, "The Gathering of the Elders," we return to the African village ethos of gathering around the council fires in order to confer with the wisdom of our Elders. Our Elders provide experience, insight, and vision. The future strength of the Xodus depends on our reconnecting and building on their wisdom. We "stand on the shoulders of the Ancestors" — a common proverb in Africa denoting the significance of remembering and honoring the life contributions and experiences of one's ancestors.

Notes

1. Jacquelyn Grant, *White Women's Christ, Black Women's Jesus* (Atlanta: Scholars Press, 1989); and "The Sin of Servanthood," in *A Troubling in My Soul* (Maryknoll, N.Y.: Orbis, 1993), 199–216.

2. Kelly Delaine Brown, "God Is as Christ Does: Toward a Womanist Christology," *Journal of Religious Thought* 46, no.1 (Summer-Fall 1989): 8.
3. Katie G. Cannon, *Black Womanist Ethics* (Atlanta: Scholars Press, 1988).
4. Katie Cannon, "Hitting a Straight Lick with a Crooked Stick," in *Black Theology: A Documentary History, Vol. 2: 1980–1992,* edited by James H. Cone and Gayraud S. Wilmore (Maryknoll, N.Y.: Orbis, 1993), 305.
5. Ibid., 304.
6. Ibid., 303.
7. Ibid., 305.
8. Ibid.
9. Delores Williams, *Sisters in the Wilderness* (Maryknoll, N.Y.: Orbis, 1993), 213.
10. Ibid.
11. The two ideas of solidarity and ongoing challenge to sexism are part of the collegial conversations between Karen Baker-Fletcher and me, especially during a conference on multiculturalism where Karen spoke on "The Womanist Contribution to Multiculturalism," California State University at Northridge, November 1993.
12. Toinette Eugene, "Moral Values and Black Womanists," in *Black Theology,* 2:310.
13. Ibid., 312.
14. Ibid.
15. Marcia Riggs, "A Clarion Call to Awake! Arise! Act!" in *A Troubling in My Soul: Womanist Perspectives on Evil and Suffering,* edited by Emilie M. Townes (Maryknoll, N.Y.: Orbis, 1993), 74–75.
16. Ibid., 75.
17. Ibid.
18. Frances Wood, "Take My Yoke upon You," in *A Troubling in My Soul,* 39–40.
19. Ibid., 44.
20. Ibid., 45.
21. Ibid., 40.
22. Ibid., 42, 45.
23. Cornel West, *Race Matters* (Boston: Beacon, 1993).
24. James H. Cone, *For My People: Black Theology and the Black Church* (Maryknoll, N.Y.: Orbis, 1984), 137–38.
25. James Cone, *Martin & Malcolm & America* (Maryknoll, N.Y.: Orbis, 1992).
26. Cornel West, *Prophetic Fragments* (Grand Rapids, Mich., and Trenton, N.J.: Eerdmans Publishing and Africa World Press, 1988), 45–48.
27. Dyson devotes an entire chapter to "Sex, Race, and Class: Two Cases," in *Reflecting Black: African-American Cultural Criticism* (Minneapolis: University of Minnesota Press, 1993), 167–79.
28. Haki Madhubuti, *Black Men: Obsolete, Single, Dangerous?* (Chicago: Third World Press, 1990).
29. Haki Madhubuti, ed., *Why L.A. Happened: Implications of the '92 Los Angeles Rebellion* (Chicago: Third World Press, 1993).
30. Dwight N. Hopkins, *Shoes That Fit Our Feet: Sources for a Constructive Black Theology* (Maryknoll, N.Y.: Orbis, 1993), 49–83 (chap. 2).
31. Ibid., 191–94.

32. A marvelous word that Karen Baker-Fletcher borrowed from Toni Morrison's *Beloved* and has developed into a womanist theological category. Karen Baker-Fletcher uses the Morrisonian paired phrases "dis-remembered" and "unaccounted for" as a way of describing the womanist search for engaging "in a process of rememory in part by remembering and reexamining African American myths." *A Singing Something: Womanist Reflections on Anna Julia Cooper* (New York: Crossroad, 1994), 200.

33. Renee Hill, "Who Are We for Each Other? Sexism, Sexuality and Womanist Theology," in *Black Theology,* 2:349–350.

34. Ibid., 347.

35. Emilie Townes, "Living in the New Jerusalem: The Rhetoric and Movement of Liberation in the House of Evil," in *A Troubling in My Soul,* 86.

36. Ibid., 86–87.

37. Toinette Eugene, "Moral Values and Black Womanists," 313.

38. Townes, "Living in the New Jerusalem," 89.

39. Williams, *Sisters in the Wilderness,* 204–10.

The GATHERING
of the Elders

Council of Ancestors: African American Male Bodies

istory sometimes flows in violent eddies and swirling currents. The historical stream of time that created a "New World" for European immigrants swept African American men and women into places of profound exploitation, sacrifice, and yet unquenchable love. While Europeans were fleeing from religious tyranny and oppression, they set themselves as masters and mistresses of dark-skinned slaves. Former peasants, outcasts, and even prisoners could become the rulers and dominators of black-skinned bodies in the "New World" of America. The domination that was achieved over the minds and bodies of enslaved Africans was never as complete as slavers imagined, but it was systemic, pervasive, and effective in perpetuating itself from 1619 to 1865.

In order to understand the Xodus Journey in its African American specificity, it is important to see how male bodies have been perceived historically. While African American male bodies are sites of labor, instruments of pleasure, or vengeful entertainment in the contemporary postmodern world, we must look at the interaction of three factors in this historical investigation: (1) how Black bodies were understood by whites, (2) how Blacks imaged ourselves, and (3) the role religion played both positively and negatively. We embark on an ideological excavation of the social discourse of institutionalized slavery from which negative images of the Black body were constructed and exploited.

One must also understand how African American persons extracted meaning from those exploitive practices, sometimes even wresting positive body-valuations from the degraded and stereotyped bodiliness of white construction. The role that religion, particularly Christianity, played in constructing both the negative discourse of exploitation by the exploiters and a positive reaction to that exploitation by the exploited cannot be overemphasized. I shall examine in a detailed fashion representative documents for their theological, christological, and ethical implications. Part of the analysis will show how certain myths of Black manhood (Sambo and John Henry) have functioned in an ambiguous way for African American male bodyself imaging. Part of the Xodus reconstructive and corrective task of these ambiguous legends requires a grounding in the positive power of the High John de Conquer legend and the historic revolutionary Nat Turner. In conclusion I shall present a way that African American males may move toward bodyself affirmation. Such an affirmation is already part of the current Africentric movement in intellectual, educational, and church circles. Africentricity is really a cultural and spiritual Xodus away from European-dominated Space. African American males must join the Xodus Journey, which requires a reinvigorated sense of body-selfhood as we construct a Space suitable for the flourishing of the bodies, souls, minds, and spirits of all African peoples.

Do They Have Souls?

Notions of converting "heathen" Africans to the "superior" religion of Christianity animated the missionary justification for slavery. Even as early as the late fifteenth century, noted historian Albert Raboteau has discovered, a Portuguese historian named Gomes Eannes de Azurara was providing a theological justification for the enslavement of Africans.[1] Azurara noted that the enslavement of African bodies was for their "greater benefit . . . for though their bodies were now brought into some subjection, that was a small matter in comparison of their souls, which would now possess true freedom for evermore."[2] Notice that Azurara implies that bringing bodies under "subjection" recognizes the matter of taking away someone's bodily freedom, but that such denial of bodily freedom is to be considered secondary in value to the greater benefit of possessing "true freedom for evermore" by converting to Christianity. Such a theological construal assumes three things that were to become fundamentally important to Christian justification for the enslavement of Africans:

1. *The soul is eternal.* The soul in its natural state is sinful, separated from God, threatened by eternal damnation, and requiring salvation. Such salvation is the freeing of the soul from the bounds of sin. Therefore Christian salvation is a salvation of the soul, and not of the body.

2. *The body is a container for the soul.* It may be detained or brought under the subjection of whip, chain, and slavery. The body is not as important as the soul, since it is the soul that is saved from damnation and judgment.

3. *Slavery is theologically justified* because it brought the bodies and souls of heathen Africans to Christians for the purpose of converting them.

Azurara's text is representative of how both the souls and bodies of Africans were evaluated from a purely Eurocentric value system. In another quote, Azurara constructed an implied hierarchy of culture in which African bodies were placed at the level of beasts:

And so their lot was now quite the contrary of what it had been; since before they had lived in perdition of soul and body; of their souls, in that they were yet pagans, without the clearness and the light of the holy faith; and of their bodies, in that they lived like beasts, without any custom of reasonable beings — for they had no knowledge of bread and wine, and they were without the covering of clothes, or the lodgement of houses; and worse than all, they had no understanding of good, but only knew how to live in bestial sloth.[3]

It is apparent in the above quote that African bodies and souls were placed on a lower level than European human beings in Azurara's Eurocentric valuing. Such judgmental notions as having "no knowledge of bread and wine," being without "covering of clothes," or "lodgement of houses" can be translated as meaning that Africans did not adhere to European ideals of proper food, clothing, and shelter.

Notions of bestiality that connected Africans with having no understanding of "the good," however, require a more finely nuanced reading of what "the good" was understood to be in this time. Azurara's quote itself suggests that at least part of his meaning of "the good" is "neither bestial nor slothful." What is unclear is whether Azurara meant to say positively that working hard and behaving as "reasonable beings" do (knowing how to feed, clothe, and shelter themselves) is what the good is. While it might seem that I am stretching a point about something we would now generally concede was a racist understanding of Africans, I assert that such notions still have currency in the marketplace of contemporary social values. The degradation of African customs, clothing, food, and relaxed attitudes toward work ("laziness") still infect the body politic of contemporary white Americans. So while most Americans might disapprove of the kind of rash religious judgments Azurara made, they practice his social-customary condemnations of the descendants of Africans in their everyday lives. The site whereby such condemnations are projected is the African American body.

White Americans struggled throughout the period of enslavement in the United States about whether it was proper to Christianize Africans. Azurara disconnected the subjection of African bodies from the question of whether Africans had souls, for he apparently held that Africans did possess souls. Americans seemed to sense that both proselytizing and baptizing Africans implied that they possessed souls worthy and equal to white souls, a socially dangerous proposition. It was dangerous because it implied that by possessing souls equal to whites', Africans might deserve the physical freedom of whites. Americans connected soul freedom to bodily freedom in a way that Azurara did not.

Arguing for the proposition that Africans possessed both souls and bodies, Anglican bishop Edmund Gibson instructed his slaveowner charges of the American colonies to

> Encourage and Promote the Instruction of their Negroes in the Christian faith . . . to consider Them, not merely as Slaves, and upon the same level with Labouring Beasts, but as Men-Slaves and Women-Slaves, who have the same Frame and Faculties with yourselves, and have Souls capable of being eternally happy, and Reason and Understanding to receive Instruction in order to it. [4]

Such an imperative must be understood as set against the prevailing contrary opinion about the state of Africans as persons. For many in the early American frontier, the only Africans who could be considered not as beastly, crude, possessing no soul, and having no rational capacity were those native-born in America. So-called "imported Africans" were considered unreachable. Native-born Africans, however, were often raised as Christians. Accordingly, Christianity itself had to be modified to accommodate the egalitarian evangelical nature of Christianity, which implied that all persons had souls and bodies of equal merit. Such a view of Christianity contradicted the view institutional slavery held that Black bodies were beastly property and that Black souls were not worthy of serious theological consideration.

By the mid-eighteenth century, with the swelling tide of the Great Awakening arousing the revival of both Black and white souls, Christianity had accommodated itself to the socioeconomic realities of slavery by insisting that Christianity made slaves better slaves. Such a stance effectively separated the salvation and freedom of Blacks' souls from the release of their bodies from physical bondage. Thus, by the mid-eighteenth century, Americans had finally achieved the theological justification necessary to ensure institutional longevity of slavery by separating soul freedom from physical bondage. The Portuguese had settled for the same thing comfortably in the late fifteenth century!

African Americans in slavery, however, understood the function of Christianity as that of "releasing the yoke" and "setting the captives free." Former slave Henry Bibb's critical letters to his former master, Albert Sibley, from Canada in 1852 demonstrated a sophistication in Black theological reasoning unexpected by whites. Bibb based his criticism of Sibley on the latter's avowed high standing in the Methodist church as a teacher of the Bible. Bibb held up a radically different understanding of Scripture than did Sibley, and so doing, stood the contradictory propositions of "slaveholding religion" on its head. Speaking about how he and his brothers had run away from bodily and mental bondage after serving for more than twenty years "without compensation," Bibb asked:

> Is this compatible with the character of a Bible christian? And yet I suppose that you, with your man robbing posse, have chased them [the brothers] with your dogs and guns, as if they were sheep-killing wolves upon the huge mountain's brow, for the purpose of re-capturing and dragging them back to a mental graveyard, in the name of law and slaveholding religion. [5]

In this quote Bibb reversed the implied perception of a slave body as a beast represented in the phrase "sheep-killing wolves." Instead of representing his brothers and himself as brutal "wolves," he morally reproved white males with dogs and guns as being evil hunters in the phrase "man robbing posse." The evil these hunters represented, for Bibb, was their acting on behalf of what was the accepted law and "slaveholding religion" of the United States. Bibb attacked the Methodist church with his own biblical exegesis in the following:

> Oh! what harmony there seems to be between these twin sisters: the Fugitive Slave Law and the Methodist E. Church — Listen to the language of inspiration. "Feed the hungry, and clothe the naked:" "Break every yoke and let the oppressed go free:" "All things, whatsoever ye would that men should do unto you, do ye even so unto them, for this is the law and the prophets."[6]

Notice how Bibb used a combination of prophetic injunctions with the Golden Rule to make his point. Bibb identified slaves as being the same as the oppressed of biblical injunction. Having drawn this similarity, Bibb demonstrated how even the central moral teaching of Christianity — the Golden Rule — could be applied to condemn the institution of slavery. Bibb went on to present his most devastating critique of the Methodist church:

> While on the other hand your church sanctions the buying and selling of men, women, and children: the robbing men of their wives, and parents of their off-spring — the violation of the whole of the decalogue, by permitting the

profanation of the Sabbath; committing of theft, murder, incest, and adultery, which is constantly done by church members holding slaves and form the very essence of slavery. Now, Sir, allow me with the greatest deference to your intelligence to inform you that you are miserably deceiving yourself, if you believe that you are in the straight and narrow path to heaven, whilst you are practising such abominable violations of the plainest precepts of religion.[7]

What is particularly striking about these passages from Bibb is his ability to self-consciously contrast the perceptions of beastliness projected on African descendants with his jeremiad against the moral repugnancy of slaveholders. In a profound way Bibb's insistence on the biblical phrase "break every yoke, and let the oppressed go free"[8] reveals an understanding of the connection between physical bondage and the yoking of the mind. He insisted that slavery was a "mental graveyard," a willful destruction of "social happiness,"[9] as well as a cruel institution that had broken the physical constitution of his mother. Bibb built a kind of legal case against Sibley and wove a mantle of accusation against the abusiveness of slavery: mental, emotional, physical, and spiritual. Finally, Bibb demonstrated the connection between the tenets of "slaveholding religion" and the psychic-physical abuse of Black bodies.

Sambo the Entertainer

The peculiar exploitive twist of African American male bodies may be revealed in the three-hundred-year career of the entertainer figure of Sambo. While Black female bodies were often forced to submit to the desires of white males for sexual "entertainment" in violent rape, Black male bodies entertained through self-ridicule, jokes, tomfoolery, and dancing. The degradation of both genders was related in a profound way to construals of maleness and femaleness. The reputed virginity and vaunted social construct of sexual "purity" and "true womanhood" attributed to white women were degraded in Black women by systematic rape, involuntary concubinage, and the loss of sexual control over their own bodies. The qualities of power, control, reason, and social poise attributed to white male slaveholders (remembering that even poor white males were exempted from this dignity) was denied Black males in the childish, emotional, and silly behavior of the Sambo character.

Even the naming of a Black clown character shows a process of systematic humiliation of African maleness. Sambo was the name settled upon through the eighteenth and nineteenth centuries for male slaves who danced and clowned for the entertainment of whites. Several names were regional favorites: John, George, Pompey, Sam, Uncle Tom, Uncle Remus, and Rastus. For female slaves certain names became fashionable, such as Diana, Mandy, Dark Mear, Brown Sugar, Auntie, and Aunt Jemima. The familial title Uncle or Aunt was given to slaves who had a hierarchical relationship to the masters.[10] The name Sambo apparently has West African roots, having a neutral meaning for the Hausa people ("second son," "name given to anyone called Muhammadu," and "name of a spirit"), a connotation of disgrace and shame for the Mende and Vai peoples, and even a meaning of "one in power."[11] Evidently the derogatory naming of Sambo arose from both English culture, where "Sam" was a name used often for a comic, and Spanish culture, where "Zambo" refers to "a person who is bowlegged or knock-kneed," or "a type of monkey."[12] The reference connecting Black male bodies and enforced comical behavior to that of a monkey was intentional. Europeans had called Congolese Africans "macaques," or rhesus monkeys, as a way of deriding their humanity. Such naming questioned whether Africans could be considered fully human, and misnamed their bodily movements as less than human.

Was Sambo a real flesh-and-blood character? Through a strange mixture of contempt and admiration — since whites enjoyed seeing their slaves dance, sing, and "make merriment" — the Sambo character became a perverse sociocultural product. Even in the early 1700s the dancing of slaves "made us pastime," according to the captain of a slave ship.[13] Viewing the obvious joy of the dancing captives, several captors noted with delight that these slaves demonstrated pleasure, satisfaction, and a good nature — suitable qualities for slaves! The Sambo figure was a blend of bodily gyrations, mimicking sounds, and rollicking laughter, observed by white captors and attributed to a stereotyped African behavior.

Whites were strangely drawn and repulsed at the same time by the ecstasy of the dances, the fervor of the humor, and high volume of African laughter. Even into the eighteenth and nineteenth centuries, the "passionate guffaw" of Blacks puzzled, delighted, and offended whites. For whites accustomed to puritanical notions of moderation, seriousness, and restraint, "the black laugh appeared . . . too vigorous, too unrestrained, and connoted frivolity and immediacy."[14]

The stereotype of the African male as a clown, a performer, a figure whose sole purpose in life was to entertain whites, "took root in white consciousness in the pre-Revolutionary period."[15] Those Blacks who seemed to have a talent for provoking the humor of whites were carefully cultivated and employed in the popular shows of that time. Legendary figures such as "Old King Charlie" and "Reverend Jonathan Todd" were known to entertain white adults and children for hours at a time.[16]

Sambo did not become a permanent part of North American culture until the character was written into the structure of traveling shows, light operas, and comedies. From the late eighteenth century into the mid-twentieth century, Sambo was in fact a blackface caricature of African males performed mostly by whites. While Southern whites had slaves to entertain them, the blackface white male was introduced in the North.[17] Dressed in outlandish costumes, speaking in exaggerated dialect taken to be that of a "Negro," the minstrel became a permanent fixture in American entertainment. Often minstrel shows would ridicule black illiteracy by giving the character the name "Professor," and denigrate black intelligence with long discourses such as the following:

> I hab come, as you all know, from 'way down in ole Warginna, whar I studded edicashun and siance all for myself, to gib a corse of lectures on siance gineraly, an events promiscously, as dey time to time occur. De letter ob invite I receibed from de komitee from dis unlitened city, was full ob flattery as a gemman ob my great discernment, edication, definement, and research could wish.[18]

Eric Lott believes that Sambo minstrelsy owed much more to the Punch-and-Judy and British clown tradition than to the animal tales and trickster traditions of African origin.[19] Lott claims that the two most highly recognizable figures on stages — the plantation rustic Jim Crow and the urban dandy Zip Coon — owe much of their bluster, exaggeration, and bravado to popular southwestern mythological figures such as Davy Crockett and Mike Fink performed with an exaggerated Negro dialect.[20] This ridiculing of Black males, according to Lott, allowed whites a "black mask . . . to play with collective fears of a degraded and threatening — and male — Other while at the same time maintaining some symbolic control over them."[21]

Lott provocatively suggests that the exaggerated bodiliness of the Sambo minstrel — especially dressed in a long, loudly colored tailcoat — implied white males' obsession with a "rampageous black penis."[22] In language colored by a cultural anthropologist's sensitivity to symbolism, Lott says:

> As [Ralph] Ellison puts it, "The Mask was the thing (the 'thing' in more ways than one)." Bold swagger, irrepressible desire, sheer bodily display: in a real sense the minstrel man *was* the penis, that organ returning in a variety of contexts, at times ludicrous, at others rather less so.[23]

If Lott's provocation is moving in the right direction, then it would be fair to say that the Black man represented by white men playing Black men was a "man on display." This male, on display for public consumption and amusement, provided a kind of ultimate symbol of the Black male body and of Black sexuality. It was a sexuality that was bold and threatening on the one hand, and laughably ridiculous on the other. The clowning and dancing dimension of performance took the fearful threat away, removing dignity and authenticity at the same time.

Blackface comedy was met in the Black community with ambiguous feelings. During the period of slavery, Joseph Boskin has noted, humor was an acceptable way for whites and Blacks to lessen the tremendous social chasm between them. Using Sigmund Freud's concept of humor as "wholly a social process wherein the shared experiences of the participants enable them to aggress and/or regress together,"[24] Boskin claims that humorous interchanges acknowledged whites as possessing a superior social location while at the same time "blacks were able to develop a repertoire of retaliatory humor to partially offset their situation."[25] If Blacks were allowed a "safe space" through clever forms of retaliatory humor, then we are left with the question of whether the Sambo figure could articulate that kind of humor. For this author it is apparent that Sambo's antics and humor were designed specifically for white amusement by his long articulations of exaggerated self-deprecation. Further, the figure of Sambo, created with greasepaint and burnt cork, provided too small a space for a satisfactory retaliation against white racism, even if some Blacks were playing out African trickster tales, which were then symbolized as tales of Sambo.

Black ambiguity toward Sambo, Jim Crow, Zip Coon, and the host of clowns became more complex from the late nineteenth century into the twentieth century. On the one hand, by the turn of the century the minstrel shows opened up opportunities for Blacks to compose original ragtime music. On the other hand, because the blackface style — with its exaggerated facial painting of white and red set against a charcoal black — was hegemonic, Black troupes were forced to wear the black makeup.[26] A strange phenomenon developed where authentically Black performers had to imitate white males in blackface imitations of Black life.

The celebratory physicality of African dancing and its enormous creative energy could be subtly introduced into the dancing of clown minstrelsy by Black performers. Blacks refined clown performance by adding "splits, jumps, and cabrioles."[27] Black minstrels wove current innovations such as the "jog, buck-and-wing, Virginia 'essence,' soft shoe, and stop-time dance" into their shows.[28]

If we examine the popularity of radio's "Amos-'n'-Andy" in the 1930s and '40s, the antics of Jimmy Walker in television's "Good Times," the recent swagger of Martin Lawrence in "Martin," or the antics of Urkel in "Family Matters,"[29] we see the Sambo character still very much alive and well. While minstrel shows were labeled as racist and eliminated in the 1960s, it is apparent that the residue of a centuries-old caricature remains firmly planted in the American mind. When white Americans are drawn to Black male (or female, for that matter) entertainers, most often it is their self-deprecating, exaggerated dialect, bright, mismatched clothes, and swaggering bodily movements that keep them popular. Such characteristics are the archetypal qualities of Sambo, who lives on as an enduring symbol in the entertainment world.

Moving beyond analyzing the entertainment world, there is a surprising retention of Sambo's threatening/ridiculous sexuality in whites' perceptions of Black males that deserves our attention. We must dig underneath the apparent presence of integration at job sites and examine the fabric of white-Black relationships. Contemporary Black males are stereotyped into two possible roles in our relationships with whites. We are perceived as either threatening because our language, gestures, bodily movement, and demeanor are not submissive and entertaining, or as funny because our bodily movements and humor remind whites of Sambo. Both of these perceptions are at the same time strangely attractive and repulsive to most whites. The underlying truth is that Blacks, male or female, are perceived as threatening to whites because we perceive ourselves as genuinely equal, whether we act in a threatening manner or not.

The Sambo, if we take Lott seriously, was a penis walking around on stage who yet symbolized reassuring control of that penis. If we examine the stereotypical reactions most African American males receive from whites, then it is not an exaggeration to claim that even now we are perceived to be threatening penises who need white control. African American males who are outspoken and not "funny" are ostracized from white society and "proper" Black middle-class society as being "too radical" (read "threatening"). The purported sexual prowess of Black males, more fiction than truth, becomes the invisible "spook sitting at the door" of every encounter with whites.

If Sambo is indeed a permanent fixture in white America's social mind, then it is up to African Americans to reconfigure that image in ways that are helpful to us. We must put together the shattered pieces of humanity that make up the traditional Sambo in a new fashion. Surely we must eliminate most of those pieces! We would have to eliminate his servile, self-deprecating, self-ridiculing speech and mannerisms. Our deconstruction would have to challenge both white Americans and Black Americans to debunk, unmask, and disentangle[30] the web of manipulative cultural production that has kept Sambo alive as a "funny" man.

After deconstructing the traditional Sambo, a positive reconstruction could use his qualities of humor as a way of blunting the threatening power of outspoken Black male presence. A new Sambo construction would hide allegedly threatening qualities behind swagger, outlandishness, and outrageous bravado. Sambo as a genuine psychological mask seems necessary for most whites who grasp at the idea that the United States is no longer racist. A mask, or masking behavior, seems appropriate if there is no other means for getting at the truth of racism's persistence. A sharply critical social rhetoric and critique of racism that is simultaneously humorous may provide a significant contribution toward a new view of African American maleness. Such qualities have surfaced momentarily in many of the comedians who came to the fore in the 1960s, such as Richard Pryor, Redd Foxx, and Bill Cosby. The ribald, hit-and-miss, exaggerated comedy of the controversial TV program "In Living Color" reveals that African Americans may yet be discovering how to reconstruct Sambo in a way that addresses white racism. If Sambo is a permanent fixture in American consciousness, for good and for ill, then intelligent African Americans will have to wrest some hidden positive potential meaning out of the archetype in order to flourish and live liberated lives.

John Henry the Worker

The legend of John Henry has actual historic roots in the late nineteenth century. Briefly retold, John Henry was a miracle-baby who was born with "a hammer in his hand." Able to do a "man's day of work" at an early age, he astonished his parents and community with outstanding feats of strength. After he left home, John Henry's feats of strength and endurance multiplied. Once he single-handedly turned the paddle wheel of a steamboat that had broken, bringing the passengers safely to shore after turning the wheel through a long, foggy night. Another time John Henry laid more track than any other worker in a day's stretch. The climax of the legend, of course, is the competition between John Henry and a steam drill to see which one would tunnel through a mountain first. The rapid blows of John Henry's hammer proved more powerful than those of the machine, but in the end, "He laid down his hammer and he died," as the concluding lyric of the folk song reports.

There are profoundly christological overtones in the John Henry legend that cannot be ignored. Positively, John Henry was a kind of Black Suffering Servant whose work was aided by supernatural strength. Born with miraculous power in his body, John Henry used his hammer as an instrument of creativity. In the paddleboat incident, his physical power became a force of deliverance, saving lives.

There are negative christological overtones as well. Instead of Christ as a conquering hero riding on a white horse (as in the Book of Revelation),

John Henry wielded a hammer. John Henry's hammer, however, did not strike blows for the freedom and justice of his people. Instead, John Henry's power was subjugated and made into an instrumentality of American industrial progress. The train was the primary symbol of nineteenth-century progress in the legend of John Henry, requiring the absolute, unswerving power and devotion of all of his life energies. As Christ died for our sins so that we might live, John Henry died opening up a way through mountainous obstacles so that the railroad could move forward. John Henry's supernatural energies are controlled, tamed, and channeled by the greater unseen power of American might, which required that he become the sacrificial lamb in this legend.

Unlike the passion of Christ, John Henry's sweat, lifeblood, and body did not regenerate after a period of time. John Henry did not rise again. His power, his talents, and his contribution were used up in one final glorious display, tunneling through a mountain. His "great heart" is mentioned near the end of the legend as being "broken." Yet the rending of his heart did not result in a cosmic release of resurrective energy. John Henry simply laid down his hammer and died.

John Henry is a repressive myth, a legend of a curbed passion with his Black physical powers safely corralled into a final moment of servitude, and then thrown away. John Henry as Black Suffering Servant dies for the Almighty White Man/Master whose invisible presence and will demands the ultimate sacrifice without uttering a word. This Master God demands the price of a supernaturally powerful Black male's giving up his life in order to do "the Master's will" (a favorite phrase in Black gospel songs).

John Henry as Suffering Servant suggests a perverse social interpretation of what theologians call subordinationist Christology, where Christ submits his life to the overwhelming will and plan of God the Father. In the legend of John Henry the will and plan of the White Master/God is to go to any means and any length necessary in order for the railroad to have transcontinental access. John Henry is but a tool in the hands of this master, a means whereby the grace of industrial progress might move everlastingly toward the eschaton of Universal Profit. There can be no hope for John Henry's life, for his life does not belong to him, just as Christ's life did not belong to him, but to God (in a subordinationist Christology). Such a construal of Christ tends to turn God into a cosmic tyrant, demanding the sacrifice of "his" only Son. It instrumentalizes Christ's life, turning all of the choices of Jesus of Nazareth into the preplanned moves of a holy automaton. Similarly, John Henry's choices for serving and saving other lives while ultimately giving up his own are never called into question, since they appear to be following faithfully some great hidden plan. John Henry's self-sacrifice, however, does not lead to a glorious resurrection and reappearance — he just dies. It is a tragedy. The subordinationist Christ *does* rise again, and there is a sense of God's ultimate justice. Where is God's justice, God's power, and God's vindication for John Henry?

In our contemporary world we are given mighty examples of African American males who display supernatural physical strength. From the high leaps of "Air" Michael Jordan in basketball to the rocketlike speed of runner Carl Lewis, African American males are given much encouragement to develop their physical prowess for the purpose of athletic fame. One popular TV commercial proclaims that "Bo knows." The athlete referred to, Bo Jackson, has played professional baseball and football. He is also skilled in track and several other sports. Jackson was severely injured in the hip during a football game, and authorities predicted that his sports career was finished. He had given his mind, body, skill, and style to several different arenas of athletic prowess and had become a symbol of excellence. Yet with this injury, and the resulting artificial hip implant operation, he was condemned to the ignominy of a great "has been." Unlike John Henry, however, Jackson did not stay "dead," but pushed himself beyond the normal limits of human endurance, pain, and exertion to come back recently as a designated hitter for baseball's White Sox team. He hit a home run the first time he returned to bat! So the legend of Bo Jackson is ongoing. Will his resurrection be an inspiration for other injured persons who have been cast away as useless, or will he give up his life tragically, as the John Henry legend grimly proclaims? Will he break the self-sacrificial model of Black male achievement glorified in John Henry and become a new, more satisfying myth?

Deeper questions are suggested beyond the current resurrection of the highly marketable Bo Jackson. Even if "Bo doesn't know" everything, why is it that he, like John Henry, has been required to be a supernatural sacrificial hero? What inner compulsions, fears, and needs drove Jackson to arise from the tomb of anonymity, or was it just that there was so much money to be gained if he tried? If Jackson had tried and failed, or if his current try turns into a failure, would it reinforce the power of the John Henry legend, especially for African American males? These questions can lead us into a deeper need for a critical deconstructive strategy whose aim is to destroy the strongholds of the White Master's financial will in order for African American bodies to be given respect and esteem outside of their instrumentality. African American males cannot wait for the White Master to deliver our bodies to us, for "He" is never finished, until our energies, strength, and productivity have been exhausted. Our bodies must be reclaimed as sacred Space belonging to none other than God, ourselves, and our communities.

In order for a reconstructive effort to begin, a few examples from African American male history may be chosen to provide a sturdy foundation. This particular foundation will be built on the imaginative trickster legend of High John de Conquer and the visionary revolutionary leader Nat Turner.

High John de Conquer

High John de Conquer is a uniquely African American mythological figure. Although his legend was conveyed originally in Black oral culture, the pre-eminent cultural anthropologist and folklorist Zora Neale Hurston took down several tales attributed to High John as narrated to her by Aunt Shady Anne Sutton. Hurston believed that the figure High John de Conquer provided an enduring gift of laughter and "source of courage" to the United States.[31]

High John de Conquer had a supernatural beginning, arising from the sorrows, pain, and enslavement of his African children in America. Hurston writes about High John's origins this way:

> High John came to be a man, and a mighty man at that. But he was not a nat-ural man in the beginning. First off, he was a whisper, a will to hope, a wish to find something worthy of laughter and song. Then the whisper put on flesh. His footsteps sounded across the world in a low but musical rhythm as if the world he walked on was a singing-drum. High John de Conquer was a man in full, and had come to live and work on the plantations, and all the slave folks know him in the flesh.[32]

The invisible/visible incarnational element of High John has obvious Christlike resonances. High John's power was enfleshed for the slaves, who recognized him as a man who worked and lived with them on the planta-tions. They recognized the presence of High John through his "sign," which was "a laugh, and his singing-symbol was a drum-beat."[33] The laugh and the drumbeat were taken as symbols of the irrepressibility and unquenchable qualities of High John by the slaves. White slavemasters misunderstood both signs, however. For them, the laughter of slaves was a sign of their happy-go-lucky, good-natured, and childish character, while the drumbeat was a sign of impending insurrection, unrest, and trouble. High John symbolized a quality of character that could "beat the unbeatable," that was "top-supe-rior to the whole mess of sorrow" in the slaves' lives.[34] The laughter and the drumbeat were but signs of the presence of these courageous qualities, which the slaves took to be the presence of the spirit of High John.

High John was a spirit within the slaves that arose from Africa. In Hur-ston's account, "Distance and the impossible had no power over High John de Conquer."[35] Thus High John responded to the cries of oppressed Africans.

Like the Jesus of the Gospels, "He came walking on the waves of sound. Then he took on flesh after he got there [America]."[36] High John rode the "waves of sound" of African pain and hope, following the slave ships by flying over them "like the albatross" riding the winds. Further, High John's presence was meant to be hidden from the ears and eyes of whites. After all, "They were not looking for any hope in those days, and it was not much of a strain for them to find something to laugh over."[37] One of Aunt Shady Anne's stories of High John had him acting in the trickster tradition of the Br'er Rabbit tales. High John stole one of the master's favorite young pigs to eat. Even after the master caught him preparing the pig, High John pleaded that the cooking pig was really an "old weasly possum" too sickly for the master. After the master insisted on eating with him, High John slyly responded, "Well Massa, I put this thing in here a possum, but if it comes out a pig, it ain't no fault of mine."[38] The master was taken with High John's humor and laughed in spite of himself. At the end of the tale the master repented of his selfish use of pig meat, and occasionally served all the slaves "at the big house after that."[39] John's courageous action of stealing the master's favorite food — note that stealing from a master is not morally condemned — opened up an opportunity for a change of heart in the master's actions toward the entire slave community. John was not a liberator here, but a cajoler, and through his mastery of sly humor he enabled the slave community to survive with a higher quality of life. In this tale High John did not alter the structure of slavery, but changed the heart of the oppressor.

In another tale High John took the slaves on what we would today call an out-of-body experience. High John convinced the slaves, who were scared of running away, by saying, "Just leave your work-tired bodies around for him [the master] to look at, and he'll never realize youse way off somewhere, going about your business."[40] Finally, with "Old Massa and Old Miss" sitting on the veranda of the "big house," High John told the slaves to "reach inside" themselves for the fine spiritual clothing they would need for their journey: "Just reach inside yourselves and get out all those fine raiments you been toting around with you for the last longest. They is in there, all right. I know. Get 'em out, and put 'em on."[41]

To their delighted surprise, the slaves reached inside themselves and found not only fine clothes, but the musical instruments they would play on their journey. High John proceeded to take them on their journey riding on a gigantic black crow so large that "one wing rested on the morning, while the other dusted off the evening star."[42]

High John took them across oceans, into hell, and finally up to heaven before they returned. Hurston compared the mythic scope of their journey in search of their freedom "song" to that of Jason in search of the golden fleece. Finally escaping from hell, they rode the devil's two fastest horses, Hallowed-Be-Thy-Name and Thy-Kingdom-Come, up the mountain into heaven. In heaven they found the spiritual refreshment and glorious melodies of the song they had been searching for. In heaven, promenading between Amen Avenue and Hallelujah Street, they encountered the rich harmonies of divinity sung and played on glorious golden instruments. The journey to heaven came to a beatific climax when they were called before Old Maker, who in front of "His great Workbench,"

> made them a tune and put it in their mouths. It had no words. It was a tune that you could bend and shape in most any way you wanted to fit the words and feelings you had.[43]

Upon their return, which was rudely initiated by the harsh hollering call of "Old Massa," the slaves immediately began to return to their former depressed state of mind. High John, however, reminded them of their transcendent journey, their supernatural enjoyment and refreshment, and of how the master was not to be told: "Us got all that, and he [the master] don't know nothing at all about it. Don't tell him nothing. Nobody don't have to know where us gets our pleasure from."[44] After hearing these words, the slaves rejoiced in their secret, and in finding out how to access inner joy and strength despite the harshness of slavery. Breaking out into singing, they noticed how even the day seemed shorter and the heat seemed more bearable after this experience.

In this tale we see that High John enabled the African slaves to own their interior spiritual resources in order to survive the harsh oppression of slavery. The oppressor was not changed, the system of slavery was not altered, but the slaves were transformed.

The most interesting thing about High John, according to Aunt Shady Anne, however, was his role in the emancipation of the slaves. Aunt Shady Anne said that High John had told Black people "one hundred years ahead of time" that freedom would one day arrive.[45] She laughed at young Blacks attributing emancipation to the Civil War; according to what her mother had told her, "John de Conquer had done put it into the white folks to give us our freedom, that's what."[46] Although "old Massa fought against it," the inevitability of freedom was assured for all those who believed in High John's word. For Aunt Shady Anne, "the war was just a sign and symbol of the thing"[47] — the "thing" being High John's accurate foretelling of freedom's coming one hundred years before it actually occurred. With freedom's coming, Hurston reports that High John "could retire with his secret smile into the soil of the South and wait."[48] Living in the secret dwelling of a special "root," those who reverence High John's power remember and honor his empowering contributions.

It is important to notice that, unlike the first two tales, this spiritual teaching or "knowing" attributed to High John implies that while High John the trickster could change the hearts of individual masters or enable the slaves to access powerful inner resources to survive slavery's cruelties, his final intention was to free the descendants of Africans from their bondage. In this way High John was a powerful liberator figure. He is a figure that requires theological analysis, appreciating the fact that he is a genuinely positive, African American liberator Christ-figure. Moving in ways that were invisible to oppressive masters, High John lived as Jesus did, incarnated as a living, breathing member of a suffering segment of humanity. High John "retires" into the earth waiting for a time when he might be needed again. Is such a moment now?

Nat Turner

While many historical figures could be used as notable examples of the interaction of religion in the souls and bodies of African American males, the story of Nat Turner is quite provocative. By his interpretation of dramatic visions and portents, Turner believed himself to be an apocalyptic prophet wreaking a just verdict on slaveholders. He led an insurrection in which fifty-seven whites were killed and more than one hundred slaves were killed in response. His life's mission was consummated by his reluctantly following what he took to be heavenly signs of the impending doom of slaveholders in which he and a small band of followers slaughtered white men, women, and children. While such an account might seem the height of violent religious fanaticism, it is worth looking at the deeply religious response of one Black man to the horrors of enslavement.

Turner, according to Gayraud Wilmore, had discovered the revolutionary empowerment of the biblical God who "demanded justice." To "know him and his Son Jesus Christ was to be set free from every power that dehumanizes and oppresses."[49] In relationship to the denied manhood of all male slaves, Wilmore suggests that Turner's violent turn provided a radical solution that by its bloodshed seemed to match the fanaticism of slaveholders in maintaining the systematic denial of what has been taken as "authentic manhood." If slaveholders projected an image of manhood that conveyed the impression that authentic masculinity meant violently dominating the will, body, and soul of whoever one wished to dominate, then Turner's insurrection was an act of tragic vengeance. Turner believed himself to be a prophet. If Turner's insurrection was not merely an act of vengeance in order to authenticate white norms of maleness, but the act of a religiously inspired prophet of divine wrath and justice, then we ought to examine the ways in which Turner's religious consciousness eventuated in armed insurrection.

In Nat Turner's confession to Thomas R. Gray in 1831, Turner indicated that his mother perceived him to be a person "intended for a great purpose."[50] The practice of discerning God's will through signs was part of his mother's religious practice and that of the slave community. As Turner told it, as a child of "three or four years old" he was overheard telling other children of an event that had occurred before his birth. This occasion was taken to be a confirming sign of Nat's prophetic calling, a calling that the slave community had been alerted to in his infancy by observing "certain marks on my head and breast."[51] While the white confessor Gray insultingly denounced such discernment as "a parcel of excrescences . . . ," it is important to note that the African slave community carefully observed and interpreted marks on the body as signs of one's spiritual life purpose. Such observation and interpretation were considered unworthy of serious attention by whites, but were taken (and in some quarters is still taken) seriously by Blacks. While it is beyond the scope of this chapter to reveal the detailed links between these practices and traditional West African religious beliefs, such a connection is distinctly implied. Several West African traditional religions profess a profound reverence for the connection between bodily marks, blemishes, and the shapes of these marks with spiritual knowledge, prophecy, and direction. The theological basis for such practices lies in the claim that the presence and influence of spirits make physical changes apparent to those "who have eyes to see."

Turner was considered a precocious child and was taught to read and write by an indulgent master. His ease at grasping intellectual matters, his lively imagination, and restless energy made him something of a legend within the slave community. Through it all he maintained a strong self-discipline of prayer and fasting, withdrawing from others to meditate on things that he had read in the Bible and elsewhere. During his periods of withdrawal he began to manifest a visionary capacity that he called "communion with the Spirit," sharing insights gathered during these times with both slaves and whites who believed that his "wisdom came from God."[52] His sense of a divine promise and purpose in his life increased, and he "began to prepare them [other slaves] for my purpose."[53] Although he tried to run away from both his "purpose" and an overseer, a vision directed him to return to the plantation. This caused quite a controversy among the slaves, who "murmured against" him and questioned his "sense." The struggle about his visionary capacity and the spiritual destiny of leadership was a tremendous source of inner conflict for Turner, a conflict that found its resolution in a famous vision.

The climactic vision became the impetus driving Turner out of the indecisiveness of inner turmoil toward insurrectionary action. The vision was of warring white and black spirits "engaged in a battle" accompanied by dramatic cosmic events:

> And I saw white spirits and black spirits engaged in a battle, and the sun was darkened — the thunder rolled in the Heavens, and blood flowed in streams — and I heard a voice saying, "Such is your luck, such you are called to see, and let it come rough or smooth, you must surely bear it." [54]

The intensity of this vision caused Turner to withdraw even more from daily living with other servants. It suggested that he was to become a leader of a violent occurrence involving bloodshed between Blacks and whites. It also suggested that it was his destiny to face this battle, come what may.

Turner's second vision was of lights in the sky that had been misnamed by "the children of darkness." These lights were revealed to Turner, in his own words, by the Holy Ghost standing in the heavens:

> "Behold me as I stand in the Heavens" — and I looked and saw the forms of men in different attitudes — and there were lights in the sky to which the children of darkness gave other names than what they really were — for they were the lights of the Savior's hands, stretched forth from east to west, even as they were extended on the cross of Calvary for the redemption of sinners. [55]

This vision suggests a conflation of the redemptive outreach of Christ on Calvary's cross with the redemption of the enslaved. The hands of the Savior, instead of being pinned down on a cross and subjected to bodily torture, are reaching out from one end of humanity to another, "from east to west."[56] Yet this vision caused Turner such confusion that he prayed for further interpretive guidance and understanding. The guidance came from dramatic natural signs that he found in the fields and woods of his plantation. The first sign was of drops of blood "on the corn as though it were dew from heaven." The second sign was more enigmatic, of "hieroglyphic characters, and numbers, with the forms of men in different attitudes, portrayed in blood, and representing the figures I had seen before in the heavens."[57] Finally, Turner had a third vision, which revealed the meaning of these "miracles" to him:

> For as the blood of Christ had been shed in this earth, and had ascended to heaven for the salvation of sinners, and was now returning to earth again in the form of dew — and as the leaves on the trees bore the impression of the figures I had seen in the heavens, it was plain to me that the Savior was about to lay down the yoke he had borne for the sins of men, and the great day of judgment was at hand. [58]

The impression this revelation had on Turner caused him to proclaim it to white and Black alike. It even had a transformative effect on a white man whom Turner had told about the vision, causing the man to pray, fast, and bleed for nine days.[59] This white man now forsook his previous cruelty and insensitivity.

While apocalyptic imagery was a standard part of some preaching, it is also apparent that Turner believed himself to be the one called to proclaim the imminent End. Further, this End was intimately connected to a war between white and black in which blood was to be shed in great profusion. It ought to be noted also that the powerful imagery of the Book of Revelation has always been attractive to Black preachers from slavery until now. Notice, as well, how the visceral imagery of blood and dew are tangibly connected to the redemptive activity of a coming Christ. The Christ who had "borne the yoke of sins" for all persons was now about to return in blood-judgment. Yet Turner did not act, waiting for other signs.

Three years later Turner had a profoundly apocalyptic vision in which a serpent was loosed and social relationships were reversed:

> On May 12th 1828, I heard a loud noise in the heavens, and the Spirit instantly appeared to me and said the Serpent was loosened, and Christ had laid down the yoke he had borne for the sins of men, and that I should take it on and fight against the Serpent for the time was fast approaching when the first should be last and the last should be first.[60]

This was the moment when the visions became connected to what Turner knew he must do. The calling to "fight against the Serpent" became a symbolic representation of Turner violently confronting the entire system of slavery. The purpose of this fight was not bloodshed, but the reversal of the roles of first and last. The struggle was against bodily enslavement, and for freedom. Turner's serpent, an image in Christianity of evil or even the devil himself, symbolized white slaveholders. The serpent also symbolized what must be defeated in order for freedom to be attained. This final vision became a way of gathering together the meaning of all the previous ones, galvanizing Turner to realize that now he had been summoned to physical combat in order to attain liberation, and that the liberation he sought was a part of an apocalypse, that the Great Judgment was going to be bodily combat with those who enslaved Black bodies. It brought together biblical eschatological imagery with a perceived calling to physical combat in order to attain liberation.

Turner waited another three years before an eclipse of the sun (August 1831) was taken to be the sign calling for action. Calling his closest disciples together, they partook of a "last supper" in which Turner recalled the purpose of all the visions and of their great calling to "strike a blow for freedom."[61] That midnight the "Judgment Day" began.

While it would be much easier to simply dismiss all of the previous visions, signs, and interpretations as indicative of the rantings of a dangerous fanatic (and that is what most people, especially whites, have done historically), there is more here than meets the eye. Nat Turner's plot failed to free the slaves, and even caused a wave of repressive legislation to be enacted across all Southern slaveholding states. Turner's name became associated with all that the slaveholders feared, because his acts made it clear that there were at least some Blacks who would rather die fighting for their freedom than live enslaved.

Turner's uncompromising struggle to follow his spiritual destiny deserves to be recognized as a prophetic sign even now. It suggests that the One who made the universe and all creatures has inspired some brave souls to fight for their freedom against injustice. For courageous persons, the violent and confrontational aspects of religious inspiration become embodied in action. Their visions become the impetus for bodily striving against subjection. They will not shirk from using their bodies in the struggle. They will fight with their bodily strength even unto death rather than live under a system of bodily subjection. Prophets such as Nat Turner refashion vision away from privatized experiences into inspirational calls for embodied liberating struggle. While others preach words describing the glories of a disembodied heaven, prophets on the order of Turner march, burn, and, if need be, take lives in accordance with their heavenly visions of freedom. Such prophets own their bodies fully, for in the physical confrontation with oppressive force the power of physical subjection is broken.

Xodus Journeying

Some one hundred and thirty years have passed since the official end of slavery. We live almost three decades removed from the agitation, bloodshed, inspiration, and dreaming of the civil rights revolution in our own century. The historic leap we are required to take between Nat Turner, High John, and ourselves is a gigantic one. Yet most in the various African American communities of the United States are still suffering from the continuing effects of racial discrimination, exploitation, and class and gender discrimination that have affected our existence since the Middle Passage. There is a sameness to Black existence that transcends the specific historical differences between slavery and our time. In the midst of conflicting voices — some calling for accommodation and sociopolitical retreat, others calling for a separate nation, and many others demanding economic and political empowerment — the movement of Africentricity is a call to Xodus. Malcolm X, newly rediscovered hero of our nihilistic age, speaks the words of Black rage in a voice strangely relevant for one slain three decades ago. Yet the thundering confidence and searing social critique of Malcolm X's speeches have enthralled a new generation of young African Americans.

Africentricity is a pan-African struggle to remove European and American cultural imperialism from its ideological centrality. Cain Hope Felder has accurately named Africentricity as corrective historiographic recovery of the pieces of African history that have been misnamed, neglected, stolen, or whitewashed. Felder questions whether there is a common African cultural heritage to be appealed to, and condemns as outright racist those whose Black nationalism casts Africans as superior in some fashion.[62] Africentricity, when understood to be a move toward correction of historical errors, is a firm basis on which future creative work may be done. It is proactive without vilifying any other race or group of individuals,[63] and is a movement toward creating a Space of our own outside the dominance of Euro-centrism. This Space of our own must include a new vision of African American masculinity and embodiment.

What will be the constitutive elements of an Africentric Xodus vision of maleness and embodiment?

This chapter has named four principles based on a careful balance between deconstructing and reconstructing three legendary figures and one historic African American male. These four principles are a fundamental part of any future Xodus work:

1. Our Bodies for Our Communities (John Henry Reconsidered)
The physical power and seemingly supernatural strength of our bodies is not to be degraded into an instrument for entertainment or the economic gain of other peoples. Primarily, African American male bodies ought to be committed to the rebuilding of broken humanity, for recapturing inspiring models of manliness for a lost generation of young Black males, and the creation of flourishing enterprises for the economic uplift of African American communities.

2. Humor and the Legacy of Sambo and High John   Humorous gestures and banter are but one means toward the greater goal of creatively expressing the rage that is tearing up African American communities. This rage is pervasive, for affluent or poor, because the racism that is still operative in North American culture denies African Americans ways of directly expressing disapproval, frustration, or (especially) outrage. Outrage denied becomes dangerous, whereas outrage expressed can become healing. Black male bodies that have internalized rage suffer disproportionately from high blood pressure, heart disease, ulcers, and other stress-related physical disorders. African American males on the average do not live to see their seventieth birthday; they are often dead by the age of sixty-two — too young to even collect Social Security! The internalization of rage has a long-term deleterious effect on the longevity of Black male bodies.

The traditional Sambo's antics might be viewed as a way to alleviate such bodily tension, but the cost to African American male dignity was too high. Yet Sambo's usage of humor should be given a second look. Perhaps we may yet find ways to use humor to help express rage. Humor could be a way to criticize racism without suffering racist "punishment" — meant here in the sense Michel Foucault spoke of as a means for disciplining errant members of an oppressive regime. The tales of High John de Conquer's exploits, tricking Old Massa and then making him laugh, are legendary examples of such humor. This kind of humor, which we could call subversive humor, could provide African American males with a way of articulating rage safely. In fact, African Americans have always entertained ourselves with subversive humor. Now we are called to discover new ways to articulate subversive humor as a means of changing oppressive social structures.

Finally, humor ought not be the only permissible means for us to express our rage. Black rage is as deep as the ocean over which slave ships carried our chained bodies, as wide as the vast African motherland from which we were stolen, and as rich as the chocolate-cinnamon-mocha-yellow tones that comprise our varied skin coloring. Rage will act, and it is up to us to define how it will act. It can be self-destructive or creative, transformative or genocidal. African American males must decide for ourselves, with the women and men we love, for the sake of the children we nurture, how our rage will be expressed. Such expression of rage cannot wait for a time "acceptable" to whites, but must flow through our poetry, our singing voices, our rap and hip-hop rhythms, our sermons, *and* our plans to build banks, corporations, and malls. Humor is but one means for releasing the kind of rage that must ultimately be viewed as an impetus for the transformation of African American communities.

3. Accessing Vision from Within (High John Conquering Power)

The ability to affirm one's dreams, hopes, plans, and visions cannot be found outside of ourselves, but must be accessed from within. Yet our souls, minds, and emotions are not divorced from our bodies. We are bodyselves, joined together, fused in a fashion that in many ways defies words. To access our inner "fine clothes" and "music" as High John taught the slaves to do is a matter of reclaiming something that many have forgotten in

African American communities. Yet it is not so far away in time that it cannot be remembered. The spiritual clothes and music are still resonating in our churches, mosques, and associations of uplift. The visions are still present, however muted or lost in mediocrity they sometimes have become.

Part of accessing African American bodyself vision is to renounce all sexist attitudes, behaviors, and traditions. African American males do not need to imitate any other model of masculinity, including many of the highly patriarchal African models. Instead, we must live into this new age with the women and the children we love. We ought to sort through all African models of manhood and take what we can use, discarding what we know to be harmful to the bodies and souls of women and men. We must come to a place of realization that accessing our bodyself power is affirming the bodyself power of women as well. The liberation of African American communities must be inclusive of man and women, or it will fail.

4. Bodyselves Must Unite to Fight Oppression (Nat Turner for the Streets) Part of reconstructive African American manhood must be the realization that being a "man" does not involve violent demonstrations as a show of "manly" force. Force, however, cannot be avoided if we are to realistically face the horrors of life in a world where we are still not considered human. Our bodyselves must learn that the real power of physical force is not in its careless and promiscuous demonstration, but in its ability to restrain destructive violence. Our bodyselves, united to stand with force restraining intracommunal violence, will be a power to be reckoned with. Such force will be impressive to ourselves and other communities because it will reveal the kind of self-love and self-determination that all peoples must have in order to be free. That is the kind of self-love Malcolm X spoke about, and not a violence that is suicidal. Our bodyselves fight oppression with all that is in us. Our minds, our hearts, our emotions, and whatever technological skills we possess ought to struggle for liberation. That is how the spirit of Nat Turner may be resurrected today. Such bodyself power has always been perceived as a threat by oppressors. We must not be deterred, for the stakes are too high, and the gain too precious.

In traditional African cultures the council fire represents the bringing together of the wisdom of the Elders with the vigor, impatience, and restless creativity of the younger tribal members. In this chapter we have brought to the council fire of the Xodus Journey a careful analysis of the historical and mythic figures in African American history. In the next three chapters we shall bring three giants of the twentieth century to the council fire: Malcolm X, Martin Luther King, Jr., and Howard Thurman.

Notes

1. Albert J. Raboteau, *Slave Religion: The "Invisible Institution" in the Antebellum South* (Oxford, England: Oxford University Press, 1978).
2. Ibid., 96.
3. Ibid., 97.
4. Ibid., 101.
5. Letter by Henry Bibb in *Slave Testimony,* ed. John Blassingame (Baton Rouge: Louisiana State University Press, 1977), 50.
6. Ibid.
7. Ibid., 50–51.
8. Bibb repeated this phrase in two of the five letters to his former master now extant.
9. Ibid., 55. This phrase was taken from another letter in which Bibb details the specific abuses Sibley had inflicted on his family.
10. Joseph Boskin, *Sambo: The Rise and Demise of an American Jester* (New York: Oxford University Press, 1986), 34.
11. Ibid., 35.
12. Ibid., 38.
13. Ibid., 44.
14. Ibid., 66.
15. Ibid., 67.
16. Ibid.
17. Ibid., 69.
18. Ibid., 79. This was a section of a minstrel's speech from an 1855 show entitled, "Black Diamonds: or Humour, Satire and Sentiment, Treated Scientifically by Professor Julius Caesar Hanibal in a Series of Burlesque Lectures Darkly Colored."
19. Eric Lott, *Love and Theft: Blackface Minstrelsy and the Working Class* (New York: Oxford University Press, 1993), 22.
20. Ibid.
21. Ibid., 25.
22. Ibid.
23. Ibid., 26.
24. Boskin, *Sambo,* 59.
25. Ibid., 58.
26. Ibid., 85.
27. Ibid., 84.
28. Ibid., 85.
29. Urkel is a "new Sambo with a new accent and a slightly different shuffle," according to Rev. George Lakes, Jr.
30. These are the three steps of Katie Cannon's womanist deconstruction used as social-critical tools for reconstructing the African American community.
31. Zora Neale Hurston, "High John de Conquer," in *Book of Negro Folklore,* edited by Langston Hughes and Arna Bontemps (New York: Dodd, Mead, 1959), 102.
32. Ibid., 93.

33. Ibid.
34. Ibid., 94.
35. Ibid.
36. Ibid.
37. Ibid., 94–95.
38. Ibid., 97–98.
39. Ibid., 98.
40. Ibid., 99.
41. Ibid.
42. Ibid.
43. Ibid., 100.
44. Ibid., 101.
45. Ibid., 96.
46. Ibid., 97.
47. Ibid.
48. Ibid., 101.
49. Gayraud Wilmore, *Black Religion and Black Radicalism,* 2d ed. (Maryknoll, N.Y.: Orbis, 1983), 64.
50. Nat Turner, excerpts from "The Confessions of Nat Turner," in *Afro-American Religious History: A Documentary Witness,* edited by Milton C. Sernett (Durham, N.C.: Duke University Press, 1985), 89.
51. Ibid.
52. Ibid., 90.
53. Ibid., 90–91.
54. Ibid., 91.
55. Ibid.
56. Much of this interpretation arose in conversation with a colleague, Prof. Lori Ann Ferrell (8 October 1993).
57. Turner, "Confessions," 91.
58. Ibid, 91–92.
59. Ibid., 92.
60. Ibid.
61. Wilmore describes this last meal as a "supper of barbecue and brandy," which took on overtones of a Passover "last supper." *Black Religion and Black Radicalism,* 69–70.
62. Cain Hope Felder, "The Imperative for a Multicultural Christian Education Curriculum," *The BISC Quarterly* (Newsletter of the Biblical Institute for Social Change), 4, no. 2: 4.
63. Ibid., 7.

CHAPTER

Malcolm's "X"

If the Xodus Journey is to be relevant it must present a radical challenge to the assumptions of Black theology. The challenge for Black theology at the beginning of a new millennium is to envision a theological understanding of human dignity strong enough to meet the triple threat of moral nihilism, communal suicide, and social dissolution. Instead of beginning with the existentialism of Paul Tillich or the neoorthodoxy of Karl Barth, our starting point must be the streets that exploded into uprisings in Los Angeles, New York, and Atlanta in 1992. Rampant injustice and dreams deferred have reached the point of critical meltdown. The Xodus theological task cannot hide behind lame abstractions taken from irrelevant textbooks, but must face the rage, pain, and hopelessness that threaten to engulf our people. With what resources can African Americans affirm our dignity despite ongoing dehumanization?

James H. Cone's *Martin & Malcolm & America* is a prophetic summons to Black theologians to begin to mine the hidden theological riches of both Malcolm X and Martin Luther King, Jr., in order to meet the contemporary dilemmas of African Americans. Through a careful analysis of both men's lives and teachings, Cone demonstrates our need to join Malcolm's call for self-love and power with King's call for universal resistance to injustice. Following Cone's lead, in the next two chapters I shall look at the pertinent theological symbols of human dignity offered by King and Malcolm X. I interpret the primary intention and theme of Malcolm X's message to be that of promoting Black self-respect. Before we can get to the uplifting and reviving message of self-respect, however, Xodus creativity demands that we excavate the theological creativity of the "X."

The "X"

Since the "X" of Xodus is what distinguishes it from the traditional liberation narrative of the ancient Hebrews (the Exodus), it is important to evaluate how a single letter can symbolize so much for Afrikan peoples. Young African Americans tend to idolize Malcolm X as a martyred role model of rebellious, defiant Black manhood. Malcolm X was the brother who went to prison a hustler and "gangsta" (in today's parlance), and left it with a fervent religious commitment to Elijah Muhammad's Nation of Islam. The brother ascended from the depths of a criminal record to an international prophetic role, and he did it by rhetorically thumbing his nose at outraged whites. Such audacity and outspokenness cannot but be admired by those locked into seemingly hopeless patterns of criminalization, violence, and lack of opportunities for a "better life." Malcolm X proclaimed the message of Elijah Muhammad with such force and eloquence that even highly trained "Negroes" of the day had to shake their heads and laugh that anybody could "talk so!"

To extend the mythic analysis of the last chapter, Malcolm X was a combination of the folk-heroes Nat Turner and Stackolee, the "Bad Nigger."[1] Malcolm would deliberately say things to provoke whites, all with a smile and an attitude that apparently was as fascinating to whites as it was repulsive. As the mythic Stackolee could outsmart, outthink, and outmaneuver any and all Euro-American countermoves, so could Malcolm X as a debater, especially on television. His ability to drive a point home with a turn of a phrase or a witty parable made him a difficult opponent in the limited time frame of a televised debate. As formidable as Stackolee was physically, so was Malcolm X intellectually. He terrorized Euro-Americans and frightened tame-spirited African Americans by his refusal to submit to the standard (unwritten) rules and conventions of racial dialogue.

His rhetoric seemed inflammatory, prone to demagoguery rather than careful and reasoned reflection. Like Nat Turner, his language seemed to be calling for a revolt of African Americans against Euro-Americans, rather than finding a way to "get along" with them. Unlike most Negro leaders of his time who called for relatively mild concessions and integration, Malcolm X symbolized an Afrikan man utterly disdainful of everything "American." His lack of interest in integration and in being an "appointed" (by white folks!) racial spokesperson made him an anathema to civil rights leaders and liberal whites. His was a "Black first" self-identity, putting Blackness at the center of his proclamation: "I'm black first. My sympathies are black, my allegiance is black, my whole objectives are black. . . . I am not interested in being American, because America has never been interested in me."[2]

Malcolm X had not always been interested solely in Blackness. He was originally named Malcolm Little. His name change followed the Nation of Islam's tradition of taking on the "X" of anonymity as Elijah Muhammad taught all of his followers. Such a name change was a sign to the world that this Black person was renouncing a former "slavemaster name." The "X" symbolizes one's "true African family name" that had been taken from every African brought to America as a slave.[3] Adding an "X" to one's name, therefore, is a public sign, a testimony against the legacy of slavery, where freed slaves either took on the names of their former slavemasters or created new names entirely.[4] The "X" in this way is a prophetic symbol of retrieval and remembrance. Such prophetic retrieval and remembrance of one's Africanness, of one's stolen, ripped away, ripped-off cultural roots made Malcolm X a very different kind of a "Negro" than Malcolm Little.

Those who have an "X" in the Nation of Islam in our contemporary society carry on this prophetic symbolic witness. Having an "X" for a last name rather than a "proper name" is a continual social reminder of what African descendants went through here as slaves. It reminds both African Americans and Euro-Americans that we came across the Atlantic at the bottom of the boat, in stocks, stacked like cordwood. The "X" reminds all "free Americans" that for over three centuries an entire sector of its native-born population lived through a more dire "legal" fate than the one so-called illegal aliens wrestle with in contemporary society. The "X" reminds Euro-Americans that the "free passage" they provided us was really a hellish Middle Passage that took away our names and thereby disconnected us from our family traditions, cultural heritages, and sense of personal dignity. It is a miracle that Afrikans survived such an onslaught to our personhood with even a shred of self-respect, but those who made it were strong.

The imposition of an "X" is a radicalizing public act of defiance, refusing to accept as normative those European-derived common names of most Americans. It insists on the uniqueness of African American lost names. It is defiant even of most local Black community practices that conform to standard Euro-American name-domination — with interesting twists, of course. Since the Black cultural awakening of the late 1960s, an increasing number of Swahili and Arabic names have emerged. One cannot be in the presence of any predominantly African American community and not be aware that even though there are many Joneses, Smiths, and Williamses, their first names demonstrate Afrikan creativity: Twanda, LaToya, Shameka, for example.

The "X" functions, nevertheless, as a double-faced symbol of pan-Africanity, one face looking back in time toward lost tribal roots, the other forward toward a beckoning future, toward becoming Afrikan identities. We are becoming Afrikans, developing variously in our different contexts throughout the globe. There is no single Afrikanity, one Afrikan "self," no mysterious and undefinable African "essence" that we all possess. Our Afrikan identity is plural, fluid, and diverse — there are British Africans, African Americans, German Africans, and so on. The "X" reminds us that we cannot ever go back to our former tribal identities — unless we had family "griots" like Alex Haley's family, remembering enough for us to trace our roots literally back to the very tribes we came from. We are African in some sense *and* American. Which is our native soil? Is it possible for us to re-member what was so brutally stripped away from us so many centuries ago? No, we can re-member our Africanness through study and meditation, but our becoming Afrikan identities lie forward in time. We can never return to the same place in our various forgotten African motherlands that we left. Yet the "X" is not mournful of our lost tribal status and motherlands, because, as Malcolm recounted to Alex Haley: "Mr. Muhammad taught that we would keep this 'X' until God Himself returned and gave us a Holy Name from His own mouth."[5]

Malcolm X received this message as one of resurrection. He called it "the teachings that could stir and wake and resurrect the black man."[6] The "X" ought to become an important symbol of rising — Black people rising up from their somnambulant state, throwing off the mists of mental sleep to awaken to their true becoming Afrikan identities. Such a theological symbol of rising should also be understood ethically as Malcolm X's teaching about self-respect.

Self-Respect

Malcolm X has been called everything from "our shining Black Prince" to a "hatemonger." He was both greatly admired and deeply feared, and his charismatic power to sway the masses of Black folk has often distracted scholars from doing serious critical study of his thought. Like Cone, I believe that Malcolm X's view of human dignity and self-respect deserves a place alongside the respect we give to King's thought. In fact, self-respect, like King's Somebodyness symbol, articulates Malcolm's most cherished fundamental claim about the nature of human beings.

Malcolm believed that self-respect had been systematically stripped away from American Blacks by the European-American system of racism, or "the collective white man."[7] Malcolm dramatized in vivid language the way in which this "white man" had brutalized, raped, and robbed the "black man" of self-respect, pride, and dignity. In fact, according to Malcolm, the "white man" literally brainwashed African people into "so-called Negroes." The "Negro," according to Malcolm, had become sickened psychologically, spiritually, emotionally, economically, and politically by accepting self-hatred into our collective psyche.[8]

While Malcolm was a part of the Nation of Islam under Elijah Muhammad, his "cure" for Black people was theologically grounded in what he later referred to as a demonology of the devilish nature of whites.[9] In an elaborate myth known as "Yacub's History," Elijah Muhammad taught members of the Nation of Islam that the white race was a genetic mutation developed by a malevolent Black genius, Yacub. The "devil white race," in accordance to prophecy, would be destroyed by God's judgment after wreaking havoc and oppression for six thousand years on the "original people" of the earth—the Black race.[10] This apocalypse was to occur soon, therefore all Muslims were called to separate themselves from the doomed race of whites rather than integrate. In fact, Malcolm believed that integration was the deceptive solution dreamed up by "liberal white devils" to keep Blacks in bondage and subjugation. Malcolm believed that Blacks had to recognize our historic-mythic greatness as "original people" of the "tribe of Shabazz" and voluntarily separate from whites in order to gain self-respect and the independence necessary for others to respect us.[11] Malcolm wanted Blacks to awaken to a mature intelligence and moral independence from whites.[12] In this phase of Malcolm's journey, a commitment to Allah enabled him to realize a disciplined transformation of himself from a hardened street hustler and convict into a fitting role model and grass-roots leader.

Grounded in this transformative faith, Malcolm was able to find salvation in the strict moral code of the Nation. This code forbade partaking of alcohol, drugs, smoking, dancing, gambling, movies, sports, "filthy pork," and "taking long vacations from work."[13] The positive aspect of the moral code enjoined courtesy (especially to women), faithfulness to one's mate, honesty, and thriftiness. Muslims were not supposed to be insubordinate to any civil authority except on religious grounds. Further, Muslims were encouraged to be economically independent, relying on one another for all business transactions, thus developing a true sense of nationhood within the oppressive state of "devils." Malcolm preached this code as the only way that was stringent enough to concretely uplift the Black race and enable it to "clean" itself up.

Cone helps us to see that Malcolm despised the message of "turn-the-other-cheek" nonviolence as espoused by Martin Luther King, Jr. Malcolm believed that it was immoral and criminal to ask Blacks to be nonviolent because it denied Blacks a fundamental human right to defend oneself in the presence of an overtly violent attack.[14] Malcolm delighted in shocking whites with the ominous-sounding message that he believed that African Americans should protect themselves "by any means necessary," insisting that the right to do so was a fundamental modicum of human respect in "every civilized society."[15] Further, Malcolm countered the other-centered aspects of King's agape concept by insisting on the deontological necessity of self-love as a primary value that constitutes self-respect.

Self-respect, for Malcolm X, meant espousing a new gospel, Black nationalism. He constantly hammered home the point that African Americans did not "catch hell" for being Baptist, Methodist, Democrat, Republican, Mason, or Elk but because we were "black."[16] Black nationalism, for Malcolm, was both a political philosophy and a necessary religious commitment. The political philosophy of Black nationalism aimed at the following:

- Revolutionary agitation necessary to create consciousness
- Revolutionary strategies aimed toward creating a "nation"[17]
- Political independence and control of our own communities
- Cultural independence from white domination
- Economic independence [18]

From the start Malcolm called for Blacks to gain self-respect by doing for ourselves, rather than waiting for "crumbs from the white man's table." Such self-motivation enabled Malcolm to overcome the shock of being cast away from his beloved Elijah Muhammad as a traitor. Creatively, Malcolm broadened his theological vision by learning the more traditional ways of Islam, ways that transformed his condemnation of whites into more pointed accusations about racism. His moral judgment on racism enabled him to broaden his message by appealing to a pan-African, international audience.[19] Creating the Organization of Afro-American Unity (OAAU) as a political organization, Malcolm countered the apoliticism of his Nation days. The ethical aim of his last days was toward forging a solution to the race problems rather than arguing about whether his methods and ideas were better or worse than those of traditional civil rights leaders. He called for "human rights," saying that "civil rights" is too confining a term for the emerging revolutionary consciousness. His assassination robbed us of a fully developed theory of self-respect from the perspective of El-Hajj Malik El-Shabazz — the Moslem name he took after his hajj to Mecca. It is clear, however, that the direction of his thought was moving toward a pan-African, internationalist program of revolutionary human rights.

I believe that the "X" symbolizes Malcolm's journey from being the criminal Malcolm Little through Malcolm X to El-Hajj Malik El-Shabazz. Each of these name changes represented a progression from a lower sense of self-respect and consciousness to a higher sense. These name changes represent an evolution related to the kind of Journeying that Xodus Journeyers must emulate. Not all of us are going to be followers of Jesus Christ as Lord and Savior, even though I am. Many of us will not be adherents of the Nation of Islam either. But all of us can become Afrikan, even if we are asleep to that fact. Xodus invites us to Journey together toward that future that only God can know with any certainty. Yet we Journey on, each with our particular perspective and beliefs in the Divine One and Many.

Cryptosymbol? Cryptocross

The "X" or "+" is an ancient symbol in the history of religions. Pointing in four directions, it has frequently symbolized a recognition of the sacredness of the four points of the compass. In order to plumb the symbolic power of the "X," it is necessary to uncover the history of its usage, particularly retrieving the often neglected historical fact that the sign of the cross existed before the rise of Christianity. This section will: (1) examine the archaeological evidence of the "X" symbol; (2) link this evidence to ancient Jewish and Egyptian sources; (3) relate how the early Jewish Christians both continued and transformed previous Jewish and Egyptian traditions; and (4) explain what significance this archaeological-theological investigation can have for Xodus travelers.

One of the most significant pre-Christian crosses was the ankh or *crux ansata* of Egypt — the "Cross of Life" that symbolized the Maatic creativity of God.[20] Archaeological evidences of the ankh are numerous. It is one of the most frequent and easily recognizable symbols in Medu Netcher (or what Westerners named "hieroglyphics"). One of the most renowned instances of the ankh inscription is its prominence on a column of the terraced temple of Queen Hatshepsut — great "living Horus" or absolute ruler of Kemet from 1479–1458 B.C.E. [21] A famous expeditionary leader, Hatshepsut concentrated her royal energies on building up Kemet's internal superstructure destroyed in previous generations by the invading hordes of Hyksos. Daughter of "The Great Liberator" Thutmose I, Hatshepsut consolidated her father's victories by organizing commercial trading expeditions instead of military campaigns.[22] She is an important embodiment of what the ankh symbolizes, the bringing together of "feminine and masculine forces in the universe."[23] Anthony Browder notes: "Symbolically, the oval represents the womb, the vertical shaft depicts the phallus and the horizontal bar expresses the coming into existence of a new life, resulting from the union of man and woman."[24]

That the ankh would figure prominently in a temple commemorating Hatshepsut's reign as a "living god" of Kemet does not mean that it was used only as a symbol of her. In fact the ankh is often depicted as placed in both hands of a pharaoh. A recently discovered statue of one of the Twelfth Dynasty pharaohs (one of the Ethiopian or Nubian dynasties), Senwosrt I, shows ankhs in both hands, placed on his chest in a crossed-arm position.[25]

"X" and "+" signs were also inscribed in a sphinxlike statue of Serabit el-Khadem, now resting in the Egyptian Museum of Cairo. What is fascinating about this particular statue is that it confirms for archaeologists that "the simple mark of the cross is, in fact, the most common sign in the proto-Sinaitic inscriptions, occurring more than thirty-five times."[26] What this means in lay terms is that the sign of the cross was extant at least fifteen hundred years before the birth of Jesus Christ.

What is far more intriguing for Xodus creativity is that some archaeologists believe that some version of an "X" was drawn as a secret sign of Christian faith by early adherents. Graydon Snyder takes a skeptical view of such things, believing that an early, pre-Constantinian-era cross symbol lies beyond our capacity to prove or disprove.[27] Others, like Jack Finegan, hold that early Christians apparently had a vast repertoire of cryptocrosses, "essentially little pictures . . . [that] remind us of the picture writing of Egyptian hieroglyphics and suggest that this manner of writing arose under Egyptian influence."[28] He detects inscriptions following a secretive arrangement of the Hebrew letters from which the crosslike letter *aleph* corresponded to a sign of Jesus Christ. For early Christians the sign of the "X" corresponded to the Greek *chi* or χ.

Finegan's research indicates that usage of the Greek χ sign arose in Hellenized Jewish communities. In ancient Hebrew the *taw* sign was "the mark" placed on the foreheads of the anointed as a sign of divine protection.[29] In Old Hebrew the *taw* was "still written in the most elemental form of a cross down at least to the eve of the NT period, or even into that period."[30] The visual correspondences between the Hebrew *taw* (looking like a sideways cross), the Greek χ and the Latin (Roman) "X" are quite apparent. The Hebrew *taw* sign is attested to in several biblical references:

- *Ezekiel 9:4-6:* "Go through the city, through Jerusalem, and put a mark [*taw*] on the forehead of those who sigh and groan over all the abominations that are committed in it." To the destroyers the prophecy states, "Pass through the city after him, and kill; your eye shall not spare, and you shall show no pity. Cut down old men, young men and young women, little children and women, but touch no one who has the mark."

- *Job 31:35:* Job cries out in his own defense, "Oh, that I had one to hear me! (Here is my signature [my "mark" or *taw*]! let the Almighty answer me!)."
- *1 Samuel 21:12-15:* David pretends to be insane (or at least feigns the irrational behavior of a dervish) because of his fear of the king Achish, "So he changed his behavior before them; he pretended to be mad when in their presence. He scratched marks [verbal form of the *taw*] on the doors of the gate, and let his spittle run down his beard."[31]

It is apparent in the passage from Ezekiel that the *taw* was a physical sign of deliverance, exemption, and redemption. Finegan notes the influence of such thinking in the apocryphal book *The Psalms of Solomon* 15:8, 10 of the first century B.C.E., where it is said, "The mark of God is upon the righteous that they might be saved," but concerning sinners it is declared that "the mark of destruction is upon their forehead."[32] The *taw* sign has now developed into a sign of either redemption and salvation or damnation and destruction. Talmudic commentary on Ezekiel 9:4 mentions two *taws:*

> In explicit connection with Ezek. 9:4 the Talmud (Shabbath 55a SBT II 1, 253-254) also tells of two taws, and distinguishes between them as "a taw of ink upon the foreheads of the righteous," and "a taw of blood upon the foreheads of the wicked." In the same context Rab (third century) is quoted in the explanation: "Taw stands for 'thou shalt live,' taw stands for 'thou shalt die.'"[33]

The early Jewish Christians associated the *taw* sign with Jesus, the Christos or Anointed One. There is evidence of the Greek "X" in the Qumran scrolls in reference to the expected "Anointed One" or "Messiah" in the Isaiah Scroll from Cave I.[34] Even more obvious for most of us who are not experts in reading ancient papyrus or stelae (inscribed pillars of stone) is the fact that the χ is the first letter for the Greek word *Christos:* χριστος. As was the practice for Jews of marking a priest with the anointing sign of the *taw* (attested to being in "the shape of a wreath . . . the shape of a Chi χ"),[35] such a mark was carried into early Jewish Christian practice. When I look at the cross marks found in Egyptian Medu Netcher and in Old Hebrew, I take it to be a safe conclusion that early Christians developed their own understanding of the "X" along the lines of both Jewish traditions and Egyptian influences. Unlike the obvious representations of a crucifixion cross that appeared in the late fourth century, these early "X" signs had a symbolic meaning rich in the power of the previous traditions they represented.

Xodus Implications

What can we make of these scholarly musings? I take the symbol χ or X to be a rich interreligious theological symbol. It has symbolic import beyond its most obvious meaning to the adherents of the Nation of Islam. It is certain that the cross, whether upright or in an X-form, reminds Christians of what orthodox theologians have traditionally considered the central event of Christianity: the victory of Jesus of Nazareth over the power of death (not over peoples!). Before the cross Jesus was a healer-teacher-prophet-miracle worker; at the cross Jesus stood convicted of criminal charges and sentenced to death; but after the cross Jesus became the historic world-religions "founder" as Christ. The X for us who are Christians ought to be a reminder of the Christ — of the events that led up to the political conspiracy to kill Jesus of Nazareth. Within us should be an honoring of that sacrifice, of the kind of love that is willing to see a healing-salvific cause through to the end, even recognizing that the end might include death.

The cross is not a glorification of the death of Jesus, but it is, in fact, the first letter to a new language of life — "X" stands for the "Ch" in *Christos. Christos* means "Anointed One." It is a newword for Xodus travelers because *Christos* ought to embody for us what it means to be anointed in the Holy Spirit for a Journey whose end we do not see, but toward which we "walk by faith, not by sight" (2 Cor. 5:7). For those interested in a meaningful dialogue between Jews, Christians, and Moslems, such a symbol has significance when we examine its early history in relation to its current usage. If we are genuinely interested in creating an Xodus Space, archaeological, textual, and historical analysis can help us uncover vital connections between our various religious traditions that have been lost in time, forgotten or transformed in practice.

The anointing mark, ancient *taw,* or first Greek letter of Christ's name may help us to understand a new meaning of the term *messianic secret.* For Xodus seekers the new messianic secret might be the creation of a new connection with the origins and roots of religious traditions quite meaningful for us today. The new messianic secret may be the eternal Blackness we described in chapter 2 as reigning in ancient Kemetic practices. Part of our new messianic secret is reviving the ancient belief that Blackness is the doorway to new peoplehood, new personhood, and new love. Such a secret does not hide itself, but recognizes the unfortunate reality that in a white world, Blackness may be a secret of life that cannot be embraced by all . . . at least not yet. Blackness is a secret of life because it is one of the fundamental elements of humanity that has been erased or severely restricted in cultural meaning. In a world in which Euro-domination has affected even the most beautiful Blackness of Africans to the point where many do not desire to identify themselves with tribal customs, traditions, and clothing, messianic Blackness is yet to come. It is *here* and *not yet*. Messianic Blackness is the coming of Blackness, Becoming Blackness in a white world that refuses to love its own Blackness. For now, Xodus Journeyers may take comfort in the inner circle of Blackness.

What is this inner circle of Blackness I speak of? It is a deepening and broadening of the ontological symbol of "blackness" that James Cone wrote of a generation ago in his groundbreaking *A Black Theology of Liberation* (1970). Xodus must deepen Cone's analysis of blackness as an ontological symbol of oppression and solidarity with the oppressed[36] to include the ancient Kemetic notions of blackness as the primal symbol of the deep unconscious, the Universal Mind, Maat, Amenta (the underworld), and wisdom. Blackness is more than a term symbolizing the "victims of oppression who realize that their humanity is inseparable from human liberation from whiteness."[37] Blackness is a positive spiritual force operating in all of humanity, nature, and the cosmos. It is not bound only to those who are victims. For ancient Kemetic priests and scholars, one was taught to desire the attainment of Blackness as "an expansion of consciousness (inner vision), spiritual consciousness, illumination, unity with nature, an activated pineal gland, creative genius, godlike powers attained by [hu]man[s] on earth."[38] Such teaching was presented as an ethical *ought* and telos, as obligation and desired end.

The inner circle realizes that all the accretions of negative dualities pitting whiteness (as "right," "good," "pure," and "holy") against blackness (as "wrong," "evil," "dirty," and "profane") are a demonic reversal of cosmic ancient truth. In fact, in ancient Kemetic teachings the color white had little spiritual significance. Whiteness was not cast as the opposite of blackness. Other dual notions were present — male-female, light-dark, dry-wet, and so on — but these dualities were not cast in such a way that "light" or "male" were absolutely positive in force, and "dark" or "female" kept forever captive in the negative side of things. The inner circle realizes that Western Christianity has become demonic in its color symbolism. As such Western Christianity is completely out of balance. In order for Western Christianity to truly heal, it must be balanced by repenting of its negative color symbolism. In order for Western Christians to be truly "saved" they must go beyond the everyday negative colorism of Western language. White and Black Christians must go beyond the things they hear from Billy Graham, their Sunday school teachings, most of the sermons they hear every Sunday, and all of the racialist/colorist language of the news media (for example, "Black Friday" as the day when the stock market crashes).

The inner circle has no problem proclaiming that the West — and that means all of us living in the West — needs to learn to embrace divine Blackness. African Americans are not exempted from this challenge, indeed we are often the most guilty of using the language of negative racial color symbolism, to our own ironic self-negation. Anyone who has participated in a service where a singer whips the congregation into a frenzy of response during the refrain "Wash me 'til I'm whiter than snow . . ." knows exactly what I mean! Why do African Americans want to be "washed" until we are "whiter than snow"? Because our westernized interpretation of the Bible tells us so. Because white-colorized Christianity insists that it be so. Because having accepted white Christianity, our Blackness is asleep, and a people that are asleep can pray, sing, and praise in patterns that reinforce their own self-destruction. Malcolm X used to love repeating this indictment of Christianity as a "white religion":

> My brothers and sisters, our white slavemaster's Christian religion has taught us black people here in the wilderness of North America that we will sprout wings when we die and fly up into the sky where God will have for us a special place called heaven. This is white man's Christian religion used to *brainwash* us black people! We have *accepted* it! We have *embraced* it! We have *believed* it! We have *practiced* it! And while we are doing all of that, for himself, this blue-eyed devil has *twisted* his Christianity, to keep his *foot* on our backs . . . to keep our eyes fixed on the pie in the sky and heaven in the hereafter . . . while *he* enjoys *his* heaven right *here* . . . on *this earth* . . . in *this life.*[39]

The inner circle has an obligation to act as liberators of the mind and spirit, starting with our own and leaving the door open to all. (Remember that the "black dot" or "third eye" is the door to our inner Blackness.) Such an obligation is a sacred one, applying to all human beings. Indeed, I make the boldly universalist claim that Blackness is an essential aspect of humanity that must be brought to the fore. The "X" is one particularly terse sign of that inner circle's mission and *raison d'être.*

In short, the "X" symbolizes serious invitation and challenge to traditional Christian negative color-symbolism. It reverses the negativity of "blackness," which in the eyes of whites is an evil, into Blackness as a positive and essential life-affirming spiritual Space, without making whiteness emblematic only of evil. Such a reversal does not turn categories upside-down in a simplistic way, but retrieves the unjustly accused from suffering. Xodus reversal breaks down the injustice of a kind of colorist symbolism that carries over into everyday language and thereby negates the value of all those persons considered "black." But because Xodus reversal is aware of how negative colorism can affect the mental, spiritual, and emotional health of entire peoples, we will not place that negativity onto Euro-Americans ("white people"). It is too much of a burden to be ontologically condemned as morally, mentally, and spiritually inferior. It is too much of a psychic-spiritual evil to place any color symbolism on a people. No, Xodus reversal can transform the moral energies of the language of "rightness-whiteness" in such a way that all "whites" are not condemned. The inner circle understands this seemingly esoteric or mysterious truth. If the reader does not, read it again!

The taking on of an "X" name graphically symbolizes the spiritual and moral move out of European-American dominated "space" into a Space of one's own. I believe that the theological symbol Exodus is suggested. The act of Exodus (Exod. 12:31-40) not only initiated the releasing of slaves from servitude, but increased their consciousness of the powerful intervening hand of God. Our contemporary Xodus is a divine intervention within our own lives empowering us to affirm self-liberation first. Suggestive of the Hebrew Exodus, we are not awaiting Pharaoh's orders; the African American "X-People" are "coming out" of this Egypt named America . . . "land of the free and home of the brave," without requesting permission or expecting a blessing. This Xodus suggests a more massive, group-wide self-deliverance than has been experienced for more than a generation. Instead of certain chosen individuals who have become aware of the need to come out of white American-controlled space, the Xodus implies the need for the entire race to "arise" in order to flourish as human beings.

Xodus Conversion

This notion of rising out of Euro-domination has ties to traditional understandings of conversion. Xodus travelers have an experience of their Blackness that changes the course of their lives forever. Such an experience resonates with accounts of Christian conversion, where a person moves in a chronological/kairological (holy time, sacred time) fashion: (1) becoming aware of one's sin; (2) developing such awareness into a conviction about how sin must be removed; (3) recognizing that one requires something or someone to deliver one from the bondage of sin; (4) experiencing the grace of God through Jesus Christ. This pattern is apparent in Afrikan conversion experiences across a wide swath of time, from slave narratives into our contemporary age. Afrikans embrace a spirituality that welcomes the Spirit of God as a tangible experience, a "feeling that pours over me from the crown of my head to the souls of my feet." Xodus traveling translates the experience of conversion into concrete Africentric terms.

Becoming aware of "sin" for Xodus travelers means becoming aware of the ways in which Afrikans (male and female, rich and poor) are engulfed in a demonic system of whiteness/Euro-domination/oppression that has colonized both their bodies and their innermost thoughts, desires, and feelings.

Conviction is accomplished through the "hearing of the word" of Blackness. The message of Blackness is liberating because it frees Afrikans from their colonized desires (most often unconscious) to be white. Often it is the actions of persons who are controlled by Euro-domination that make Afrikans aware of our "status," precipitating our conviction experience. For me it was becoming aware of how, no matter how hard I tried to dress, act, and behave like a "professional" (read "middle-class, unthreatening, white male"), I would always be viewed by my Euro-American "superiors" as either a reflection of them (when they were younger, of course) or as a threat to be handled. As a threat I mean that I was viewed as "too loud," not "cooperative," and (the worst insult of all for Euro-dominated values) "not a team-player." This meant that I was "cut out of the loop" and left to put things together on my own. In other words, I was being disciplined in the famous way that Michel Foucault speaks of discipline as a rationalized means of power controlling populations.[40] Foucault speaks about such disciplinary power in this apt phrase:

> But in thinking of the mechanisms of power, I am thinking rather of its capillary form of existence, the point where power reaches into the very grain of individuals, touches their bodies and inserts itself into their actions and attitudes, their discourses, learning processes and everyday lives . . . a synaptic regime of power.[41]

The message was being broadcast to me continually. It haunted my sleep, dogged my steps by day. I could not escape it because it was a part of every interaction, spoken and unspoken. The message was: "Conform or leave." I left. I X-scaped.

For Xodus travelers the need for deliverance can come through many avenues. Malcolm X had to be in prison, in trouble, and out of options before he came face-to-face with "himself" as a colonized Negro. The someone or something that delivered him was Elijah Muhammad's teachings. For me and the Christians who will read this, our first deliverance came through hearing the word of Jesus Christ, accepting it, and becoming Christians. But Xodus Space requires a second deliverance — or at least an extension of the first. The second deliverance is the hearing of the word of Blackness, which is a cry to leave Euro-dominated Space and return to God's affirmation of your Afrikan self. The second deliverance is a message of liberation — self-liberation — where the fog of Euro-domination is finally recognized in all of its demonic proportions. It is a deliverance because after it occurs, one is no longer bound by the mental, cultural, and spiritual shackles of Euro-dominators. It is an inner move beyond Euro-space, a stepping outside of that space of domination that has shackled our imagination, will, drives, and creativity.

The second deliverance is necessary for Afrikans in particular, but I believe that it is necessary for all who live in our age of technological Euro-domination because every nation is being influenced by the demonic value system of Euro-domination (i.e., the belief that materialism is salvation; that success requires a heartless attitude toward suffering; that conformity to "the way things are" is essential to be successful; that our clothes, houses, cars, and so on are the evidence of being "civilized"). The second deliverance provides teaching, preaching, and information that inspires Xodus men and women to arise and come out of Euro-space . . . forever.

For Malcolm X, a spiritual experience took the form of a vision of Elijah Muhammad coming to him in his prison cell. He had a vision of "a light-brown-skinned man" sitting next to him in his cell during prayer to Allah.[42] This experience was so profoundly moving for Malcolm that it changed the course of his life, turning him from a convict into an international symbol of Black manhood. For most Christians who are Afrikan this spiritual experience comes as a kind of numinous encounter with Jesus Christ. My first deliverance was like that; a moving presence filled my heart and mind with a powerful sense of love that I had never known. But the second deliverance, for me, was a spiritual encounter with my hidden self/soul. Initially it emerged as a potent righteous rage against Euro-domination, but it quickly became a celebration of Blackness and the awakening of a sleeping Afrikan identity.

I have noted that my experience has been duplicated, to various degrees and shades of intensity, by others who have become Africentric, from students to professional colleagues. I am glad for that initial potent righteous rage because it empowered me: to become unafraid of the systemic discipline and punishment tactics, to name those tactics as demonic, to bring up out of my unconscious experiences of injustice and inhumanity suffered at the hands of Euro-dominators that had been suppressed for years, and to consciously "exit." I am free of whiteness! To God be the glory!

I rejoice for the celebration of Blackness and awakening of Afrikan identity even more than for the rage because it is the positive force that holds me as an Xodus traveler. Without the celebration I would have no reason to do anything, but would constantly be at the mercy of whatever recent demonic thing Euro-dominators had "done to me." Rage, by itself, can make us view ourselves only as victims and not as overcomers. But celebration enables the Spirit of God to enter our hearts in a new way, a "baptism in the Holy Ghost" way. Such baptism fires our imaginations with visions of what can be, and fills our days with hope rather than despair. Out of that celebration I have become aware of the power of my Afrikan self/soul, akin to being born again. I am born again; out of the waters of adversity and the fire of oppression, a new Afrikan self/soul has arisen. No longer bound by desires that it has accepted as "true," the Afrikan self/soul is open for divine instruction and divine teaching. No longer affected by the scowls of disapproval by Euro-dominators, a reborn Afrikan self/soul can rise above Euro-Space and create a Space of our own.

Xodus Space is the psycho-spiritual Space that reborn Afrikans are creating with every new act of defiance, every new book, every new piece of art or music. It is a Space beyond the control and gaze of Euro-domination because it is God's Space. It is rooted in God, founded in God, and maintained by God. It is a gift of grace to Xodus travelers for the time being, but it is not closed to anyone. The only way one can recognize it, however, is to hear and receive one's own Blackness.

Xodus Resurrection

In Christian theological language, Xodus represents the dead and crucified historical-cultural personhood of African Americans "rolling away the stone" of Euro-heteronomous imposition, rising to a new self-affirming life. It is the resurrection of a psychoculturally dead people. But unlike traditional evangelical Christian teachings that emphasize the salvation of individual souls — accepting Jesus on an individual basis and having an individual relationship with God — Xodus insists that the salvation of this resurrection must be a group experience. Salvation, for Afrikans, must become something beyond religious dogma or creed. It must directly address the cultural death of our people. Xodus offers a profound social application to the doctrines of salvation — liberating one's self from the shackles of Euro-dominated death — and resurrection — the release of our inner captive so that we might rise to new life as self-affirming Afrikans. The inner captive is finally free because the inner captive is finally awake. Being awake, the inner captive may now be transformed into a self-affirming Xodus-liberator.

If such particularizing of traditionally Christian language seems to negate the purported universal significance of Christian salvation and resurrection teachings, one must remember that the real scandal of the gospel for early followers was the notion that the almighty, high, and omnipotent God would take on the limitation, weakness, and frailty of human flesh. To particularize Christian salvation and resurrection with an Xodus flavor is more in the spirit of the early Christian scandal of God embodying God-self (the doctrine of incarnation), than are any long-winded, boring dissertations on the universal significance of Christ. Jesus Christ embodied God. For Christians, we embody Jesus. That means, for Afrikans, that Jesus and God are "Black." To say "God is Black" is to make a particular theological statement about God's incarnation. It is not to negate God for white folks, red folks, brown folks, or yellow folks. It is simply to affirm something that Euro-dominated Christianity refuses to entertain even to this day — that God can be, must be, and indeed is Black.

It is not my concern whether God is any other color. If God is "Spirit," then it would appear that color and race as we experience them are both embraced and surpassed by the fullness of God. God embraces every particularity and color of humanity in much the same way God embraces and surpasses the most brilliant display of colors, textures, and smells in the vast flora and fauna of a tropical rain forest. God embraces our many colors, textures, and differences, surpassing our understanding because we are only one color, one texture, one "race" at a time. But if God is truly God, then we must allow God to be Black as well as all the other possibilities. God is colorful, not colorless. God loves the rich diversity of shades, hues, and tinctures of colors, from vivid brilliance to shadowy drabness. God is the consummate artist, we are but God's wondrous canvas. To paraphrase 1 Corinthians 12, Can the vivid orange and red foreground colors say to the misty background shadows, "You are not as important as we because we stand out, and you do not"? Is not the canvas the handiwork of the artist? Are not the shadow and background as necessary for the full beauty of the canvas as the brilliant foreground images?

In a very naughty yet sincere way, Xodus journeyers carry on the tradition of the scandal of the gospel in an Africentric fashion by insisting that God is Black. God's Blackness is a pertinent sign of the times that a new *kairos* is under way. Now is the time for Blackness to arise. Under the banner of the "X," Xodus-liberators have been given an inner mission. It is not a mission of conquering, subjugation, and destruction, but one of building up the ruins, setting free the captives, and awakening those who have been asleep for too long. We join all the New Joshuas who are shouting down walls of injustice by singing the songs of ancient truth. Black truth will not be dismissed or erased any longer. Black truth has arisen, it will not die again.

Notes

1. James Cone calls Malcolm X the "Bad Nigger" in his *Martin & Malcolm & America: A Dream or a Nightmare* (Maryknoll, N.Y.: Orbis, 1991), 38–57 ("The

Making of a 'Bad Nigger' [1925–1952]". The "Bad Nigger" is another type of Black male image; the Stackolee myth is of unbridled, bold, almost criminally destructive Black maleness.

2. Ibid., 38, taken from Peter Goldman, *The Death and Life of Malcolm X,* 2d ed. (Urbana: University of Illinois Press, 1979), 6.

3. Malcolm X and Alex Haley, *The Autobiography of Malcolm X* (New York: Ballantine Books, 1965), 216.

4. Herbert G. Gutman uncovered and described a complex and intriguing legacy of Black self-naming in his book *The Black Family in Slavery and Freedom: 1750–1925* (New York: Vintage Books, 1976).

5. Malcolm X and Haley, *Autobiography,* 217.

6. Ibid., 216.

7. Ibid., 290.

8. Ibid., 279. Cf. also Malcolm's exposition of the "hateful self image" in *Malcolm X: The Last Speeches,* ed. Bruce Perry (New York: Pathfinder, 1989), 166.

9. *Autobiography,* 179.

10. Ibid., 179–83.

11. Ibid., 277, 297, 300.

12. George Breitman, ed., *Malcolm X: By Any Means Necessary* (New York: Pathfinder, 1970), 9.

13. Ibid., 241.

14. George Breitman, ed., *Malcolm X Speaks* (New York: Grove Press, 1965), 22.

15. David Gallen, *Malcolm X as They Knew Him* (New York: Carroll & Graf, 1992), 184.

16. "Message to the Grass Roots," in *Malcolm X Speaks,* 4.

17. Ibid., 9, 10.

18. "The Ballot or the Bullet," in *Malcolm X Speaks,* 38–40.

19. Malcolm X, *Last Speeches,* 158, 45.

20. The ankh is referred to in Maulanga Karenga, *Selections from the Husia: Sacred Wisdom of Ancient Egypt* (Los Angeles: University of Sankore Press, 1989); and as *crux ansata* in Graydon F. Snyder, *Ante Pacem: Archeological Evidence of Church Life Before Constantine* (Mercer, Ga.: Mercer University Press, 1985), 27.

21. Ivan Van Sertima, ed., *Great Black Leaders: Ancient and Modern* (New York: Journal of African Civilizations, 1988), 197.

22. Ibid., 13.

23. Anthony Browder, *Nile Valley Contributions to Civilization* (Washington, D.C.: Institute of Karmic Guidance, 1992), 67.

24. Ibid.

25. Ibid., 140.

26. Jack Finegan, *The Archaeology of the New Testament: The Life of Jesus and the Beginning of the Early Church,* 2d ed. (Princeton, N.Y.: Princeton University Press, 1992), 340.

27. Snyder, *Ante Pacem,* 29. He notes that "the cryptocrosses" of Guarducci (an archaeologist) were taken to be combinations of a Greek *tau* or something like an "XP."

28. Finegan, *Archeology of the New Testament,* 340.

29. Ibid., 346.

30. Ibid., 343.

31. All biblical quotes taken from *HarperCollins Study Bible,* New Revised Standard Version (New York: HarperCollins, 1993). Meanings and references to usage of the *taw* are found in *The New Brown and Driver Briggs Gesenius Hebrew and English Lexicon of the Old Testament* (Grand Rapids, Mich.: Baker Book House, 1981 reprint), 1063.

32. Finegan, *Archeology of the New Testament,* 344.

33. Ibid.

34. Ibid., 346.

35. Ibid.

36. James H. Cone, *A Black Theology of Liberation* (Philadelphia: J. P. Lippincott, 1970), 28, 120–21, 182–86.

37. Ibid., 28.

38. Richard King, M.D., *African Origin of Biological Psychiatry* (Germantown, Tenn.: Seymour-Smith, 1990), 22.

39. Malcolm X and Haley, *Autobiography,* 218.

40. Michel Foucault, *Power/Knowledge: Selected Interviews and Other Writings (1972–1977),* edited by Colin Gordon (New York: Pantheon, 1980), 39.

41. Ibid.

42. Malcolm X and Haley, *Autobiography,* 293.

CHAPTER 6

Martin's "Dream"

A s we take care to assemble an illustrious "Gathering of the Elders," it is necessary to remember properly. Never in the history of the United States of America has a human being been as misappropriated and misremembered as the Rev. Dr. Martin Luther King, Jr. In the late 1950s and early 1960s he was miscast as a "militant," "communist," and a "radical." After the rise of Malcolm X, Stokely Carmichael, the Black Panthers, and the militant Black Power movement, King was again misviewed as an "accommodator," and as "soft on white folks." Now King has become a national symbol of "racial progress" in the holiday observed in his name (which I worked hard to promote in the recalcitrant state of New Hampshire even as recently as 1988–1990 as pastor of New Hope Baptist Church). Yet as "symbol," King is left once again in the wrong historical position, this time by many young African Americans, especially strong Africentrists, who view his teachings, stance, and leadership as completely irrelevant to any contemporary agenda for social change.

King hagiographers built a mythic view of his life and teachings that King deconstructors have recently striven mightily to debunk.[1] He was not the ultimate "saint" or the craven "sinner" that clashing headlines would have us believe. He was a profoundly militant Christian who truly believed that the teachings of Jesus Christ about love and justice could be successfully combined with the American creedal statements about the equality of all human beings. Such a stand was militant because King did more than believe — he successfully organized, promoted, and marched with the

93

thousands of African Americans, Jews, Euro-Americans, Native Americans, and others who demonstrated, shed blood, and even died for the civil rights movement (1955–1970) because they were inspired by his message.

King was a prophet because he dared to stand up and "cry out" to the United States of America about its injustices. His voice, rich in the sonorous tones of the best in "Black Baptist rural South oral tradition,"[2] caused southern segregationists to shudder when they heard that he was coming to their town. His was a voice that could move hearts, minds, and bodies against evil. He used this gift until his life was cut short by an assassin's bullet in 1968.

Finally, Martin Luther King was a striving human being more aware of his frailties, weaknesses, and faults than most. His sermons are filled with admissions of his weaknesses, in language both obvious and veiled. Recent allegations that he "cheated" in his dissertation and that he led a profligate life of sexual infidelity only serve to demonstrate that making an idol of the man can only serve a system of Euro-domination, because what is made into an idol on one day can be destroyed as inadequate, false, and dangerous on another.

For the purpose of bringing his insights to the Council Fire, I will focus on the often misunderstood preeminent symbol of King's public theology, the sign that for many in contemporary African American communities represents King's "accommodated" status as a national hero: the Dream. The Dream must be cast as it relates to the more comprehensive symbol of Somebodyness. The Dream and Somebodyness will be presented in terms of their theological grounding, fundamental ethical aim, and capacity to envision a more radical affirmation of one's humanity. I shall conclude with suggestions on how these two symbols may be applied to the contemporary task of constructing an Xodus.

The Dream

The Dream was never about accommodation or capitulation to the good intentions of Euro-Americans. The Dream is a symbol of fierce utopian hope for those who have fought their entire lives for the freedom of all citizens of the United States, but especially for Black folk. Such hope is not something to be trifled with, because such fierce faith is based on a determined resolve to believe in God's ability to transform seemingly unmovable "mountains of evil" — as King might have put it. Such faith is not "soft" on Euro-Americans but makes an ultimate demand on Euro-American dominators that they live up to the highest ideals of their public creeds and national principles of governance. Only if we study the Dream carefully, and demystify its usage as a social opiate intended to make "the Blacks feel good," can we uncover its revolutionary potential for the creation of Xodus Space.

The first important thing to note about the Dream is that it developed over a period a time. King was developing his ideas about the Dream as early as June 1961 in a commencement address at Lincoln University. In the address entitled "The American Dream," we find a carefully reasoned exploration of what the Dream meant to King.[3]

In the first paragraph of the speech, King noted that "America is essentially a dream, a dream as yet unfulfilled." This sentence was striking because it demonstrated both a hopeful stance toward American self-identity and a critical stance about the fulfillment of that identity. This dialectic, or yes-and-no position, could easily be glossed over if we do not take the time to examine what King said about the "American dream."

King described the essence of the American dream in the following words: "It is a dream of a land where men of all races, of all nationalities and of all creeds can live together as brothers."[4] Where had King derived this interpretation of the Dream? No documents state "the American Dream" in that way, nor do any official records insist that all Americans ought to "live together as brothers." King found support for his universalizing theological interpretation in the Preamble of the Declaration of Independence, which he quoted immediately following his universalizing theological sentence:

> The substance of the dream is expressed in these sublime words, words lifted to cosmic proportions: "We hold these truths to be self-evident, that all men are created equal, that they are endowed by their Creator with certain unalienable rights, that among these are life, liberty, and the pursuit of happiness." This is the dream.[5]

Ever the careful rhetorician, King constructed the opening paragraph of "The American Dream" in such a way that he: (1) presented a dialectic of affirmation and criticism of American idealism in contrast to American practices; (2) presented a universal and theological interpretation of the Dream; and (3) tied this universalizing interpretation to one of the most cherished documents of the Founding Fathers. What is ingenious about such a considered rhetorical structure is that it introduced the listeners to the idea of affirming American idealism as a universal standard, a standard so high and broad in its implications that American practices could be criticized by it. So doing, King carefully injected his own universal theological standard of brotherhood into the Dream. In essence, he brought together American ideal notions of equality and justice as fairness of opportunity, as stated in the Preamble, with Christian and particularly African American Christian social justice ideals of brotherhood.[6]

After this ingenious first paragraph, King restated clearly in the second paragraph that the Dream had "an amazing universalism."[7] For King, this universalism was indicative of an inclusive ethic that had no racial, religious, or creedal boundaries.

For King the most amazing thing about the universalism of the Dream was the way it insured basic rights as God-given, rather than "conferred or derived from the state." He believed that this meant that "the dignity and worth of human personality" was affirmed in an unequivocating language seldom found in the social and political documents establishing the principles of statehood. Such unequivocal affirmation of human dignity insured that the norm of inclusion validates the ethical principle that "every [hu]man is heir to the legacy of worthiness."[8]

Such an ennobling and lofty social idealism was in stark and bitter contrast to American practices regarding African Americans. In his address, King now turned toward the contrast between American Dream idealism and concrete racial practices. He indicted America as having a "schizophrenic personality, tragically divided against herself."[9] Condemning slavery and segregation as paradoxes, King rapidly moved into a prophetic rhetoric of denunciation. His denunciation of America's "schizophrenia" on racial matters takes on ominous tones:

> But the shape of the world today does not permit us the luxury of an anemic democracy. The price America must pay for the continued exploitation of the Negro and other minority groups is the price of its own destruction. The hour is late; the clock of destiny is ticking out.[10]

The urgency and forcefulness of these words continue to amaze me. This is not the rhetoric of an accommodator. It is not "soft" on Euro-domination. It is provocative and commanding. This is the language of prophecy, combining an economic metaphor of price with one of time — the "clock of destiny." Yet it is not a rhetoric of hatred. It is no blanket condemnation of all Euro-Americans. Indeed, inscribed within the text is a sense of "Us-ness," a "we" that includes African Americans, Euro-Americans, and other "minority groups" not specifically named. From this small excerpt from one of King's speeches, we can readily discern the contours of his style and substance. His was a theologically informed vision that both proclaimed inclusion as the highest and most ideal form of American justice, and practiced inclusion as its substantive program. We do not find "them" and "us" distinctions in King's language, only a common enemy that all of "us" must fight . . . together.

King believed that the American dream required a world perspective in order to be properly understood. This world perspective was a recognition of the ways in which modern technology has made the entire world into a "neighborhood." This proximity is indicative of the theological-ontological insight that "all life is interrelated."[11] The world perspective would relativize the "American dream" by making it cognizant of "the larger dream of world brotherhood."[12] So the Dream, if we continue to capitalize it as an Xodus newword, is much more than merely an affirmation of the American dream of a good life, material wealth, and the pursuit of happiness. The Dream, for King, involved a recognition of the ways in which air travel has connected residents of cities all over the globe in a closely tied network of interchange. Travel had brought King and his wife into direct contact with the hunger, poverty, and dire conditions of the majority of people living in Calcutta and Bombay, India. Such personal experience of the suffering of others around the world reminded King of the ways in which the destinies of all nations are tied together. Thus King could not rest easy while he knew that millions were starving. He wrestled with the moral dilemma of America spending "more than a million dollars a day to store surplus food in this country," insisting that the same food could be stored "free of charge — in the wrinkled stomachs of the millions of people who go to bed hungry at night."[13] Such sensitivity was not based on a softhearted sentimentality, but on a mystical sense of connection with all life.

Martin Luther King's Dream, at its core, was a vision of interrelationship and connection. This vision of interrelationship and connection is my interpretation in contemporary inclusive language of King's "larger dream of brotherhood" of which the "American dream" was an important exemplar. This vision included the following aspects:

- *All life is interrelated.* King supported this insight by noting that life is an inescapable network of mutuality that was tied into a single garment of destiny.
- *Whatever affects one directly affects all indirectly.* This is the profound moral insight of the impossibility of any action having only a single and individual effect. I call this the Vision Imperative.
- *I can never be what I ought to be until you are what you ought to be.* This is a restatement of the Vision Imperative that reinforces the idea of the interrelated structure of reality.[14]

The following paragraphs of "The American Dream" reinforced the fundamental theological and ethical foundation of the vision of interrelationship and connection. King noted three additional aspects of making the "dream" of America a reality:

1. *Moral and spiritual progress must keep abreast of massive scientific and technological change.* King was greatly concerned about the gap between the technological and scientific creativity of human beings

and their lagging ability to keep up morally and spiritually with what they had created. With alarm King noted that "the means by which we live" were outdistancing "the ends for which we live." He was afraid that without proper spiritual progress, the world was rapidly approaching the point where we would be "ending up with guided missiles in the hands of misguided men."[15] It is important for us to note that King was not against the "progress" of science and technology per se, but against our contemporary inability to march alongside of such "progress" with increasingly meaningful and insightful spiritual knowledge.

2. *We need to get rid of notions of inferior and superior races.* Debunking and refuting all theories of supremacy — Black as well as white — was one of the hallmarks of King's thought. He did so with finesse, attention to current anthropological writings, and a sense of the flow of history that had established notions of racial supremacy.[16]

3. *The American dream can be implemented by the continued "creative protest" of nonviolence.* While I have already provided a description of nonviolence in *Somebodyness*, for this current work it may suffice to say that nonviolence was more than a strategy for social change — it was a revolutionary lifestyle and philosophical-theological commitment for King. King believed that nonviolence provided the moral resources to fight American "schizophrenia" because it sought to "secure moral ends by moral means."[17] This moral resource made it ethically superior to Machiavellians who believed that any means might be used to secure a moral end. It was a moral means to a moral end because it refused to allow hatred to provide the motivational power to move masses to fight for their freedom. Instead, nonviolence relied on the notion of agape as an energizing force that transformed its practitioner as it transformed the society. (I shall say more about this later.) Further, King believed that nonviolence had practical resources that disarmed one's opponent because it aroused conscience in the opponent, "exposed the moral defenses" of the opponent, and thereby broke down the opponent's morale.[18]

The import of the Vision Imperatives of interrelationship and connection for Xodus reflection can be enormous. King takes away the power of hatred as a motivating force by emphasizing nonviolence. Yet nonviolence is not a passivist, do-nothing alternative. It is a dangerous choice because one puts one's life in the hands of one's opponent, knowing full well that one's life might be taken. It takes more than "foolish courage" to maintain that such a way of believing and acting has the potential to change society. It takes fierce utopian hope, a hope based on more than meets the eye. Such an issue is a matter of faith, but more importantly, it is a matter of organization and planning on a massive scale.

If the Los Angeles Rebellion of 1992 had been carried out by a systematic, sustained, massive, and organized campaign of the same sort as those led by the Southern Christian Leadership Conference (SCLC) in the 1960s, real national attention would have been brought to bear on the problems of African Americans and urban residents. Instead the Rebellion became a "riot," a thing to be controlled and handled, and now most people have all but forgotten it. Fierce utopian hope fires the imaginations, emotions, and bodies of Xodus travelers so that we are not afraid to march en masse into a drug-infested area to "take back our streets."[19] The drug dealers, who could have mowed these brothers down with their heavy arsenal of Uzis, packed up and left instead. Such victories, while symbolically meaningful, are not long-lasting, because those same crack dealers simply moved to another block or another area of the 'hood. Without a massive, nationwide, organized campaign, the limited victories of these nonviolent Xodus-style demonstrations will have no long-term impact except in symbolism and media hype.

In addition, Xodus vision requires a Pan-African perspective, an international grasp of the ways in which what happens to one nation affects the situation of all. Martin Luther King's call for a world perspective still rings true today. His internationalism had a particular interest in the people of "the South," the darker-skinned peoples in poverty-stricken quarters of the world. It is a little known fact that King was interested in the freedom movements abounding in Africa from the late 1950s on. King was Pan-African before the term attained its current popular status. His Pan-Africanism ought to be understood as part of his concept of a larger dream, what I have called his vision of interrelationship and connection.

Pan-African Vision

In an early unpublished text entitled "The Birth of a New Nation," King tied his personal interpretation of then-current moves throughout Africa to overthrow colonial powers to the Exodus narrative in the Bible. The text was transcribed from a recorded sermon, so there is a contemporaneous and folksy quality to King's rhetoric not often found in most of his formally edited publications. The sermon related the then-current struggles of Africans to give birth to new nations with the struggles of Moses and the Hebrews to attain the freedom implied by their Exodus deliverance. King tied these current historical struggles for freedom with a universal story of the human quest for freedom: "This is something [referring to the narrative of Moses as related in the movie *The Ten Commandments*] of the story of every people struggling for freedom. And it demonstrates the stages that seem to inevitably follow the quest for freedom."[20]

For the next several pages of the text, King made a case paralleling the lives of Moses and Kwame Nkrumah of the Gold Coast (now Ghana). He does not overtly mention the Moses narrative, but it is clear that he was using the Exodus story as a backdrop. For example, he described the birth, education, and rise to national leadership of Nkrumah in language parallel to that of Scripture. (Son of a poor Hebrew slave, Moses grew up in Pharaoh's court and received the finest education befitting a son of Pharaoh.) King's reference to the situation of the Gold Coast Africans was analogous to the situation of African Americans in the United States in 1955 with the Montgomery bus boycott, the first moment of the civil rights movement. King described the Gold Coast people as being "tired," as he described the Black folks of Montgomery a few years before: "And as the colony [the Gold Coast] suffered all of the injustices, all of the exploitation, all of the humiliation that comes as a result of colonialism, come to the point that the people got tired of it."[21]

King saw this tiredness, this weariness of being exploited and oppressed, as something universal. He believed that it was emblematic of something deep within human beings related to being created in God's image:

> There seems to be a throbbing desire, there seems to be an internal desire for freedom within the soul of every man. And it's there. It might not break forth in the beginning, but eventually it breaks out. Men realize that freedom is something basic. To rob a man of his freedom is to take from him the essential basis of his manhood, to take from him his freedom is to rob him of God's image.[22]

King went to great oratorical lengths in this speech to describe in detail the events that led to the liberation of the Gold Coast and the birth of Ghana. Over the next several pages unfolds a great narrative, a freedom story depicting how the people of the Gold Coast agitated against the colonial rule of Britain under Nkrumah's leadership. The narrative relates how Nkrumah and his followers first organized a Convention Party, which "started in a humble way" urging the people "to unite for freedom," but they "were slow to respond." Yet the "masses of the people were with him, and they united," becoming the most powerful and organized party ever established "in that section of Africa."[23]

Because of his influential writings on independence, Nkrumah was imprisoned for several years as a rebellious leader of "sedition." When the people grew so agitated that they were going to free him by force, the British Empire relented and let him go. After his release, Nkrumah and the people waged "continual agitation . . . continual resistance," until the British finally realized that "this nation could no longer be a colony of the British Empire, that this nation would be a sovereign nation in the British Commonwealth."[24] King reinforced his point about the importance of "persistent protest, continual agitation" as the primary reason for the success of Nkrumah, other African leaders, and the people of Ghana.

Coretta and Martin King were invited to participate in the opening ceremonies marking the birth of Ghana. The next section of the sermon describes with great relish the details of those exciting and momentous days. It is apparent that King was tremendously moved by the outpouring of feeling displayed by the people, especially after the "Old Parliament" was closed and the British Union Jack was taken down and the flag of Ghana was raised.[25] King described how he stood listening to Nkrumah tell his people that they were no longer a colony but rather "a sovereign people," and how that proclamation brought tears to all eyes. King related to these events quite personally:

> An' I stood there thinking about so many things. Before I knew it, I started weeping. I was crying for joy. An' I knew about all of the struggles, an' all of the pain an' all of the agony these people had gone through for this moment.[26]

Then the people, a new people, marched in a mighty throng through the streets crying "Freedom," as the African Americans of that time were doing in America, but in their own accent. King related thinking about hearing "that old Negro spiritual once more crying out, 'Free at last, free at last, great God almighty, I'm free at last.'"[27]

It is significant that King related feeling this way in Ghana in 1957, because he quoted this same phrase at the climax of the famous "Dream" speech of August 1963 in Washington, D.C. Was King seeing the "birth of a new nation" in Washington that sweltering summer day that reminded him of the throngs of Ghanaians he had witnessed six years before? Is it possible that King detected in the famous "Dream" speech something of similar impact for all Americans, particularly African Americans? Surely anyone who has heard that speech can feel the joy and sense of ecstasy of that moment. With Xodus eyes and ears I believe that Martin Luther King discerned an important and lasting connection between the birth moment of Ghana and that Dream moment in August 1963 for African Americans. We must make this connection clearly because the ad nauseam repetition of the King "sound-bite" saying only, "I have a dream . . ." disconnects the moment from its larger cosmic sense of freedom. The "Dream" speech was an eloquent articulation of that momentous time when some half a million Americans gathered in our nation's capital to protest racial injustice. It was a kind of epiphany, a moment of divine inbreaking into the lives of all Americans. For African Americans, it was the moment when our suit for freedom, our pursuit of American equal opportunity and its idealism of justice, came to a head. For King, standing in front of the press of so many thousands, his mind carried him back to that moment in Ghana of a nation's inauguration, back to the old Negro spiritual, and he connected all of these events together.

What fascinates me about the last section of "The Birth of a New Nation" is the way in which King urged American Blacks to emigrate to Ghana in order to perform "technical assistance" needed for its birth. He urged doctors, dentists, insurance salesmen, and others to go. African American assistance was needed because Ghana was "going through the wilderness," the "time of adjustment" that always occurs after one "breaks loose from Egypt." The wilderness, said King, had to be faced with hope because "the promised land is ahead."[28]

King used the last part of this freedom narrative sermon to make explicit ties between the birth of Ghana and the nonviolent agitation of African Americans. King made the following points:

- *Freedom is never voluntarily given by the oppressor to the oppressed.* Strong and persistent resistance is necessary for freedom to come. The oppressed must "keep on keepin' on in order to gain freedom."[29]
- *A people can break loose from oppression without violence.* King was pleased that Nkrumah's autobiography noted the importance of Gandhi's social philosophy to his movement in Ghana. Nonviolent resistance frees without humiliating the oppressor, by creating beloved community, creating redemption and reconciliation between former foes without an aftermath of bloodshed.[30]
- *Nonviolence frees without bitterness* but with a sense of hope and determination to work together for a "better world."[31]
- *Freedom never comes on a silver platter, is never easy, but requires persistence and "hardness of life."* King made parallels between Ghana's determined pursuit of new nationhood and the violent resistance of white segregationists in the South during the late 1950s. King reminded his listeners that the "tensionless period" was a period of insult, oppression, and passivity, whereas the current "period of tension" was a "period when the Negro has decided to rise up and cut aloose from that."[32]
- *The birth of Ghana told King that the "forces of the universe are on the side of justice."* The "old order" of colonialism and segregation was passing away while a "new order of justice and freedom and good will is being born."[33]

In his closing remarks King noted that "the God of the universe eventually takes a stand" for freedom and justice. He urged the listeners to "rise up and know that as you struggle for justice, you do not struggle alone because God struggles with ya', and He's workin' every day."[34] King wanted the people in that church to make a connection, a Pan-African connection that was deeper than being "black" together. He wanted those African Americans to realize their spiritual connection with freedom-seeking Africans. He wanted them to draw spiritual succor and strength from the victories of Ghanaians who had fought nonviolently for their freedom and won. The Dream is not the sole province of American materialist visions of wealth, it is connected to those divine moments when God's power floods into the sphere of human interaction, creating freedom and justice, and giving former foes the power to be reconciled.

Is such a Dream appropriate for Xodus Space? Is the language of freedom, justice, and beloved community too lame for the harsh urban realities of the coming turn of the century and millennium? At this apocalyptic moment, can we really connect with a moment of ecstatic joy such as was experienced by the people of Ghana in 1957, or in Washington, D.C., in 1963? The Dream is still important, but only if we realize its global, interrelated, and connective nature. The whitewashed (literally!), watered-down, cleaned-up, and pacified "dream" that we are fed by the media on King holidays is inadequate for Xodus because it is not the Dream. The Dream is Pan-African. It connects Xodus African Americans to other Africans throughout the world.

The Dream has recurred since King's death. One only need recount the joy African Americans felt when Nelson Mandela was released from prison, and how that release led to the free elections for Black South Africans in 1994. No one thought that white South Africans would ever peacefully (or at least relatively peacefully) submit to the will of the world and open up the democratic process to Black South Africans. Yet the "wilderness" of bringing together warring factions, of healing tribal animosities, and of redistributing the unjustly accumulated hoards of white South Africans for Blacks still awaits Mandela and the new South Africans. We experienced the joy of the birth of a new South Africa in April 1994 similar to King's experience in Ghana in 1957. Such a moment helps African Americans to realize once again the price of freedom, the high cost of justice.

The Dream is not enough, on the other hand, for those of us struggling with questions of the efficacy of nonviolence. Nonviolence "worked" as a sociopolitical strategy in the cities of the United States only when limited public-access issues were at stake in the early civil rights movement between 1955 and 1963. When the freedom struggle called for more radical economic measures, resistance hardened. The reaction of young Blacks was to turn to more violent tactics and rhetoric in the Black Power movement. The fiery language of Malcolm X, the bravado of Stokely Carmichael, and the militant posture of the Black Panthers appealed to Blacks who had tired of getting their heads beaten, their legs bitten by dogs, and their bodies assaulted by fire hoses.

Even King was compelled to step up his rhetoric in the late 1960s before his untimely death. The record shows that King and the SCLC were at a point of crisis about following the nonviolent agenda, with King insisting that he would be nonviolent even if it meant that he would do it alone. Nonviolence was never meant to be a strategy for social change practiced on an individual basis in adherence to a privatized conviction, or held only as a personal religious tenet. Nonviolence worked as a strategy for social change in the form of massive organized demonstrations. So, while we may admire King's stance for its call for holding to nonviolence as a moral principle, for all practical purposes he had already conceded that its time had come and gone by 1967 and 1968. The violent aftermath of his assassination demonstrated Black rage in a world in which the apostle of nonviolence could be violently killed. For many, King's death was also the death of nonviolence as a credible means of achieving social change.

African American nonviolence was successful as long as the threat existed of Malcolm X or Stokely Carmichael or the Panthers as an alternative "answer." To put it more directly, the guns of the Black Panthers strengthened the echoing cries of Martin Luther King, Jr. The white power structure could always turn to leaders like King as "reasonable" in contrast to the demands of those more radical. Once viewed as an extremist, King appeared to be the rational person to negotiate with when one contrasted his rhetoric of redemptive suffering and nonviolence with the fiery "in-your-face" polemics of Malcolm X.

In fact, nonviolence called for a different sort of revolution than did the calls of "Black Power," both in the ears of whites and in the minds of African Americans. In an interview with Robert Penn Warren in 1964, King noted that African Americans were calling for a "revolution calling upon the nation to live up to what is already there in an idealistic sense — I mean, in all of its creeds and all of its basic affirmations." While the Dream motivated African Americans to become more aware of our ties to global freedom struggles, inspiring connections and vision, the immediate goal of nonviolence was to become part of the American mainstream: "It is a revolution of rising expectations, and it is a revolution, not to liquidate the structure of America, but a revolution to get into the main stream of American life."[35]

What did King mean by a "revolution to get into the main stream of American life"? Our late-twentieth-century, integration-weary minds might consider this statement to be the kind of accommodationism and moderation that leads many young people to look at the Black middle class as "sellouts." After all, what King wanted did happen in a significant way, for *some* Black folks. In 1960 only 5 percent of the African American population was middle-class; by 1990 that figure had risen to 33 percent. That rise suggests that for those African Americans who were well trained and socially "ready," the integration movement was ideal. Those Blacks "made it," and "got into" the American mainstream. We ought not belittle such a massive social shift. Further, for King and those who fought hard for integration, there was a kind of optimism about being present in the mainstream — a hope that just being there would somewhere make a difference in how we were going to be treated. By the mid-1960s the "integrationists" were viewed as "reasonable" by the white power structure, the kind of Negroes that "we can work with" in comparison with the "militants."

The question for us now is, Does Xodus Space want to be "reasonable" and part of the "mainstream"? No. We want to change the mainstream so that it will have enough room for us to be Afrikan without discipline, punishment, or banishment. We want to be accepted, not accommodated. We want to change the mainstream, not be changed by it. Xodus people are the "Children of the Dream" who recognize that a revolution to enter the mainstream has become a march toward cultural, psychic, and emotional genocide. Xodus Space is the creation of a Space that affirms the Blackness of Afrikans, no matter what the mainstream thinks or does. Yet Xodus Space does not have a desire to destroy America or white people. We simply create Space for ourselves, and press to change the mainstream so that we can breathe.

I do not want us to cast aside King's thought entirely. The "new order of justice and freedom and goodwill" is a particularly positive contribution we ought to add to the creation of Xodus Space. The principles of justice, freedom, and goodwill are ethical landmarks worthy of being preserved. These are principles of relationship that open up possibilities for deeper and richer fellowship both among Afrikans and between Afrikans and the rest of the world. Xodus Space is not isolationist, merely skeptical of the capacity of those immersed in whiteness to genuinely share power — the ostensible goal of King's integration telos. Justice, freedom, and goodwill may indeed form the pillars of an Xodus Space where power might be redefined as the sharing of power that King named "integration." He defined integration as a lofty and noble undertaking, far richer than mere "desegregation":

Integration is creative, and is therefore more profound and far-reaching than desegregation. Integration is the positive acceptance of desegregation and the welcomed participation of Negroes into the total range of human activities. Integration is genuine inter-group, interpersonal doing. Desegregation then, rightly, is only a short-range goal. Integration is the ultimate goal of our national community.[36]

If most Euro-Americans had taken King's advice and positively embraced desegregation as the prelude to entering into an integrated society, we would not have the bitterness and disillusionment concerning the possibilities of integration now. Integration, as spelled out by King, was not a social program as desegregation obviously was, but a social goal — an end. Such an end, cast in the language of genuineness, sincerity, and trust, seems to be a naive dream for most of us. Such a view of integration seems almost to be ideologically utopian in the most romanticized and unrealistic sense. Yet King's concept of integration, if viewed as part of the empowering substance of fierce utopian hope, makes sense, because it provides a goal or end toward which all persons ought to aspire. Integration, if we translate it into Xodus sharing, may be a positive antidote to the *disillragedeterminassion* I spoke of in chapter 1.

Xodus sharing is realistic integration, people choosing to share power with each other, not out of conformity to a court order, but because they desire the community that comes from sharing. Xodus sharing cannot take place under the strictures of a court order or the threat of lawsuits. If people do not want to share their power, they will not, even if they disguise their actions in the form of "desegregation." Furthermore, Xodus sharing insists on the realistic appraisal by all members of the possibility of sharing. There cannot be a "genuine inter-group, interpersonal doing" between individuals who cannot get beyond their racial privileges and status. In Xodus Space all are welcomed, but realism dictates doubts about whether many will be able to stand the intensity of genuine sharing. After all, Euro-domination thrives on the pretense of integration while manipulating chosen tokens (used here in the same way that Mary Daly uses the term) to hide the absence of genuine sharing.

The only way that the Dream can become a reality is for it to be combined with another one of King's concepts: Somebodyness. A many-sided, complex, and comprehensive ideal, Somebodyness incorporates elements of the Dream into a rhetoric of embodiment — the living incarnation of Xodus Space.

Somebodyness

While King's work has been analyzed as the religious genius of a preacher, nascent Black theology, political theory, or a nonviolent ethic, a more adequate view of King's thought is as a vigorously intellectual and practical visionary concept for transforming our understanding of human dignity.

By emphasizing dignity, the essential connections betw¢
Boston personalist metaphysics, African American "dow\
spirituality, Gandhian nonviolence, and popular America
presuppositions become more apparent.[37] King's most influ¢
phrases were woven throughout the entire corpus of his tho\
variously in speeches, sermons, addresses, and writings. I \
King's most comprehensive and multivalent symbol of human   , was
Somebodyness. It is a symbol that appeared most prominently toward the
end of King's life in response to the nascent Black Power movement,
although his earlier writings also used the expression.

Somebodyness presupposes a traditional Christian view of human beings
in which every person is created in the image of God. For King, the image
of God in human beings is best understood as the indelible imprint of dignity and freedom that becomes a throbbing desire for freedom in the
oppressed who are robbed of their freedom.[38] King interpreted this inner
thirst for freedom as so profound that it demanded action to fight to regain
freedom. For King, nonviolent demonstration was the best means to attain
freedom. Thus, the fundamental theological basis of Somebodyness is that
*all human beings have been granted dignity because we are all children of
God*. Further, King construes the image of God as freedom, without which
people are left with only a throbbing desire to attain it. This desire, in turn,
energizes their struggle to regain freedom through nonviolent means.

King insisted that through the energizing force of agape the nonviolent
practitioner concretely realized the confrontational power of Somebodyness.
King construed agape as a volitional commitment to confronting injustice
with nonviolence, creating a beloved community, going to any length to
preserve community, forgiveness, and an awareness of the interrelatedness
of all life.

King's commitment to an agape-centered life enabled the fundamental
ethical aim of Somebodyness to be the self-affirmation of African American
personhood. Such self-affirmation was attained by "standing up" to the
oppressive structures of racism that depersonalize us. During an interview
in 1967, King listed four qualities of Somebodyness: (1) an internal change
in the psyche of African Americans; (2) a sense of pride; (3) an ability to
stand up; and (4) the feeling of being a human being.[39]

King viewed Somebodyness as a positive response overturning the
instilled sense of worthlessness that is our legacy of slavery. Somebodyness
demands an unshackling of our minds in order to affirm our worth for ourselves:

> The Negro must assert for all to hear and see a majestic sense of worth. There
> is such a thing as a desegregated mind. We must no longer allow the outer

$_\smile$ of an oppressive society to shackle our minds. With courage and fear-$_\smile$essness we must set out daringly to stabilize our egos. This alone will give us a confirmation of our roots and a validation of our worth.[40]

Such self-affirmation caused King to note that Somebodyness requires courage. Courage, in King's estimation, was that quality of dogged determination, perseverance, and a spirit of never giving up hope embodied in "our slave forebears."[41] In fact, for King, such courage engenders self-respect, a quality we examined more closely in the thought of Malcolm X (see chapter 5).

Finally, King believed that Somebodyness is an affirmation of the beauty of our Blackness. He chastised Black folk for using bleaching creams to lighten our skin and processing our hair to straighten it. King envisioned life as a piano with both black and white keys, where *all* the keys would be valued for their contribution in producing the harmonious music of living together. King believed that if Blacks would gain the genuine self-appreciation and self-acceptance of Somebodyness, a process could begin whereby white Americans might come to understand integration as "an opportunity to participate in the beauty of diversity."[42] Therefore, while King constructed the notion of Somebodyness from his mother's injunction to remember that he was "somebody," in his maturity he reached out to value the beauty and diversity of both Black folks and white folks. Somebodyness is a imaginative conceptual vision of human self-affirmation in spite of dehumanizing evils that perpetuate Black oppression. Somebodyness reaches outward ultimately toward the transformation of all persons.

Martin and Malcolm in Xodus

Both Martin Luther King and Malcolm X developed a broader and more radical vision of human dignity in their last days. King intensified his Pan-African commitment to a worldwide vision of interrelatedness that he felt was appropriate for the revolutionary times, while Malcolm radicalized his pan-Africanism within a context of global awareness. Both defended their core vision of love to the end. For King the other-centered, outreaching, and community-building agape was essential to the formation of Somebodyness; while Malcolm insisted, to the contrary, that Blacks could only achieve self-respect by learning to love themselves first — a difficult achievement for a race that had been brainwashed to hate everything about itself. Yet both Martin and Malcolm's symbols of human dignity insist upon:

- *a love of one's self and one's body* that originates from a life-changing encounter with the divine;

- *radical self-affirmation* that is the fruit of the life-changing divine encounter; self-affirmation that counteracts the self-hatred and depersonalization of one's past self-image produced by systemic racism;
- *a sense of pride* gained by disciplined study and analysis of one's historic past; and
- *an affirmation of Black power* as a healthy thing spiritually, emotionally, psychologically, and economically.

Xodus seekers may use these four areas as we journey toward the affirmation of our selves and our bodies, developing a sense of pride, and affirming Black power. Like King we may affirm that at its core Black power has to do with developing a profound sense of ourselves, how beautiful we are and how worthy to be loved. In a world where Black love is "unfashionable," in Toinette Eugene's phrase,[43] we must learn to love ourselves as a radical act of social change. Xodus Space may be the Space — that inner-outer, psychocultural place — where we may begin to develop the skills needed to learn such radical self-affirmation. In Xodus Space, learning the ways of brotherhood/sisterhood-in-process, we have the opportunity to creatively learn together, make mistakes together, fail together, and grow in patience as we stand up and try again.

I have no illusions about Xodus Space being a superhuman space where Super-Afrikans are acting, loving, and serving each other with no sense of greed, selfishness, envy, or jealousy. Such things are a part of what it means to be human. They are a part of the frustrating and humbling process of what it means to be alive. In order for us to plumb the depths of the vitality of life, and to see how we fit into that cosmic connection, we shall take inspiration in the next chapter from another Elder, Howard Thurman.

Notes

1. The work of David Garrow radically deconstructs "King as Saint," portraying him as a lonely, driven, and increasingly isolated leader. See his *Bearing the Cross: Martin Luther King, Jr., and the Southern Christian Leadership Conference* (New York: Wm. Morrow, 1986).
2. See my excursus on this tradition in *Somebodyness: Martin Luther King, Jr., and the Theory of Dignity* (Minneapolis: Fortress Press, 1993), 10–16.
3. In James M. Washington, *A Testament of Hope: The Essential Writings of Martin Luther King, Jr.* (San Francisco: Harper & Row, 1986), 208–16.
4. Ibid., 208.
5. Ibid.
6. Peter Paris notes that the notion of "brotherhood" is one of the fundamental social justice imperatives of African Americans; see *The Social Teaching of Black Churches* (Philadelphia: Fortress Press, 1985).

7. Washington, *Testament of Hope,* 208.
8. Ibid.
9. Ibid., 208–9.
10. Ibid., 209.
11. Ibid., 209–10.
12. Ibid., 209.
13. Ibid., 210.
14. Ibid.
15. Ibid., 210–11.
16. Ibid., 211–12.
17. Ibid., 214.
18. Ibid.
19. The One Hundred Black Men of Milwaukee did this in 1992 and 1993 as a sign of their commitment to and concern for transforming their own neighborhoods.
20. Martin Luther King, Jr., "The Birth of a New Nation," April 1957, Martin Luther King Center for Nonviolent Social Change Archives (hereafter, King Center Archives), Atlanta, p. 1.
21. Ibid., 3.
22. Ibid., 3–4.
23. Ibid., 6.
24. Ibid., 7.
25. Ibid., 8–9.
26. Ibid., 9.
27. Ibid., 9–10.
28. Ibid., 11–12.
29. Ibid., 12–13.
30. Ibid., 14–15.
31. Ibid., 16.
32. Ibid., 16–17.
33. Ibid., 17–18.
34. Ibid., 21.
35. Martin Luther King, Jr., interview with Robert Penn Warren, "Who Speaks for the Negro?" 18 March 1964, King Center Archives, 4.
36. From "The Ethical Demands of Integration," in *Testament of Hope.*
37. See Garth Baker-Fletcher, "Somebodyness: Resources for a Theory of Dignity in the Thought of Martin Luther King, Jr.," Ph.D. diss., Harvard University, 1991, p. xv.
38. Martin Luther King, Jr., "The Birth of a New Nation," pp. 3–4.
39. Martin Luther King, Jr., interview on "The Merv Griffin Show," 6 July 1967, King Center Archives, 6.
40. Martin Luther King, Jr., *Where Do We Go from Here: Chaos or Community?* (Boston: Beacon Press, 1967), 122–23.
41. Ibid., 123.
42. Ibid.
43. Toinette Eugene, "While Love Is Unfashionable: The Ethical Implications of Black Spirituality and Sexuality," in *Sexuality and the Sacred: Sources for Theological Reflection* (Louisville: Westminster/John Knox Press, 1994), 105–12.

CHAPTER 7

Common Ground

I love to take early morning walks up into the foothills of the San Gabriel Mountains, which lie just four miles from our house in southern California. It is invigorating to feel the body respond to the challenge of ascending toward the sky. This joy is both bodily and spiritual, suffusing my self with a sense of connection with the earth — its creatures, its life, and its suffering. One cannot live in southern California without being aware of the tremendous toll human beings have taken on the natural beauty and health of the earth. Only on clear winter days can one enjoy all of the beautiful panoramic views of mountains, because the brownish-gray haze of smog usually blots out all landscape vision except for those mountains closest to our home. Only on days of extreme Santa Ana winds, or after a vigorous rainstorm, or on a chilly winter day do we realize that in the San Gabriel Valley we are surrounded on three sides by breathtakingly beautiful mountains and valleys covered with a tremendously big sky.

Xodus Space contributes to a postmodern discourse dealing with issues that relate to living in a smoggy, overexploited, and threatened natural environment. Benjamin Chavis, African American social activist and recently deposed executive director of the National Association for the Advancement of Colored People, reminds us that toxic waste sites, incinerators, high wires, and factories belching pollutants into the atmosphere often surround the poorest of Black communities. Calling such phenomena environmental racism, he connects the exploitive and genocidal social practices of racist

111

discourse to the exploitive practice of environmental destruction. Such a connection is essential to the creation of Xodus Space because it reveals the ways in which environmentalism and the ecological movement must be viewed as a "Black thing." The development of an ecological ethic is an essential task to the ongoing health and well-being of Afrikans throughout the world.

This chapter attempts to respond creatively to James Cone's theological challenge as issued in *Martin & Malcolm & America* by listening to the voice of earth-loving wisdom — the voice of Howard Thurman. In Thurman we find a necessary earth-connection revitalizing for Afrikans who have been colonized by the earth-hating practices of urbanization. This earth-connection is best demonstrated in the wonderful expression "Common Ground." Resonating with theological meaning, Common Ground may represent yet another powerful Afrikan/pan-African contribution to contemporary ecological thinking. For Xodus, Common Ground helps to fill out the missing pieces of a theology and ethics based on the thought of Martin Luther King, Jr., and Malcolm X. In Christian theological language, Common Ground is a symbol we may borrow from the rich wellspring of Thurman's spiritual insights that is a distinctively African American contribution to the doctrine of creation.

Common Ground cannot be established until the religious person recognizes that the "transcendent monitor" (the transcendent aspect of humanity that rides on the horizon of timelessness and eternity) must find its stabilizing roots in the earth itself. The earth is the womb from which the human being acts as "a participant in that which sustains and supports all life on the planet."[1]

Howard Thurman presses us to realize the need for "seeking always to locate [our] profoundest religious insights in the very structure of . . . life."[2] "Life" is an enormous category for Thurman. On one hand, fundamentally life simply *is:*

> Considered in this way, we think of life without particular consciousness as we experience it or know it, but rather as rhythmic movement, as ebb and flow, as integration and disintegration, as orderliness and disorderliness. In such a view, the motion of beginning and ending has no meaning. Life simply *is.*[3]

According to Thurman, another way of viewing life is created when we begin to consider that there must be an origin, a beginning of some sort. This second sort of thinking about life is religious, as in "the creation accounts, myths, or queries," or scientific in its need to deduce "creation hypotheses" through experimentation, observation, and verification.[4] Thurman spends the entire length of *The Search for Common Ground* elaborating the ramifications of these two general areas of seeking. He revels in contrasting the Jewish and Christian myth of origins — the Garden of Eden account — with the Hopi Indian creation story of Spider Woman. Thurman sets out to reveal how such accounts are remarkable in their profound attempt to determine, from a beginning, a sense of "inherent order, harmony," and "integration." In these accounts Thurman detects the concept of intent, the idea that there is a purposiveness, a direction of creating that confirms the further religious notion of a Creator or creators.[5] Such mythic analysis and exploration is essential to Xodus journeying because as we seek a life-promoting new meaning for ourselves as Afrikans, we reach backward into mythic time as we march forward into future time. We listen to this particular Elder to provide us with clues for the Journey . . .

In the Genesis creation account as Thurman sees it, God creates order, harmony, and a sense of "community" and "tranquillity" in a succession of "days," developing matter in a progression of complexity from inorganic to organic forms. a "harmony of innocence . . . is given as a part of the givenness of the Creator to His creation" in the account, according to Thurman.[6] All this is challenged by the temptation of Eve and Adam by the serpent — the principle of "discord, disharmony," from which "dissent" arises. After the original two humans eat of the fruit of the tree of knowledge of good and evil, the "community of innocence" is shattered, leading to the necessity of Adam becoming a "responsible creature."[7] Thurman does not develop a heavy notion of a fall from grace, but rather of a fall from innocence into responsibility.

Adam and Eve are viewed as initially innocent, but with the potential for moral choices, decisions, and behavior that could destroy innocence. Thurman sees this as a "dialectical dimension" in Adam, attributing to Eve the potential for destroying innocence. By contemporary standards this assuredly is the traditionally sexist notion of blaming Eve for Adam's fall, yet the way Thurman takes on this doctrine seems to emphasize the concept of loss of innocence as leading to the development of responsibility.

By losing innocence, violating God's intention, Adam "loses his sense of community with the rest of creation." For the first time his potential for disharmony is actualized in a "volitional act contrary to the Creator's intent" that leads to Adam becoming "responsible to the Creator, for it is the Creator's intent in creating him that he has violated; now he is also responsible to himself for his actions."[8]

Putting it in a different way, Thurman notes that "in Adam innocence is given. . . . This potential is actualized without achievement or struggle." As a given, innocence is Adam's "experience of what his life ought to be and in fact is," which he "separates himself from" in the volitional act of violating the Creator's intent. Because Adam is separated from his fundamental experience of the oughtness/isness of community, "he is forced now to win it, to achieve it by his own struggle." Thurman implies that this development is positive, because there can be "no responsibility for action so long as he functions out of innocence."[9]

The Hopi Creation Account and Racial Memory

The move from an original sense of harmony, order, and community to the experience of disorder, conflict, and strife is repeated in a different mythic form in the Hopi creation account. In this story the Creator, Taiowa, existed in the First World of Tokpela, or Endless Space. Taiowa was said to exist before the First World, so that all time, form, shape, and substance "existed only in the mind of the Creator." The first act of Taiowa was to "conceive the finite, the bounded, the limited." Thisness and Thatness were the first concepts. Sotuknang was the First Being created by Taiowa, with the order as "first power and instrument as a person, to carry out my plan for life in endless space." Taiowa identified himself as Uncle and named Sotuknang Nephew. Sotuknang was commanded, "Go now and lay out these universes according to my plan."[10]

Sotuknang worked out the will of Taiowa, bringing solidness and substance to endless space, shape and form into the establishment of "nine universal kingdoms divided as follows: one each for the Creator and himself and seven others for the life that was yet to come." Then Uncle directed Nephew to divide and give form and shape to the waters, dividing them "equally among the universes—half solid and half water." Then Uncle directed Nephew to create "forces of air to surround the waters with peaceful movement." So doing, Nephew created of the forces of air a "gentle order and rhythm around each universe."[11]

Nephew, having pleased Uncle so much, was then commanded to create life in order to "round out the four parts of a universal plan," but Nephew could not do this alone. He needed someone to do this act of creating life. So Nephew went to the First World and there created "woman to be his helper," naming her Kokyangwuti, Spider Woman. She comes to life asking the fundamental question that now is embedded in human spirit, "Why am I here?" Nephew replied with this beautiful and empowering response:

> Look about you. Here is this earth we have created. It has shape and substance, direction and time, a beginning and an end. But there is no life upon it. We see no joyful movement. We hear no joyful sounds. What is life without sound or

movement? So you have been given the power to help us create this life. You have been given the knowledge, wisdom, and love to bless all the beings you create. That is why you are here.[12]

Spider Woman went forth to create life. Mixing earth with her saliva, she molded it into "two twin beings." She covered them "with a white cape of creative wisdom and sang the Creation Song over them." After doing this she uncovered them and the Twins asked the same question, "Who are we? Why are we here?" To the one on the right Spider Woman said, "You are Poqanghoya and you are to help keep this world in order when life is put upon it. Go now around all the world and put your hands upon the earth so that it will become fully solidified. This is your duty." Thurman notes that this command means that "order had to be grounded as integral in the earth." (The implications of placing order into the earth will be elaborated later in this chapter.) To the one on the left Spider Woman said,

> You are Palongawhoya and you are to help keep this world in order when life is put upon it. This is your duty now: go about all the world and send out a sound so that it may be heard throughout the land. When this is heard you will be known as Echo, for all sound echoes the Creator.[13]

The twins went forth to do as they were bid, Poqanghoya fashioning mountains and valleys, Palongawhoya sounding forth his call from which "all vibratory centers along the earth's axis resounded." When the twins had done their work, the earth "trembled; the universe quivered in tune." Then each was sent to opposite poles, one to the north, the other to the south, in order to keep the earth rotating properly. One was ordered to "keep the earth solid and firm," the other was to "keep the air in gentle motion and to send out his call for good or for warning."[14]

Meanwhile Spider Woman created everything else in nature, naming all creatures and ordering them after their own kind. She covered each with her white mantle so that they might share in the wisdom of the Creator. Then she spread them to the four corners of the earth.

Taiowa was pleased at Spider Woman's work and now felt that the time had come for human beings to be created. It is beyond the scope of this book to recount this complicated narrative in detail; in short, Spider Woman created four pairs of human beings, male and female, this time by mixing "four colors of earth: yellow, red, white and black." She covered them with the white mantle of creative wisdom. Nephew gave them the power of speech, each color was given a different language, and all were granted "the wisdom and the power to reproduce and multiply."[15]

The First People multiplied. They lived in harmony with each other and with the earth. Thurman is impressed with their sense of "inner community

— oneness of body and mind." He praises their powerful ability to communicate across their differences:

> Despite the fact that they were different colors and spoke different languages, they were one people and understood one another without speech or talking. The same was true of the birds and animals. Different forms there were, but there was one life, nourished by Mother Earth and sustained by the Sun, through which the Creator worked or created.[16]

Trouble, sickness, and estrangement did not occur until a Talker came among them in the form of a bird named Mochni. Sundering the sense of community human beings had with all other forms of life, Mochni incessantly pointed out the differences between the species, colors, and races. As differences were emphasized, animals drew away from human beings, and humans grew fearful of each other and forgot the original intent of the Creator. Instead of differences being recognized as relative, they were made into moral absolutes worthy of inordinate attention.[17]

Both the Genesis and Hopi narratives share a progression, a "common thread" that moves from "creation with the harmony of innocence" to "the loss of innocence with a disintegration of the harmony." Both creation accounts point to a "primordial theme" that nourishes an "ancient hunger" in human beings — the memory of a lost harmony. Thurman elaborates this memory further as a common experience of the human race, calling it the racial memory.[18] This racial memory (we may include this in our newword lexicon) serves as a principle of social criticism for humanity. No matter what our current experience of brokenness, strife, and sin, a sacred reminder in these creation accounts points us back toward a time when the intent of the Creator for harmony, concord, and tranquillity ordered all aspects of life. Although it exists as a dream or an echo, it remains.[19]

Yoruba Creation Legend: Earth Memory

A Yoruba creation legend serves to tie an Xodus mythic perspective to Thurman's. In a profoundly moving section of this legend, the orisha (a Yoruba deity) Obatala, the creator of earth and all its life, is descending from the heavenly realms of the orishas (which is ruled by the high god Olurun — a figure similar to Zeus/Athena in Greek mythology since Olurun is both male and female and transcends gender) and drops "the egg." The egg, given to him as a culminating gift by the orisha of divination, Orunmila, contained all of the personalities and wisdom of all the orishas. Obatala had been dropping sand, snail shells, and baobab powder onto the murky chaos of the primordial waters as he was descending. Springing from the shattered egg was the phoenix bird, Sankofa, who "flew down and attacked the sand, which flew in all directions, piling into mounds and dunes and hills." Thus it was said in the Yoruba legend that "Sankofa sowed personality into the soil from which people would come."[20] From this Yoruba legend we may take the insight that there is not only a racial memory but an earth memory of how things ought to be. There is an earth memory of the divine personality (in the sense of the monotheistic God) in all of its variety, moods, and complexity. From the community-of-gods perspective such as that of traditional Yoruba religion, the richness and power of the various orishas has been sowed into the very soil of the earth. Earth memory lets us know, as Xodus travelers, that the ground on which we walk is sacred ground because it has been infused with the personalities of the Spirit(s).

Thurman gives us insight into the ways in which we might regain lost earth memories through a concept of responsibility. He does this by noting that the series of events named *responsibility* flowed through actions that broke the original intent of community. Responsibility is the result of an act that "sets in motion elements that are dormant [the potential for disharmony] prior to the act." In one sense these elements are impersonal, yet Thurman also wants us to recognize a sense of personal responsibility, of guilt. Guilt must be purged with the triumph of goodness, of personal moral actions that recover the lost sense of grace. So, for Thurman, goodness is differentiated from innocence after innocence is lost. Innocence is "essentially untried, untested, unchallenged," but after its "violation" an effort must be made to reestablish the grace of innocence through responsibility. In goodness Thurman emphasizes that a new synthesis is achieved, a moral triumph of the quality of innocence over the quality of discord.[21] In Thurman's mind, such a triumph is necessarily an eternal struggle. It is worth struggling to achieve, even if we never see the complete triumph in an eschatological (end-time) sense because we are wrestling with those elements that prevent the realization of community.

Seeking Understanding in the Scientific Way

The other way that we seek to understand life is the scientific, in the empirically observed and verified "living structures" of life itself. Thurman is fascinated with the potential of physicists to describe the "all-inclusive immensity of the universe." He notes that one may discern an "observable stability" of structured relations, patterns, and movements that suggests an organization or design. With mystical insight Thurman observes that just as we are living in the universe, the universe lives in us, and human beings are an organic part of the universe. Within our very bodies, our organism, we experience the order and harmony of the universe. Because we are so inter-related and interconnected to the universe, Thurman pushes us to become aware of the manifestations of the sense of direction and purpose that structures life.[22]

Thurman delights in the incredible detail and precision required, the "establishing of precise conditions for the existence and maintenance of life on earth." He is not at all convinced that life is a random or chance occurrence in the vastness of the universe, but points to the peculiar confines of the "biosphere" (quoting Clifford Grobstein) by which "life 'knows' what it must do in order to realize itself, its limitations and boundaries in which it actualizes its potential or experiences community."[23]

Life, for Thurman, exhibits something of what human beings would call behavior, which is related to its environment through the interconnected elements of what is known as an ecosystem. Therefore, though the universe is vast and immense, it is also "minutely structured and coordinated, maintaining itself by a boundless energy that configures in rich variety, each configuration integrated with other units to comprise the totality of the universe."[24]

Such a way of looking at the earth as a vast ecosystem is commonplace for us in the last decade of the twentieth century. What is amazing about Thurman is that he was thinking about these things in the late 1960s and early 1970s. His intuitive mystical sense of things, that quality of connection not only with human beings but with nature and the universe Itself, helped him to realize that important relationships needed to be established between the then-brand-new insights of ecological science and the search for community.

The Prophet's Dream

As a seeker of community, Thurman in his search went beyond the first two areas of analyzing life to look at three more areas, each relating to the specific dynamics of human community: (1) the Prophet's Dream, (2) Common Consciousness, and (3) Identity. Each of these three ways of seeking is built on the concepts of community derived in the first two views.

The Prophet's dream, for Thurman, is intimately connected to the primordial dream of the creation accounts, the two relating to one another in a dialectical relationship. The Prophet's dream is the dream of utopia. Thurman has a marvelous way of describing utopia as that future community in which "the potential of the individual as well as that of society can be actualized." Utopia is that Space (to use an Xodus newword) where each aspect, each element, has identical presence and function in the fabric and flow of the community. As such utopias are "custom made . . . fashioned to order" on the if-ness of what ought to be, and not what is. It is the fulfilled community that is operating on the "as if . . ." ideal, what the "collective life of man would be like if it functioned in keeping with man's high destiny."[25]

What is this high destiny Thurman speaks of? Although he does not spell it out in this chapter of *The Search for Common Ground,* it is apparent that the high destiny of human beings is to live in the fullest sense of community — with God, each other, nature, and the cosmos. The high destiny of humanity is what he calls "the intent of the Creator in creation . . . community." The high destiny of humanity, for Thurman, lies "in the fulfillment of life at every level." Such a view of community is the "actualization of this potential . . . nourished in each expression of life." Therefore animal and plant life share this potential actualization with humanity.[26]

Thurman finds a political articulation of such a utopian view of community in Plato's *Republic*. He notes that Plato wrote *The Republic* when Athens was enduring a protracted and costly war with Sparta, and that it was conceived as a way of correcting present evils by "projecting a State in which these evils do not appear." Thurman notes that for Plato the "fundamental search [is] for justice," socially and politically defined. Plato describes and defines matters of "common interest" and ways in which the state may develop its own "function to meet the needs of its citizens."[27]

For Thurman Plato's *Republic* draws together important ideals of necessary limitation of personal freedoms in order for the community to realize the fullest potential of each individual. This is just, because justice depends on the intentional living together of groups in such a balanced and fair fashion that no group has any reason to be "happier than any other." Plato, in Thurman's view, draws a revealing analogy between the community and an individual human being, holding that each human being "is possessed of wisdom, valor, temperance, and justice." Plato assigns the first three virtues to particular classes — rulers have wisdom, defenders have valor, and "temperance belongs to all classes." Temperance is both an individual and corporate virtue, creating and preserving "harmony." Such harmony is possible only when the fullest "potentials of the State *and* its citizens . . . [are] mutually realized."[28]

Thurman notes that Plato is keenly aware of the dual potential for good and for evil in human beings. The one whose "better has the worse under control . . . is said to be master of himself."[29] What Thurman did not know, or at least did not mention, was that this high ideal of self-mastery had been derived by the Greeks from their Egyptian teachers in the phrase *maat geru,* one who has attained self-mastery. For Plato the one who is controlled by

"the worse . . . is blamed and is called the slave of self and unprincipled."
In ancient Kemetic thought the one who was not under the balanced power
of Maat was said to be ruled by Isfet — disorder, slavery, unbalance.[30] It is
difficult for me not to interject and "correct" authors, even African American
ones, when a Kemetic "truth" has been obscured and mistaken!

For Thurman the notion of justice is both "private and public morality."
Privately, the individual is asked not to deprive another nor his or her own
self of "what is his own . . . doing the thing to which his nature is best adapt-
ed." Publicly, each person "has and does peacefully what it is his right to
have and to do," filling "the place for which he is fitted." Thurman regrets
that this promotes a classist rigidity, legitimizing the status quo of hierarchical relations.[31]

Thurman contrasts Plato's *Republic* with the New Jerusalem vision of the
Book of Revelation. Like Plato's projected future world, the Christian vision
projects fulfillment into an otherworld. In fact, Thurman clearly acknowl-
edges modern notions of utopia as having been created by the apocalyptic
utopias of Christianity. Christians, seeing themselves as "pilgrims in the
world," operate within the present from this otherworldly perspective. For
all of its climactic imagery, bizarre metaphors, and drama, Thurman notes
that the utopian apocalypse of the Revelation "is not open to all," but is profoundly discriminating. Not everyone is saved. Not everyone can have "all
their radiant possibilities available to them." It is at this point, the point of
exclusivity and discrimination, that Thurman declares that all utopias have a
tragic flaw.[32]

For Thurman utopias are a necessary part of human sociopolitical imagining, the stuff of which social dreams are made, but must not become actual or concrete. The utopian community, when left in the realm of dreams,
enables humanity to envision what things could be like *if* . . . Their function
is to draw out the ways in which we might "fashion a world in accordance
with [human] needs, . . . hopes, . . . destiny." Utopias, for Thurman, must
remain the stuff of dreams, drawing us into higher hopes and better living,
not into a frozen, structured institutionalization of "the dream."[33]

Such a view has important ramifications for Xodus seekers because we
are the Children of the Dream — that utopian dream of brotherhood, hand-
holding, and equality that our parents believed in and that Martin Luther
King articulated with such biblical eloquence. Utopia, for Thurman, functions in a manner analogous to the way love functions with justice for
Reinhold Niebuhr. From Niebuhr's early *An Interpretation of Christian Ethics*
to his version of a medieval *summa, The Nature and Destiny of Man,* love
always functioned as an ideal that transcended the social-conflictive capacities of justice, yet was required as an ideal in order for justice to incarnate

itself as complete justice. In Niebuhr's writings love is said to draw justice to the best realization of itself. Utopias are necessary ideals for Thurman in order for human potential to be more fully realized. Without them humanity's ability to envision is crippled, and the capacity to put into practice better and higher moral principles is forever precluded. Thus, one way we might interpret Thurman's insight is that community in actuality needs the ideal power of utopias in potentiality. Xodus creativity ought to embrace utopian envisionment as necessary for developing any capacity to envision a life beyond the confines of domination, particularly Euro-domination.

Affinity of Consciousness

Thurman is also interested in the ways in which the mystical connection and sense of community humans ought to experience with all of creation might be discerned in "levels of communication that tend to make for harmonious relationship."[34] Building his thesis on a notion of affinity, Thurman builds a tie between creation accounts of all forms of life sharing an original harmony, and the idea of affinity of consciousness: "What men have discovered through the ages is that not only is there an affinity that the mind has for the external world, but also that there is an affinity between man's consciousness and the many forms of consciousness around him."[35]

The purpose of a concept of affinity of consciousness is to help make human beings more aware of its existence. Thurman claims that as we become more aware, the more we discover that our own sense of self is becoming "greatly enlarged, and all of life seems to be more intimately a part" of us, and we a part of life. The notion of affinity bears close scrutiny, because it is a central ideal in the thought of Howard Thurman. "Affinity," according to Webster's Dictionary, in its second and forth senses means the following:

> 2. a condition of close relationships; conformity; resemblance; connection; as, the *affinity* of sounds, of colors, or of languages. . . .
>
> 4. a resemblance in general plan or structure, or in the essential structural parts, existing between species, languages, etc., implying a common origin.[36]

In a very real sense, then, Thurman presents both the mystic's language of union and a metaphysical articulation of the guiding assumptions of the affinity of consciousness underlying all created life. Life shares a fundamental, structural connection, a resemblance based on its common origin in the mind and creative activity of the Creator. But in Thurman it must be remembered that the act of creation is not over or complete, it is a process. Life itself is "seeking to realize itself . . . in the process by which potentials are actualized." In families as in members of the same species, this process of actualization takes place as the generation of new life insuring the continuation of the species. Each individual form goes beyond its solitariness because "in it [the solitary form of life] life itself may not be defeated." So Thurman sees community as the consummate action of affirming affinity of consciousness and insuring the continuity of life.[37]

Thurman delights in tales of harmony, albeit sometimes shared in fleeting and transitory moments, between animals and human beings. He relishes the harmony that existed between a curious baby playing in her backyard and a rattlesnake, or a tale of Ernest Hemingway's way of understanding bears.[38] Thurman inserted these tales into the text not to demonstrate his mystical propensity (although they do reveal it quite forcefully), but to demonstrate that an affinity of consciousness exists between human beings and other life forms, an affinity that we ought to become aware of, cultivate, and cherish as divine moments of communication. Thurman self-consciously debunks the idea that human self-reflective consciousness is somehow morally superior to the consciousness of other life forms. He sees such valorizing of human intelligence as erecting a "great wall between man and other animals" that feeds a sense of separateness. This sense of separateness, in turn, fuels a conceit that human beings are necessarily "over against nature." Thurman does not deny that a separateness exists, only that it is absolute. What connects our consciousness with other forms is life itself, "always seeking to realize itself in myriad forms and patterns of manifestations."[39]

Thurman affirms that there is a ground of unity between humans and other forms of life that is expressed in symbolic forms beyond oral language. He does not claim to understand how these things are accomplished, but affirms the necessity of eliminating the doors of fear that preclude in our minds the possibility of harmony with animals and other forms of life. Thurman is insistent that our life will be reinvigorated or, as he would put it, made "vital" by having "the experience of being consciously in touch with other forms of conscious life" surrounding us.[40]

Bodies, Selves, and Identity

Building on his previous ideal of tearing down walls of absolute separateness between different forms of life, the final seeking for Common Ground is that of identity. Thurman begins this search with a probing query into the relationship of the self and the body. We are "not alien to life," but are creatures "grounded in the life process." We cannot isolate ourselves from it; in fact, through our bodies we participate "completely in the life process, and it [the body] is nourished and sustained by ancient processes as old as life, and set in motion before any awareness of or knowledge about them [those ancient life processes] was in evidence."[41] The body is coextensive with our self, our intimate dwelling place, our domain.

For Thurman it is essential to realize how connected our selves are to our bodies because when one desires to break the will of a person, that innermost province of selfhood, one often resorts "to direct and violent cruelty upon" the body. The aim in such practices is to compel the person to "abdicate" his or her body to the torturer, thus making the person an "alien" in his or her own house. Such torture disembodies us and makes us, to a certain extent, "beingless" in Thurman's mind.[42]

Human beings are experiential creatures. All experience, says Thurman, becomes the "raw material for harmony, for order, and the individual stands ever in immediate candidacy for such fulfillment." Because Thurman is persuaded that the human life is a journey into life and a quest for community within ourselves, care is essential to actualization of our potential.[43] This is why, according to Thurman, it is so damaging and damning to the self of African Americans to be placed as "outsiders" and "second-class citizens." It cuts into the life process of both those who are afflicted and the state itself, in Thurman's view.[44]

Contrasting the plight of the American Indian as the insider forced to become an outsider in his or her own territory, with that of the African slave who was forced to sever all ties to tribal land, territory, and home, Thurman reveals how our Black bodies are tied to the land. Slave bodies were things to be possessed and owned, just like the land. Thurman, however, turns this idea on its head and states that the slave (as a thing to be possessed and owned) was indeed a part of the land, a crucial ground of community. In Thurman's mind, three currents of life enabled the slaves to survive and sustain themselves: (1) a tendency toward wholeness by which families, love, and life were sustained and nourished despite harsh realities; (2) an all-encompassing spiritual dimension that could reach the native soil of the human spirit; and (3) aggression, whereby the drive and urge for community seeks to nourish its own and reject or expel intruders. I find it fascinating that Thurman noted that aggression was a necessary element in the formation and maintenance of community; this implies that aggression cannot be ignored or repressed. Although Thurman does not elaborate fully the implications of naming aggression as an aspect of community, Xodus conceptuality must do so in our era of increasing misunderstanding of how to address violence and aggressive instincts. Aggression must be named for what it is, recognized, and then channeled into creative power.

Thurman praises the efforts of African Americans of the 1950s through the early 1970s to throw off their collective subjugation. He offers laudatory remarks about the ways in which even in the most ravaged areas of the segregated South, African American communities managed to create a strong sense of caring among ourselves — parenting all of the children, extending hospitality to any stranger, constantly identifying with each other. Yet because the very bodies of Black folk remember slavery and the cruelties of the segregated system,[45] Thurman also presents a compelling case for why Black people could no longer be at the mercy of any white person, and why our potential had to be demanded. Thurman uplifts the teachings of Dr. King as the highest example of what the civil rights movement meant. But Thurman also goes on to present in a persuasive fashion the profound necessity for engaging in our own form of separate consciousness through the Black Power movement. For Thurman there had to be a distinction between the voluntary and deliberate separateness of Black Power and the coercion of segregation. Calling it a "new mood," Thurman assessed both the strengths and weaknesses of the self-imposed cultural exile of Black Power, saying that it provided: (1) a basis for identity with a cause and a purpose more significant to them than their own individual survival; and (2) a feeling of membership with others of common values with whom they can experience direct and intense communication.[46]

Yet for all of his understanding and appreciation of the positive gains of the Black Power thrust, Thurman ultimately evaluated the "new mood" as a "stop-gap halt in the line of march toward full community, or, at most, a time of bivouac on a promontory overlooking the entire landscape." Ever constant in the call for a community greater than the self-exile of Black Power, Thurman affirms that Blacks have now "found our own sense of identity," and that from that "established center" we may at last "function and relate to other" people. Having lost our fear of white power and coercion, Blacks ought not to separate ourselves "behind self-imposed walls."[47]

Xodus Earthseed

How does Xodus respond to such a charge? Do we simply dismiss Thurman as a mystic visionary of a previous age whose words and thoughts no longer have meaning for us? Do we dissect Thurman's corpus, carefully excising what we do not like, and paint him as an Xodus radical?

Thurman's insights continue to have meaning for us, especially as we travel in Xodus. Thurman was a religious genius, deeply rooted and grounded in the creative wellsprings of spirit drawn from Afrikan traditions. As with every figure, some things are more meaningful to our Journey than others, but the core of Thurman's writings should remain present with Xodus travelers, even as we seek to find ways to affirm our Afrikanness and our common life with others. At the core of all of his writings, meditations, and prayers is a desire to develop an awareness of one's personal center, that inner space of communion with the depths of spirit, the "luminous darkness" of the self and God.[48] Thurman's book titles alone are indicative of the kind of concern he had for developing one's inner space: *The Inward Journey, Deep Is the Hunger, Disciplines of the Spirit, Meditations of the Heart, The Creative Encounter*. He was deeply concerned that human beings learn to draw upon the powers of God made available to the heart hungry for truth, hope, peace, and goodness. We cannot appreciate the profundity of Thurman's Common Ground unless we understand the inner and personal context of concern that he always addressed. He was determined that the self be founded on a powerful awareness of our capacity to determine the true and the good from within us, unswayed by the external distractions and petty "carking cares" (one of his favorite phrases). Rather, having firmly grasped the true and the good within ourselves, we can organize our lives around those things, not allowing ourselves to be swayed or turned away.[49]

The symbolic power of Common Ground is quite meaningful to the creative flow of Xodus Space as a corrective to those places of exclusivity and the excluding tendencies that utopian enterprise might encourage. Xodus Space is utopian. It is *here* and *not yet*. Its hereness is a presence of the will, a cultural edifice built in the hungering heart, in the inward journey of the self. But Xodus Space is not an institution, nor should it ever be concretized into rules and laws, frozen into dry Do's and Don'ts. To do so would be to limit its luminous darkness, to blur the subtle distinctions between cultural things of the spirit and cultural artifices preserved in museums.

Thurman's Common Ground reminds us that it is much easier to reconstruct walls of division and separation than to keep down the walls recently removed. If Xodus Space is going to be meaningful, it must be able to hold within itself an ability to address and nourish the Blackness of Afrikans (which is synonymous with the cosmic inner blackness of all humanity) and the Common Ground of all life.

Thurman's affinity of consciousness is a concept too powerful for Xodus people to ignore because it emphasizes our kinship and connection to the earth. We share Common Ground with the earth. We are God's "earth creatures," according to Phyllis Trible, created from the dust of the earth and the breath (in Hebrew *nephesh*) of God. To use the theo-poetry of science fiction writer Octavia Butler, we are Earthseed.[50] As Earthseed we are rooted, grounded, and shaped by the Common Ground from which we spring. Butler pushes Thurman and Xodus thought to realize that just as the earth and God Shape us, so we Shape[51] earth and God in an ever-changing, ever-adjusting process.

Both Common Ground and Earthseed are process metaphors, not static but dynamic. They remind us of the quality of ever-transforming living symbols that best express our vital who-ness and what-ness. In our human bodies we are Earthseed; in our very flesh we share Common Ground with each other, despite our differing colors, sizes, and shapes. Cultural differences cannot be so absolute as to erase our fundamental affinity. We share the breath of life with all living creatures. So we *are* Common Ground, Earthseed, fashioned from the stones, the rocks, the trees, the water, and the energy of the stars that lies in the earth. As Earthseed, we *are* Common Ground because we share the sacred Space of the earth, whether we can get along with one another or not. We are Common Ground because when the rocks cry "Glory, Hallelujah!" we ought to be aware of their praises to the Creator even without "understanding." Our affinity to the earth and all that lives on it is more powerful than our species differences. Through an Earthseed understanding of Common Ground, Xodus Space can offer a powerful ecological metaphor of connection to the ecological movement, drawn out of our own Councils of Ancestors.

The Council Fires may now be doused. . . . A new dawn is arriving. The Xodus is coming!

Notes

1. Howard Thurman, *The Search for Common Ground* (Richmond, Ind.: Friends United Press, 1986), xvi.
2. Ibid.
3. Ibid., 29.
4. Ibid., 30.
5. In "The Search into Beginnings," ibid., 12–13.
6. Ibid., 14.
7. Ibid., 14–15.
8. Ibid., 15.
9. All quotes in this paragraph, ibid.
10. Ibid., 15–16
11. All quotes in this paragraph, ibid., 16.
12. Ibid., 16–17.
13. All quotes in this paragraph, ibid., 17.
14. Ibid.
15. Ibid., 16–18.
16. Ibid., 22.
17. Ibid.
18. Ibid., 23–24.
19. Ibid., 24.

20. As told to David Anderson, *Sankofa, The Origin of Life on Earth: An African Creation Myth* (Mount Airy, Md.: Sights Production, 1994), 17.
21. Thurman, *Search for Common Ground*, 26–27.
22. All quotes from this paragraph are from "The Search in Living Structures," ibid., 31–32.
23. Ibid.
24. Ibid., 32–33.
25. All quotes here from "The Search in the Prophet's Dream," ibid., 42–43.
26. Ibid., 46.
27. Ibid., 46–47.
28. Ibid., 47–48.
29. Ibid., 48.
30. Maulana Karenga, *Selections from the Husia: Sacred Wisdom of Ancient Egypt* (University of Sankore Press, 1989).
31. Thurman, *Search for Common Ground*, 48.
32. Ibid., 51–52.
33. Ibid., 55.
34. "The Search in the Common Consciousness," il id., 57.
35. Ibid., 57.
36. *Webster's New Twentieth Century Dictionary of the English Language: Unabridged Second Edition*, vol. 1 (New York: World Publishing, 1960), 32.
37. Thurman, *Search for Common Ground*, 57–58.
38. Ibid., 57–58, 64.
39. Ibid., 63.
40. Ibid., 62, 75.
41. "The Search in Identity," ibid., 78.
42. Ibid., 79.
43. Ibid., 80.
44. Ibid., 87.
45. Ibid., 92.
46. Ibid., 102.
47. Ibid., 103–4.
48. Howard Thurman, *The Luminous Darkness: A Personal Interpretation of the Anatomy of Segregation and the Ground of Hope* (Richmond, Ind.: Friends United Press, 1965, 1989), 110–11.
49. These insights are found throughout Thurman's corpus, but especially in *Deep Is the Hunger: Meditations for Apostles of Sensitiveness* (Richmond, Ind.: Friends United Press, 1951, 1990), 15, 88.
50. Octavia Butler, *Parable of the Sower* (New York: Four Walls Eight Windows, 1993). Butler develops an intricate theology of God, humanity, and earth in this fascinating science fiction morality tale of survival in an apocalyptic future.
51. "Shape" is an Xodus newword that means "the way in which we consciously manipulate, form, fashion, and utilize concepts." This Xodus idea is in conformity with Octavia Butler's notion of "shaping," but is more self-conscious about the limitations of our ability to actually "manipulate" God than is Butler.

PART III

XODUS SPACE: Afrikan Ecclesiology

CHAPTER

Rap's "Angry" Children

There is an upheaval from the city streets. It is accompanied by a heavy drumbeat and lightning-fast staccato lyrics, sporting a gangster's hat and an "in-yo'-face" attitude. I speak of the preeminent art form of the urban streets in the last two decades of the twentieth century, rap music, rhapsodized as "traditional African American popular music" by its supporters.[1] In his book *Reflecting Black* (1993), cultural critic Michael Eric Dyson has elevated rappers to the honorific titles of "cultural griots, urban griots dispensing a message of prophetic criticism," and "peripatetic preachers."[2] Nevertheless, except for the engaging philosophical critique of Cornel West in his book of essays *Prophetic Fragments,* rap has been a taboo subject for serious theological and ethical reflection. Untamed, fractured, and idiosyncratic, rap has captured the imaginations and hearts of sectors from all races and classes in so-called Generation X. Like it or not, rap has become the preeminent street form of countercultural art and discourse for contemporary African American youth.

Locating rap as a countercultural art form indicates something about who is analyzing rap, who is listening, and which culture rap considers against itself. I am an almost-forty-year-old, middle-class, professional African American Christian male who, besides being a professor of ethics, is a musician. As a middle-class professional I can understand how rap might be viewed as "dangerous" and "subversive," as undermining the kinds of language values, work ethos, and view of life that support middle-class culture. Fortunately that is not my only view of rap. As a musician who composes,

131

performs, and enjoys many diverse styles of artistic expression, I view rap as an innovative ultra-postmodern avant-garde form. As a musician I deeply respect and even revel in the aggressive expansion of sonic and lyrical terrains that typifies rap. So one cannot enter into an analysis of rap without a "confessional" locating one's own interests and limitations.

Tricia Rose's preeminent analysis of rap, *Black Noise* (1994), reminds us that rap is *ghettocentric* because it is an honest, specific, and localized cultural production.[3] To be ghettocentric is to be conscious of all that is going on around you, to be "conscious" of the "hard-core" ways, wiles, temptations, traps, pleasures, and beauty of "da streetz." If rap represents "ghetto-centricity" (a phrase from Nelson George's *Buppies, Baps, and Bohos* [1989]), then it ought to be a valuable tool and necessary resource in reconstructing Black theology in this second generation as a countercultural discourse. Rap's intensely localized and specific cultural location — the "streets" — challenges Black theology and ethics to reevaluate our sources with the disturbing question, What are most Black theologies centered in? Are Black theology and ethics "Afri-middle-class-centric" without recognizing that by being thus, we eliminate "the street" as a serious source of correction and inspiration? If we are, then is rap's ghettocentric stance troublesome because it is counter-Afri-middle-class-centric? Rap's "anger" points an accusing finger at all values that displace and replace the values of the streets.

A Critical Conversation: Rap Hermeneutics 101

There are so many forms of rap that to make blanket congratulatory remarks or condemning criticism is to demonstrate how little one really knows about it. Furthermore, rap has evolved into such a major cultural force possessing a lyrical power capable of criticizing the United States that it has become one of the favored targets of major politicians who cite it as having a negative influence on their "children." One need only remember the attention raptivist (a newword meaning a rap artist who is also a social activist) Sister Souljah received from then-candidate-for-president Bill Clinton for her off-the-cuff (and ill-considered) remark about taking a "week off to kill white people" to realize that rap is being "heard," even if it is not understood.

Xodus takes the voices of these "angry children" as a sign of the times, as something that must be included in our constructive task. Since this section of the Xodus Journey seeks to find ways of making Xodus more concrete, various forms of rap are analyzed as they relate to ways in which

Xodus travel and, specifically, the construction of an Afrikan ecclesiology can be encouraged. To begin Afrikan ecclesiology with an examination of rap pushes Xodus creativity to articulate a critical frontier for both second-generation Black theology in North America and for the future vitality of Black churches. It reveals, as well, a novel hermeneutical decision about ecclesiology in general: any Afrikan ecclesiology created must look outside the walls of church buildings toward the larger community of Afrikans first, rather than looking toward finding ways to reiterate and reinforce the classic marks of the church as postulated by the Nicene and Apostolic Creeds of a different millennium.

It was the rap group X-Clan that first articulated the name, idea, and conceptual suggestion of "Xodus," in one of their albums. Filled with theologically inflected poetic lyrics, the album "Xodus" carries a message of spiritual revival. It calls for a spiritual return to "home," to Afrikan cultural and spiritual values. X-Clan uses remarkably biblical imagery in its call for the Journey home, inviting listeners to "board the Cosmic Ark" and "ride the waves of Sound." It is one of the originating sources of what I eventually came to call Xodus creativity. Reinforcing a theme from their first album, X-Clan calls for Afrikans to go "to the East Blackwards." The East becomes a compass-symbol of the direction of origins, of the way toward which one must Journey spiritually, culturally, and psychologically. X-Clan proclaims the message that it is in the movement of the Afrikan mind back to the East that we attain "Blackward" awareness. In true postmodern fashion, X-Clan leaves a silence concerning what the "West" represents; the word never appears. The unspoken West may be interpreted as the "whiteward" space that we now ought to leave. But X-Clan does not state this overtly, leaving that space, that silence, to be felt in between the pounding of drums and the whirling cadenzas of synthesizers. So doing, X-Clan's "Xodus" acts as rap prophecy, calling the people back to their origins in the Blackness of our being. Yet all rap is not as psychospiritually prophetic as that of X-Clan. Much of rap has little to do with poetic prophecy.

In order for us to examine rap with a comprehensive enough perspective, it is necessary to create a hermeneutic sufficiently flexible for successfully negotiating rap's deeply contradictory energies and lyrical terrain. I am going to combine the interpretive methods of two intellectual giants, David Tracy and Cornel West. Tracy offers a conversational hermeneutic, something that he calls critical correlation, as part of the way that rap as a social text ought to be analyzed. Critical correlation insists on the necessity of having a "dramatic confrontation" that moves toward "mutual illuminations and corrections," and even dares to believe that a "possible basic reconciliation between the principal values, cognitive claims, and existential faiths of both a reinterpreted postmodern consciousness (in our case "rap" is a postmodern consciousness) and a reinterpreted Christianity" can occur.[4]

Too many church people, particularly African American preachers who are put off by the nastier side of rap, tend to overlook the possibility that *rap may have something important to say to all of us, especially those who represent Jesus Christ to our communities.* If Black churches become open to the possibility that rap may provide insights, clues, and direct/indirect access to areas of Black culture that are inaccessible to most Christians, then perhaps we (and I am a part of that "we") might learn from rap. Such a learning means, on the one hand, that we are willing to engage in learning the world of rap — going to the extreme length of learning to understand exactly what rap "words" mean, what values are being portrayed, and to read between the lines of those "words" to "hear" the young people. On the other hand, it also means that we expect rappers to take the church more seriously, and not use it only as a butt of crude jokes or dismiss it altogether.

Tracy's more recent text *Plurality and Ambiguity* moves beyond the strictures of a revisionist method and model to the more flexible approach of conversation.[5] In a conversation we expect to be challenged, to give and take, to move back and forth with freedom and fluidity. Tracy states it beautifully when he notes that in a conversation there is a sharing of narratives through which the participants "expose their hopes, desires, and fears." Mutual self-revelation occurs in which both parties adhere to the "hard rules of complete honesty, respectful listening, courteous response, correction and defense of opinions, necessary confrontation, a willingness to endure conflict, and an openness to changing one's mind if convinced by the evidence.[6]

Rappers and Black churches need to come into conversation with each other because Afrikans living in the United States are listening to both voices. We must learn from each other, be challenged, defend, argue, and change ourselves when the evidence suggests that former ways may not forward the liberation, salvation, healing, and uplift of Afrikans (and of all people).

Conversation is not enough, however, because something else must be established before conversation can take place. Here Cornel West is enormously helpful in naming one of the fundamental existential crises of being "Black" in a white world (especially in the United States): *We face namelessness and invisibility that demand that we create and maintain a capacity for self-validation and recognition.* West calls this a "diasporan problematic" — meaning that throughout the African global diaspora Afrikans face the same structures of invisibility and namelessness. He refines this problematic in a philosophical manner, restating it as a lack of Black power to "represent themselves to themselves and others as complex human beings, and thereby to contest the bombardment of negative, degrading stereotypes put forward by white-supremacist ideologies."[7] In this sentence we can obtain a useful and liberating norm for evaluating and interpreting all statements, from rappers or anyone else. Either the Black churches are representing Afrikans in a resistant mode, casting down the degrading stereotypes that whiteness promulgates, or they are unconsciously validating them. Either rappers are representing Afrikans in a resistant mode, or they are unconsciously promoting images and symbols of Black folk that legitimate white supremacy.

The plumb line is cast for judgment in West's Norm of Representation. If we use it carefully as a norm of discernment, it can clarify issues that otherwise might become confusing, with opinions breaking down along generational lines of musical taste. To apply West's language a bit more, both Black churches and rappers are "black cultural workers" who ought to be working at a "politics of representation" whose

> main aim is not simply access to representation in order to produce positive images, of homogeneous communities . . . nor is the primary goal here that of contesting stereotypes, . . . [but to] constitute and sustain discursive and institutional networks that deconstruct earlier modern black strategies for identity-formation, demystify power relations that incorporate class, patriarchal and homophobic biases, and construct more multivalent and multidimensional responses that articulate the complexity and diversity of black practices in the modern and postmodern world.[8]

A politics of representation that has the triple task of deconstructing and demystifying former Black strategies for "getting over" and their power relations, and constructing a Space for the many-sided and many-dimensioned responses that Afrikans represent to ourselves and others is consonant with the primary mission of Xodus.

In a very real sense rap as preeminent cultural art form is representational. It represents the world from three modes of Black representation; it is ghettocentric, streets-conscious, and survival-oriented. These three modes are distinctively "Black" in culture, even when re-presented by Euro-American rappers such as the Beastie Boys, Snow, and House of Pain, because there are categories of analysis, expression, and creativity that originally arise from the ghettocentric, streets-conscious, and survival-oriented modes of representation Afrikans devised. Further, rappers recognize and revel in the uniqueness of their form of representation. There are no other forms of Afrikan expressiveness whose sole purpose and end is to articulate these three modes. Nobody else takes "the streets" as seriously. Nobody else praises "the 'hood" with such fierce intensity. No one else seems to express the rawness of survival, in the language of survivors, as do rappers. Therefore one of the phrases long favored by rappers to encourage one another in this expressive task is "Represent!"

As a musical form rap fundamentally "re-presents" and re-creates using fragmented re-presentations of formerly whole works. In a distinctively afri-centric fashion, rap lives on the delicious samples of the entire musical history of Afrikans here in the so-called New World. A sample is a musical phrase, an interesting chunk of another work that is placed into a computer loop and repeated over and over again, thus forming a new independent art form. The rapper then places lyrics over this sampling. Rap re-presents blues riffs, rock-and-roll bass and guitar licks, and favorite soul grooves of the Motown era. Progressive rappers like Queen Latifah have integrated Jamaican reggae, dancehall, and "rub-a-dub" sing-rap styles into more traditional African American sampled rap. Recent rappers such as A Tribe Called Quest have begun to reinvigorate the entire rap musical scene by sampling jazz standards. Quincy Jones has used Ice-T and other well-known rappers on his adventurous jazz/multistyled albums, and Miles Davis's last album before his death literally fused cool jazz with rap to form the beginnings of cool bop. So, from a purely musical analysis, rap has re-created and re-presented older forms of Black music into a new form of life.

Rappers also enjoy re-presenting English, creating new forms of the language. Combining words or altering formerly accepted spellings of words are favorite rap methods. For instance, a new southern rap group named itself Outkast and its first album "Southernplayalisticadillacmuzik." Ice Cube's breakaway album of 1990 was entitled "Amerikkka's Most Wanted." One cannot help but notice how the intentional misspelling Amerikkka gives linguistic and visual presence to the "KKK" in the middle of the word. Without having to explain himself, Ice Cube ignites a rhetorical revolution, re-signifies pure, righteous, and virginal "America" into murderously racist, genocidal, and Black-hating Amerikkka. Such a country is not "land of the free, home of the brave," but is the spawning ground of racist mobs who masquerade as preservers of the old order — the KKK.

Rap subverts traditional understandings of English by creating a constantly expanding dictionary of rap terms that bend English. Rap English, or Rap-talk, twists and re-presents English into a language that only those initiated into the rap world can understand.

If rappers are re-presenting the Black flavor of life in a language that intentionally subverts traditional understandings of the English language, and we take seriously Cornel West's claim that pan-Africans must find a voice that re-presents our experience to ourselves and others, then rap must be carefully analyzed for what it is re-presenting. If rap is re-presenting us, then how well does it do this task, or does it need to be radically revised? Likewise, why is rap the major force of re-presentation for young African Americans when Black churches have long considered such things to be an aspect of their mission? Answering these questions requires that we clarify the different forms of rap in order to more effectively appraise its re-presentational power and to aid the process of critical conversational correlation.

Typology of Rap

In my examination of rap I have discerned five major musical and lyrical types. Each of these five can be presented with a view toward describing its musical forms, ethical norms, and views of God and humanity. Further, the types can be articulated in light of their liberative potential or lack thereof. The continuum of liberating-nonliberating is the axis of discernment on which all ethical evaluations will be posited. The five types are:

1. *Gangsta rap.* The most popular type, gangsta rap has provoked the most outrage and controversy. While it is national in scope, its home base is the West Coast, particularly Los Angeles. Gangsta rappers considered here include Snoop Doggy Dogg, Eazy E, Ice-T, Ice Cube, Tupac Shakur, Yo Yo, and Conscious Daughters.
2. *Revolutionary rap.* Africentric in content and insurrectionary in intent, revolutionary rap mounts a full-scale call for the destruction of the dominant powers controlling the United States. It appears to have been superseded by gangsta rap since the 1992 Sister Souljah controversy. Revolutionaries include Sister Souljah, Public Enemy, Arrested Development, Paris, and some of the lyrics of Tupac, Ice Cube, and Ice-T.
3. *Sexual play rap.* Sexual play rap focuses on expressing sexual pleasure, sensuous acts, and romantic desires. Naughty, playful, sometimes obsessive, and even dangerously exploitive, sexual-play rappers must be subdivided into two camps: the players, who tease and are "naughty" — Salt-n-Pepa, Heavy D and the Boyz, and Wreckz-N-Effect; and the exploiters, who explore lurid, objectifying, and phallocentric realms — 2-Live Crew and D.R.S. (Dirty Rotten Scoundrels).
4. *Crossover rap.* Apoliticized and "nonthreatening" to the power structures of the Westward people, crossover artists emphasize partying, good times, and innocuous subject matter in their lyrics. While other rap types have also "crossed over" and been exploited by the musical mainstream because of their popularity with the curious children of

the dominant culture, crossover is distinctively depoliticized in relation to other types. Artists that are primarily crossover include Fresh Prince and Jazzy Jeff, Kid-N-Play, L. L. Cool J, Snow, and the Beastie Boys.

5. *Inspirational rap.* These rappers have a street-smart awareness that enables them to criticize what is happening on the streets. Their intent is to direct and inspire young people to a different direction. Inspirational rappers include Queen Latifah, Hammer, and various Christian rappers such as MC R.G., LA J, and Disciples of Christ.

Limited space allows for an extensive evaluation of only one type, gangsta rap, while sexual, revolutionary, and inspirational rap will be referred to from within the following re-constructive Xodus theo-ethic. Further Xodus conversation with rap will take place in my next book.

Gangsta'z on the Loose . . . Sex, Drugs, and Parties

Gangsta rap has recently become the most marketable form of rap, gaining a wide and diversified audience. Arising from the West Coast, particularly greater Los Angeles and Oakland, it is ghettocentric music to an extreme degree, representing the inner thoughts, motives, values, and norms of the streets. To enter the world of gangsta rap one must allow oneself to enter the rhythms, noises, and danger of the streets. To be "ghettocentric" is to be conscious of all that is going on around you, to be conscious of the hard-core ways, wiles, temptations, traps, and pleasures of the streets. Gangsta'z (as they like to spell it) are ghettocentric because the core of their music and message arises from their articulation of street life, street ways, and street values. Conscious Daughters, a female rap duo, define being "conscious" as possessing knowledge of the streets and knowing how to use the skills one learns from the streets:

> "Conscious" is just conscious of the street, because everybody always says, "They know where the clubs are, they always get the records first, they know, always know what's goin' on, and they are hip to what's happening." So reality is around the way we live, and we stay on that level.[9]

Gangsta rap believes itself to be re-presenting "reality" because of its ghettocentricity. "Reality" means current events, questions, problems, and local gossip of the streets. "Reality" means knowing "the flava" — the "flavor of the month," or what is fashionable at the moment. Arising from frenetic dynamism of "hip-hop" culture,[10] "the flava" is the continually changing trend, the fashion, the message that is central to "the street." But to know "the flava" this month does not guarantee that one will know "the flava" next month. To know "what's happenin'" requires a constant vigilance, allegiance, and loyalty to the streets. Eazy-E, one of the premier gangsta rappers, represents this dynamism in both hip-hop culture and gangsta rap by continually asking the question in one of his raps, "Do you know what's goin' on? If you don't, you betta' ask somebody . . . you betta' ask somebody."

The knowledge of parties, clubs, and general events that the Conscious Daughters speak of is supplemented in the lyrics of male gangsta'z by an articulation of the ways of being a street hustler, gang member, and drug peddler. Eazy E and Ice-T are the "founding fathers" of West Coast gangsta rap, both turning their gang experience as drug hustlers, pimps, and gang members into a profitable trade. The reality these gangsta'z speak of includes the feel, smell, and taste of what it means to use your "Glock" (a semiautomatic handgun popular on the streets). Although both deny having killed anyone, their lyrics provide a personal witness to the harshness of murder and the loneliness of the streets. Ice-T is an "O.G.," "original gangster," who describes what he remembers, not what he imagines. Gangsta'z place great value on being "O.G." For example, Eazy-E bitterly criticizes equally successful Dr. Dre (former co-member of the group N.W.A. — Niggaz with Attitude) for not being "O.G." In his interview with the informative rap magazine *The Source,* Eazy-E accuses Dre of hypocrisy:

> Dre comes out on his record [the best-selling *The Chronic*] tellin' me where I ain't from or what I am. Don't talk about me where I'm from if you ain't never been there. I'm from the streets of Compton with an ID that says so. Dre's claimin' he's from a place he ain't really from, a place he packed his bags and left. He ain't never gang-banged or sold dope. Never, never in his life.[11]

Gangsta'z like Eazy-E, Ice Cube, Dr. Dre, and Snoop Doggy Dogg intersperse their lyrics with references to times when they are under the influence of marijuana — a.k.a. "the Chronic," "Endo," or a "Blunt." Snoop Doggy Dogg's refrain, "Rollin' down the street, smokin' Endo, sippin' on gin and juice . . . with my mind on ma' money and ma' money on ma' mind," represents the pervasiveness of marijuana as a recreational drug. Yo Yo, a female rapper associated with Ice Cube, proudly asks for her fellow partiers to "take a hit and pass the Blunt." As a theological ethicist I would venture to say that a mixture of a sincere desire for transcendence and an opiatelike escapism is probably involved here. So pervasive is its usage, so uplifted is the presence of "the Blunt," and so enraptured are gangsta'z with the high they achieve from marijuana that one is compelled to speculate that the usage of marijuana here ought to be interpreted as a powerful determination to achieve and maintain transcendence . . . by the fastest means possible. Getting high is also connected with having multiple sexual encounters — which might be seen as another form of seeking an ecstatic transcendence.

There is a certain spiritual element induced by drugs, a capacity to experience one's thoughts, feelings, and senses on a heightened level. We would be remiss not to remember that the Rastafarians call smoking a rolled marijuana cigarette "taking the Chalice." In this pan-African New World faith, smoking marijuana is incorporated into the highest sacred moment of the ritual of communion with the Divine. Many native peoples throughout the globe induce altered states of consciousness by use of peyote or opium as part of their religious rituals.[12]

How does an Xodus ecclesiology view the religious usage of drugs? While other persons writing from another Xodus perspective in the future may understand the religious usage of drugs positively, I cannot as a Christian. From a Christian point of view, drug usage is unnecessary for communion with the Divine, and perhaps dangerous to one's health. It is difficult to quantify or evaluate drug use and drug addiction from an abstracted religious viewpoint if one is cognizant of the devastation, loss of human resources, and loss of life that drugs continue to cause within Black communities.

Certainly we ought to recognize that the Divine placed all things on this earth for some good purpose and use. If we affirm the goodness of all created things, then the opium poppy, peyote, and marijuana plant ought to be affirmed as having a place in the divine order of things. The usage of pain-reducing and even hallucinogenic drugs for the alleviation of unbearable physical suffering certainly ought to be affirmed, although confined to particular limited conditions. Furthermore, God has placed a multitude of herbs, roots, and plants throughout the world for the flourishing of our overall physical, mental, and spiritual welfare. It is clear that smelling, tasting, and imbibing various herbs and plants does produce a heightened sense of profound spiritual connection with the divine. Traditional peoples throughout the world have maintained this kind of earth-wisdom more than the so-called modern West has, although renewed interest in "alternative therapies" is a move to reclaim what has been neglected, dismissed, and forgotten. From the viewpoint of a theologically informed medical ethics, African Americans have lost much of the traditional earth-wisdom of our African ancestors and also suffer from not having proper access to legitimate and safe drugs used for medicinal purposes. It is important not to condemn any herb or plant, just its abuse. A proliferation of drug abuse within Afrikan communities in North America threatens to destroy any hope of a promising future. How can Christians respect the usage of drugs as a part of one's religiosity when such a difference may mean affirming the usage of drugs in ways not directly associated with healing?

As a Christian I believe that we have access through prayer to the elemental and consciousness-expanding power of the Holy Spirit. Christians believe that prayer opens individuals and communities to the power, presence, and promise of God. The abuse of "the Chronic" on the streets is not comparable to the religious usage of drugs. One can be aware of the dangers and joys of the streets without being "high," but perhaps one cannot glorify the power of lethal weapons, uplift the beauty of gunfire, and write songs about murder unless one is "high"! In that case the use of "the Chronic" is a way of numbing the pain caused by the horror of taking life, an escape door to a fantasy world of illusions, good feelings, and irresponsibility. Because we are dealing with human beings who are caught up in the overwhelmingness of the streets, it is important to analyze their situation with a view toward how drugs enable coping. Further, because "slinging dope" — rap English for selling drugs, especially crack cocaine — is usually represented as part of the way gangsta'z make their money, gangsta rap does not present a united critique of how the infestation of crack is destroying Afrikan communities. So "the Blunt" is uplifted as a positive "high," while the real drug enemy, crack, is present throughout the range of gangsta lyrics without being condemned. This represents an ambiguous response to a real problem for most gangsta rappers. How can it not be represented in a morally ambiguous way since so many gangsta'z represent themselves as the ones who have profited from crack addictions? Smoking marijuana must appear to be a "safe" high in comparison to the self-destructive spiral of addiction by which crack imprisons its victims. Crack, as an addiction, seems to be the ultimate imprisoning doorway to transcendence.

Conversely, I believe it necessary to remind Christians that many of our churches are not places of liberating transcendence, but are the well-groomed halls of holy escapism. Within these walls we preach a message in which young women and men acquainted with the streets find it hard to discern any meaning or relevance. How can a young person who has witnessed the murder of a best friend, a lover, or a baby have any patience with a simplistic declaration of forgiveness and reconciliation? How can young folks whose lives are severely constricted and controlled by the flow of drugs and guns to support that "trade" find the boring reiteration of gospel pablum enough to feed their starving souls? The churches of Jesus Christ need to transform the dry-bones gospel of simple salvation into a fully fleshed-out call for spiritual revival and liberation on the streets. We must brave the same dangers and foes as our children do every day if we are to expect them to listen and believe what we preach. The message of the gospel must deliberately find its way out onto those same killing streets that threaten the future of Afrikans, or young people will continue to smoke dope and get high, laughing at the gospel of Jesus Christ as the nonsense of weak-minded chumps. If we do take Jesus Christ's power onto the streets, then we have the opportunity to challenge the evildoers on their own turf and be heard, even if the message is not accepted. If we challenge the streets in the safety of books, church services, and prayer meetings, we are not facing the evil, but running from it. The simple truth is that there is no safe place to be now. Either we stand up to such evil or be destroyed by its undermining, corrosive influence.

Woman-Degradation and Responses

The most infamous aspect of gangsta lyrics is their negative labeling of women as "bitches" and "'hoes" (whores). In this regard it is difficult for Christians who believe that all of God's children are created in God's image to extend a level of understanding. The only way that such a degrading image of womanhood could be fostered with such casualness would be for it to be profitable — and Afrikans do not own the distribution networks that control the recording industry. Euro-Americans own such networks, and have greatly increased their profit margins by widening the marketing of rap (particularly gangsta rap) to a young Euro-American audience. Is this new demographic group, primarily male and between the ages of sixteen and twenty-four, interested in describing women — particularly Black women — in degrading terms? One must wonder about such things when the cover of Snoop Doggy Dogg's hit album *Doggystyle* portrayed Black women with snouts, tails, and on all fours (does such a prone position imply that these Black women are viewed as ready for sexual activity?). Are gangsta rappers really part of a larger cultural force in Amerikkka that works both consciously and unconsciously in capitalist institutions for the simultaneous exaltation of whiteness and degradation of anything Black? If calling Black women disparaging names is not a concerted manifestation of a conspiracy to destroy the minds, hearts, and pride of Afrikans, then what is?

At a recent peace gathering in Los Angeles (June 1994), a woman carried a placard that summarized the criticism we need to make about degrading lyrics: "Martin Luther King and the Civil Rights Movement did not die for you to call yourself a 'Niggah' on stage, or a woman a 'bitch.'" To call any woman such a name cannot represent us, because it can only serve to divide our strengths and put us on the defensive. Such language may be expressive of what some women present themselves as being, especially in poor neighborhoods where desperate women may look upon rappers as wealthy and as easy sources of income in exchange for sexual favors. If that is the kind of woman that most rappers attract, then rappers need to reexamine their presence and influence. Most women do not present themselves as sexually ravenous whores who would do anything for money or drugs, as many rap lyrics suggest.

The presence of woman-degrading language in gangsta rap is of such long standing that women rappers have begun to react. In her song "Mackstress," Yo Yo calls on women to become counters of the male "Mack Daddy" or sexual player. Instead of allowing herself to be "played for a 'ho," the Mackstress takes on the aggressive and dominating attitude of a Mack Daddy in female form. Further, a Mackstress uses words likes weapons, directing them to destroy targeted representatives of the "System" like police, informers, and so forth.[13] Salt-n-Pepa deride women for allowing themselves to be called "bitches" and "'hoes," describing in lurid terms the ways in which women's sexuality is a power that cannot be denied or degraded.[14] Queen Latifah's hit "U.N.I.T.Y." harshly criticizes the street usage of the term "bitch" over a delightfully positive reggae sample. Throughout the course of her rap, Latifah asks over and over again, "Who you callin' a bitch?" She challenges her male listeners with the provocative refrain, "I'm not a bitch, you're a 'ho."[15] By this, Latifah re-signifies the word 'ho to mean that male gangsta rappers make prostitutes of themselves by using female-degrading language in order to make money. If that is the case, then Latifah represents the cutting edge of criticism where a negative word is re-signified by the objects of its negativity into something more universal. On an MTV special about gangsta rap, Ice Cube, one of the most flagrant users of the "b" word, recently stated, "Anybody can be a 'bitch,' not just women." It is unclear what he means by that. What is clear is that some rappers are wrestling with the overwhelmingly negative response to their usage of those words to describe females.

One group of women has decided to cash in on the interest, naming themselves H.W.A. (Hoez with Attitude). H.W.A.'s debut album is a compilation of their "street philosophy" on the positive aspects of being a "'ho." They make strong distinctions throughout the album between street-smart, sexually irresistible "'hoes," and street-stupid, too-trusting "bitches." This distinction is far too subtle to be meaningful for this author! I am not certain that women rappers taking unto themselves the name "Hoez" (as a positive way of being female) is going to transform the negative valence of the term. I believe that Queen Latifah's strong critique of woman-degrading language is more transformative and liberating.

Christians in general and Black churches in particular ought to have a great deal to say about woman-degrading rap lyrics because rap helps to shape cultural attitudes toward women. But how can Black churches really mount a sustained critique of woman-degrading rhetoric when so many preachers and churches devalue women on a regular basis? Women report being amazed at how their preachers speak of women in their own congregations as "bitches"! How can a leader in the Black church stand against that in which he is deeply invested?[16] Xodus Space is that Space-within-Black-church in which such a critique may be mounted, from within. Those pastors, such as Marvin McMickle of Antioch in Cleveland, Ohio; Charles Adams of Hartford Memorial in Detroit; Calvin Butts of Abyssinia in Harlem; and Cecil Murray of First A.M.E. Los Angeles (to name but a few), who are already denouncing sexism in their churches and in rap lyrics, are exemplars of this aspect of Xodus Space.

In light of the horrifying fact that some rappers like D.R.S. (Dirty Rotten Scoundrels) spend entire songs describing the torture and dismemberment of women as a sexual act, Xodus Space must speak out now! Such atrocities must be called "by name" (an important African Americanism). We must call demonic pleasures out "by name" and rebuke them "in the name of Jesus," sending them back to the hellish pit from whence they have arisen. We cannot converse with demons; we must command them from the spiritual place of authority that we possess. We must stop ignoring the negative influence of such lyrics on African American male-female relations; we must call it "by name" and address it.

Black churches have a powerfully prophetic role to play in this regard, in reconstituting Black sexuality beyond the oppressive woman-degrading constrictions of gangsta rappers. We must move to address *us* in a way that uplifts the positiveness and beauty of sexuality rather than its exploitation as a way of making money. I would call such a reconstitution a positive sexual ethic. While I write of it as a committed Christian, I would expect that Xodus Space would desire the contributions of other religious and philosophical views of sexuality. This is my contribution to that ongoing process of Xodus Space-making.

Positive Sexuality in Xodus

As a Christian I view sexuality as a positive intimate aspect of the human being. Human beings are created in God's image (Gen. 1:26-27). Our genders as male and female are part of a divine plan that rejoices and revels in the differences and similarities we manifest as female and male. There has been little theological speculation on what being created "in God's image" means in relation to our sexuality. Standard Christian orthodoxy (in the Western world) has traditionally believed that we are created in God's image most clearly in regard to our capacity for self-consciousness and reason. I want to open the category up a bit more and suggest that part of our being created in God's image has to do with being created as sexual creatures. Human beings have sexual relations with one another as an expression of their capacity for feelings, loyalty, pleasure, and play. We are not merely reasonable — we are also playful, pleasure-seeking, desirable, and emotive creatures. Why should such aspects of humanity not also be connected to our being created in "God's image?" Is not God the creator of pleasure, desire, and emotion as well? Why do we constrict our divine spark to the realm of intellectual activity? I believe that we do so because these other forces — desire, emotion, pleasure — are so potent, so awesome, and so prone to getting out of control (that is, beyond the regulating power of reason) that traditionally we have believed them to belong anywhere but to God's image. Yet if we are to begin to refashion our understanding of human sexuality, as Christians we ought to begin with a "new revised standard version" of the image of God. Being in God's image means that we embody the fullness of Divine Personality. Divine Personality is not just reason, but desire, pleasure, ecstasy, and sensuality. God delights and enjoys. God is pleasure. God is more than strict rules that dictate a series of "No's!" Rather, God is the Source and Author of human capacities — all of them, including the capacity for sensuality, sexual ecstasy, and pleasure. If we can make this leap in our theological dogma, we find ourselves in a completely new and open Space: an Xodus Space of positive sexuality.

Positive sexuality is affirming of our God-given sensuousness. We are creatures who are capable of experiencing delight through our senses, sexually and nonsexually. We revel in the smell of a rose, the softness of grass under our feet, the warmth of a fire on a cold evening, and the wetness of water when we swim or bathe. Traditional Christianity has failed to take into account these sensuous experiences as part of the image of God. When we begin to see the connections between our fundamental sensuousness and the expression of intimacy through sexual acts, we can see the importance of speaking about the topic of sex as a sacred act, and not as "that dirty thing."

Positive sexuality holds the communion of two human beings in sexual intercourse to be so sacred that it cannot be left open to the abuse of non-commitment. Instead of preaching a simplistic message of abstinence (even though such a message does need to be central to those young people who abuse sexual intercourse), we need to teach our young people about the sacredness of sexuality. Sacred things are holy, set apart from everyday usage. Sexual intercourse is the fullest, most powerful, most spiritually ecstatic expression of our basic God-given sensuousness. It is on a continuum with basic delights in smelling roses, touching hands, and so forth.

Therefore sexual intercourse cannot be undertaken as a part of a "scorecard" kept to tally how many times one has had sex (as is the case among some high school students today). It is a sacred act, set apart from normal intimacies, touches, kisses, and caresses, to be kept precious and singular. It is to be shared with one special person, and not a means of experimentation. One does not need to practice it to be proficient; one simply needs to understand that it is so powerful and so sacred that it must be kept as something done between covenanted partners and not impassioned experimenters. One can never learn more about oneself through sexual intercourse with just anyone; it is a joining of more than body. In sexual intercourse two human beings express the communion, the commingling, of their souls in a physical sign of their love for each other. In the language of a positive sexual ethic, sexual intercourse is the most sacred act undertaken by our God-created, image-of-God sensuality.

To emphasize such things may lead some to believe that we are not expressing strongly enough the need for abstinence. A positive sexuality is supportive of abstinence, but distrusts the negative approach often taken by traditionalists. New ceremonial rituals of abstinence are springing up across the United States in which rings are exchanged, vows taken, and a community of support is affirmed and nurtured. Such rituals are tremendously important and are in concert with the theological ethics of an Xodus positive sexuality. Xodus travelers must encourage such programs and press toward the creation of new ways for unmarried young people to socialize, enjoy one another, form bounds, and develop relationships while teaching about the sacredness of sexuality.

At the turn of the century "Daddy" King, father of Martin Luther King, Jr., wrote about the ways in which church picnics and socials formed the major part of official courting between potential spouses. At such picnics the elders of the community, those church mothers and fathers who were known as "pillars," could serve as chaperones without necessarily being intrusive. Things were kept public, out in the open. Young people today have too much unsupervised, unchaperoned time, and then regret the consequences later on. Instead, churches ought to help develop social times when relationships can flourish and be nurtured under the caring, unobtrusive eye of the adults, mentors, and elders of the community. Such a suggestion may seem terribly old-fashioned, and not "cutting edge" at all, but I believe that Xodus Space ought to be at the forefront of such ideas.

What does gangsta rap, or rap music in general, have to do with an Xodus positive sexuality? The crude, abusive, and negative sexuality of gangsta rap have provoked creation of an Xodus positive sexuality. The "Streetz" (as some rappers spell it) are not going to wait for unanimity of response from all churches, but will go on abusing and mistreating both females and the males who participate in its "me-first" ethos. Xodus positive sexuality responds to the street with something meant to attract rather than dismiss, to invite rather than to condemn, and to call forth the best in all of us rather than catering to our basest fears, loathings, and cravings.

Sexual Players

Sexual-play rappers such as Salt-n-Pepa present an ambiguous picture of sexuality when we contrast their ideas to that of an Xodus positive sexuality. On the one hand there are the players who present as wonderful the bodies, muscles, and strength of Black women and men, as in Salt-n-Pepa's rap songs. Their recent hit "Whatta Man" has a refrain praising a steady-thinking, family-values-yet-sexy man in the words, "Whatta man, whatta man, whatta man, whatta mighty good man!"[17] On the other hand, another rap song on the same album speaks about men as a "weakness" because the very sight of such brothers sends these women into such an ecstasy that they cry out, "You make me wanna shoop."[18] In the video of this particular rap, every time this refrain is reached the duo make suggestive pelvic gyrations that make it clear that to "Shoop" is to have sexual intercourse. Tricia Rose interprets the sexual teasing and play of Salt-n-Pepa as indicative of Black women's right to enjoy themselves and to resist sexual objectification by males at the same time. She cites the lyrics and video of the song "Shake Your Thang" as representing a powerful "defiance of the moral, sexual restrictions on women" through slapstick teasing of male desire, enjoyment of their own bodies, and disregard for conventional interpretations of their actions.[19] Shaking one's "thang" is a female celebration of their own bodies as sites of enjoyment rather than objectified sexual leering.

Male sexual players Wreckx-N-Effect, in a similar fashion to Salt-n-Pepa, praise the bodily attributes of women in their hit "Rumpshaker," but in a more objectifying manner. With an irresistibly danceable beat, Wreckz-N-Effect plead in Rap-English with gyrating women to have sexual intercourse:

All I wanna do is zooma-zoom-zoom zoom [with the video camera] *and a Boom-Boom — Just shake your rump!*[20]

While the element of playfulness and enjoyable sexual interplay in both Salt-n-Pepa and Wreckx-N-Effect may be interpreted as exploitive of women's bodies — Black women's bodies in particular — it is important to distinguish between Black women enjoying their bodies to the beat of music and men finding those gyrating bodies sexually stimulating. Salt-n-Pepa enjoy themselves, Wreckx-N-Effect are enjoying an "other." The ambiguity of

Black women and men acting sexually in the public sphere is a legacy of the purported "oversexuality" or "demonic propensity" for lust, which has been attributed to African people by Euro-Americans. Black males might learn something from players like Salt-n-Pepa about how to *enjoy* our sexuality publically, regardless. Such a view cannot be gained while male sexuality remains constructed along the lines of other-centeredness and objectification. Recent developments in the men's movement are promising in this regard, with men attending retreats in the woods and mountains, learning how to touch and enjoy our own bodies. Yet such retreats are prohibitive in cost and beyond the easy access of most men, particularly Afrikan males.

What unites these two very different kinds of sexual-play rap groups is their ambiguous connection between appreciating the sexiness of bodies and impulsive sexual acting-out. They do not have the dangerous levels of sexual objectification, pushed to an abusive level of sadomasochistic violence and phallocentrism, of sexual-exploiters such as 2-Live Crew, D.R.S. (Dirty Rotten Scoundrels), and the women in H.W.A. (Hoez With Attitude). That kind of sexual-rap music addresses female bodies as the "object" of male sexual release, presenting a philosophy of "Hoe-dom" that glorifies the power of women to get what they want from men by being sexually available to them.[21]

Xodus positive sexuality does not support such an ethic of sexual impulsiveness. Every time we view a sensuously attired body, or the walk (or rump-shake) of a well-endowed physique, we are not automatically required to move toward sexual intercourse! If that were the case, the sacred act would be cheapened. If the visual stimulation of a beautiful, sensuous body (female or male) necessarily drives us to have sexual intercourse, then it is no longer a positive sacred act we are addressing, but a release of biochemical instincts akin to the mating of dogs or cats in heat. Xodus positive sexuality insists that because our sexuality is connected to and on a continuum with our God-created and endowed image, then sexual intercourse can never be merely a release. It must always be an expression of Godly Sensuality and God-endowed pleasure. There is a cosmic spiritual gap between the kind of biochemical release of sexual instincts praised in sexual play rap and the sacred act of Xodus positive sexuality.

Blacklight Raptivism and the Xodus Journey

The "Angry Children" of raptivism (rap activists) are prophets and streetfighters, revolutionaries whose message calls for a return to African traditional ways. They present a kind of "practical Afrocentricity 101," as it were, and strong declarations of the beauty of Blackness. They critique Black Churches in a way that Xodus theo-creativity can use to forge "Blacklight." When Black folks hold up the light of God, it is Blacklight — Black truth and experience revealed as a prophetic knife, cutting away the centuries-old accumulated hypocrisies, denials, evasions, and lack of accountability that have sustained Euro-domination and all dominations. Xodus Space holds up Blacklight as a way of undressing the airs of naked Euro-domination, patriarchy, classism, and all the other isms that rule and ruin our lives. Blacklight is revelational. Sojourner Truth and Harriet Tubman, W. E. B. DuBois and Booker T. Washington, Martin Luther King, Jr. and Malcolm X, were its agents in history. Blacklight is universal in its outreach and application but particular in that it is revelational-prophetic power wrapped in Black flesh.

The searing knife of Blacklight is most clearly enunciated in the raptivism of Sister Souljah. A radical Christian, Sister Souljah decries the sentimental "forgive everybody" Jesus of Europeans, demanding that Jesus must be understood as "Justice" in her powerful lyric "My God is a Powerful God."[22] Sister Souljah's message is a call to arms, encouraging Afrikans to become "Souljahs" ("Soldiers" in rap-talk) like herself, who are psychologically prepared, physically disciplined, and emotionally fit for making a war against Euro-domination. The war that Sister Souljah proposes we wage is not one that requires guns or rifles but a unified commitment to the flourishing of Black life.

Paris, another profoundly influential raptivist, widens the religious parameters of Revolutionary Rap to embrace Islam. A follower of the Nation of Islam, Paris calls himself the "Black Panther of Rap." In a 1994 album, *Guerilla Funk,* Paris joins Ice Cube in naming "America" in the intentional re-signified re-presentation of *Amerikkka,* a nation whose political-economic heart is centered in the racist philosophy of the KKK. In keeping with the kind of sustained criticism of Christianity as a "white man's religion" that we have already examined in Malcolm X, Paris notes on the liner notes of the album that Christianity was fashioned into a perfect tool of oppression by white supremacists. Decrying Amerikkka as practicing a "false Christianity," Paris goes on to write out an ingenious historical denunciation of Christian imperialism as beginning at the Council of Nicaea in 322 C.E.:

At this conference, *European images* replaced *African images* of the Madonna and Child. Above the crucifix, the words, "*In Hoc Signo, vinces*" were written, which means "in this sign . . . you will *conquer.*" And that's just what white supremacists did around the world, armed with a gun in one hand and a falsified Bible (there are over 125 *versions* in existence) in the other.[23]

Paris is tremendously concerned with the psychological impact that the imposition of whiteness on Jesus and God has had and continues to have on Black self-image and self-respect. Paris also calls for non-white peoples around the world to "Wake Up! We're at war!"[24] Crediting all of the critical insurrectionary content of his lyrics to Allah, noting (again on the cover of the album) "All praise is due to Allah!" Paris foresees a violent apocalyptic struggle where Afrikans finally awaken and rebel with weapons as a sign of their hard-won right to respect themselves. So while Paris is a follower of Allah and Sister Souljah a follower of Jesus Christ, both are united in envisioning a revolutionary apocalypse to free Afrikans from the death-dealing embrace of Euro-domination.

Arrested Development provides a pan-African and Africentric alternative to the apocalyptic message of raptivists like Sister Souljah and Paris. Their alternative message of revolution begins with a return to traditional African spirituality. They espouse ways of knowing the Earth — touching it, being "in touch" with it, and naming this contact "good" in their teaching "Children Play with Earth."[25] Arrested Development is both traditionally African in spirituality and intensely political, decrying the political passivity of traditional "Baptists" in "Fishin' 4 Religion." The lyrics demoan boring expressions of faith in which preachers enjoin the congregation to pray for the strength to cope rather than the power to change unjust systems.[26] Their prophetic message comes in a profoundly biblical analysis:

The Government is Happy with
    most Baptist Churches,
Cuz they don't do a Damm Thing
    To try to Nurture,
Brothers and Sisters in
    The Revolution
Baptist teaches dying is
    the Only Solution.
Passiveness causes
    others to pass us by.
I throw my line til I've
made my decision, until then I'm
still fishin' 4 religion.[27]

How can Xodus travelers and the Xodus church use the Blacklight prophecies? What enlightenment and wisdom can we take from these "Angry Children" whose voices have an edge that Christians are not accustomed to hearing? I think that we can grow by incorporating several aspects of Blacklight raptivism.

First, we can make sure that the anger, rage, and passionate social intelligence of Afrikan young people are not dismissed or ignored as we seek to build Xodus Space. There is a real power, street power, in those lyrics — even the ones with "dirty words" that we often are afraid to hear. Second, Xodus Space must envision itself as open to the spirituality of Christians, Muslims, traditional African spiritualities, and the nonreligious. I write as a Christian, but Xodus Space deals with all Afrikans, therefore we must take care not to exclude other spiritualities from the revolutionary praxis that Xodus creativity is processively making. Since Xodus Space is about promoting Blacklight revelation, it ought to believe humbly that the God who has inspired such a revelation is bigger than denominational and doctrinal differences. Third, Xodus Space must never separate personal spiritual empowerment in the Holy Spirit from its enabling power to organize and energize social change. That is why Blacklight raptivism is so critical of privatized "shouting" and services that do not explicitly connect the empowerment of God with the need to struggle for justice. Fourth, we must learn to build a positive sexual ethic that enables affirmation and positive feelings about the sacredness of our sexuality while providing a wise counsel of restraint from uncovenanted sexual encounters. Finally, we ought to revisit some of the rap-English terms for their creative capacity to help us reconstruct old, irrelevant understandings of Christianity. While the scope of such a project is ongoing, in the next few pages I will focus on developing an Xodus rap-ethics that concentrates on the rap-word "ruff" as a point of creative departure.

Ruffness, Defiance, and the Souljah Imperative

If it ain't rough . . . then I can do without it
If it ain't rough . . . just kick it to the curb
If it ain't rough . . . then I'll just do without it
If it ain't rough . . . it's gettin' on my nerves[28]

On February 3, 1994, Connie Chung's "Eye to Eye" weekly news/journal/gossip show carried an interview with notorious rapper Ice-T. Carefully trying to maintain the purportedly objective standards of journalism, Chung was at once fascinated and repulsed by this contemporary rap superstar. The interview detailed his Horatio Alger-like rise from being an "O.G." who hustled, sold drugs, and pimped to a multimillionaire living in an expensive penthouse with an imposing North Hollywood view. What captured my attention about their encounter was the way that Ice-T seemed perfectly at ease with his "in yo' face" rhetorical style. In-yo'-face is a rhetoric of the streets, standing at the crossroads between the "dozens" game of insults we all had to endure as kids, the bravado posturing of a "toast" — another Black street form of parading one's accomplishments — and a sly strategy of reverse morality. For instance, to be "ruff" in the language of rappers is to portray an unvarnished, survival-oriented, sexually proficient, and street-wise stance toward life, otherwise known as "hard-core." To present it as "sweet" or "soft" is to miss the essence of the strenuous, dangerous, and yet peculiarly vibrant context that makes the 'hood a place you would never want to leave. As such, hard-core, in-yo'-face rap-English posits being "ruff" as an essential, positive, and admirable character trait that any true member of the 'hood ought to wear as a badge of honor. It is a virtue according to rappers.

Ice-T claimed to present/re-present various rap stories where the crimi-nal, the gangsta, and the various negative words about women ("bitch," "'ho," and so on) never come out as winners in the end. Ice-T saw himself as a griot of bleak remembrances, all designed to teach young people to see through the seeming seductiveness and glamour of the O.G. lifestyle to its violent, self-destructive reality. He proudly stated something that made me pause because it portrayed the ruff quality so highly prized by rappers: "I'm a role model to them kids." "A role model?" asked an incredulous Connie Chung. "Yeah, the only kind they can hear. The only kind they would respect. I'm the kind of role model that can get they respect, you understand?" Ice-T stated, eyes flashing . . . in yo' face all the way!

Ice-T symbolizes for most people everything our mommas told us a Black man ought *not* to be. He boldly speaks about having many women — some-thing any self-respecting brother ought to know simply reinforces percep-tions of Black male bestial-sexuality. He calls himself an "O.G.," seemingly glorifying the criminal element in our community that is often portrayed by the mass media as larger and more prevalent than it actually is. He calls him-self a "niggah" proudly, defending the term as a way of honoring what has previously been a degrading racial epithet used by whites to dehumanize Blacks. According to Ice-T, "since they [whites] are going to call us that, and we are that anyway, no matter who we are or what we got [in material pos-sessions, fame, influence, education], then I call myself a niggah." Connie Chung asked whether such self-naming didn't buy into racialist attitudes still prevalent in many sectors of the country. Ice-T's response was telling: "I don't care what white people think. It doesn't concern me. . . ."

I began to ruminate on the way that young Blacks in the 1960s called themselves "Black" proudly, taking a former insult out of white mouths and placing it in Black mouths as a precious utterance of honor. Could this be what rappers such as Ice-T and Tupac Shakur (whose best-selling album is entitled "Strictly for My N.I.G.G.A.Z.") are doing? If so, are they not forcing African Americans to cross over into an undiscovered country of rhetorical-moral freedom? Imagine what this could mean, that young African American rappers compelled the entire American community to deconstruct the final insult to Black humanity — the final insult, the "N" word, a word so assiduously avoided by white liberals proud of their shed blood, sore feet, and bruised social standings because they had "marched with Martin" in Selma, Birmingham, and Washington, D.C. — the word whose very utterance can cause mature, highly educated Black persons to break out in rage, defiance, and a sense of frustration about "the state of things" in the '90s. The "N" word has always symbolized the subhuman status a dominant race has reserved for a subordinated race. And now, how is it that young Black kids want to call *themselves* this word? Is it the end of decency, morality, our heritage, our self-respect? Or is it the crossing over into an undiscovered country where Black people finally do not care what white people think about us, or whether they approve of us, or whether they have meaningful commentary about our habits? The cavalier manner in which Ice-T curses at people who take offense is a demonstration of a new defiance on the horizon.

I don't believe I could ever call myself a "niggah" with the kind of bodacious pride many rappers do. I am hopeful, however, that I might learn something from their new defiance. There is something positive about rappers' sense of detachment from a dominant cultural-moral system that keeps African Americans constantly seeking approval, permission, and encouragement from whites (whether these whites be liberal, conservative, or just plain "dangerous"). It is indeed a "ruff" thing to affirm oneself as a niggah with pride, knowing that the "N" word is a scandal, shame, and symbol of the continuing legacy of racism in America. It is ruff, but useful for prying open the subtle ways that the dominant morality of the U.S.A. continues to operate in a mode of control and domination over the actions, language, and public presentation of African Americans. Rappers don't "give a Thang" (Queen Latifah's revised expression of exasperation) about how they are perceived or received by white Americans. They know that a majority of their fans are white kids interested in relating to the 'hood any way they can. They know that their message, rhythm, and "flow" (a multivalent expression that has to do with the interaction between a vibe in the rhythm and rap lyrics and the interpretation-reception of that message by the listeners) creates controversy because it subverts customary modes of being and acting publicly as a Black person. But they don't care. Why? Because they are "ruffnecks," ragamuffins, bad, packin', jackin', O.G. Niggaz who glorify all things apparently un-American, un-Christian, and immoral. But America, most of

Christianity, and dominant morality have either conspired to silence or collaborated to erase and efface these Black persons from the so-called mainstream. So they rejoice in being ruff and real, hard-core without apology.

Sister Souljah's imperative, to becomes souljahs ("soldiers" in rap English) who wage "war" against the system of erasure and degradation of European derivation, must be applied to our own sexism. Our sexism is the private-sphere war that threatens the liberation of our community as deeply as does the racism of the public sphere. As womanist ethicist Katie Cannon suggests, the "war" is on at least three fronts — race (public), sex (private), and class (an elusive mixture of both spheres). Until the Sepia male is willing to engage on all three fronts, rather than concentrating all of his attention on the public sphere, he is not really willing to be a souljah.

What is the best response for the church, particularly Black churches? We need to bring a ruff gospel message of how Jesus hung out with the rappers, dope-slingers, and those considered the "bitches" and "O.G's" of his time. Jesus reached out to the unreachable and somehow made a difference in their lives so that after they had encountered him, they moved into a different, higher "flow." A ruff gospel must move beyond the walls of church buildings out into the crack-houses, the hallways, and the street-corners of need. It must have the freshness, quickness, and hard-core ability to "tell it like it is" . . . in the name of Jesus the Liberator. A ruff gospel must learn to heal broken spirits *and* sidewalks, mend torn hearts *and* communities, and save souls *and* addiction-wracked bodies. A ruff gospel is being proclaimed by a few (oh so few), but not enough preachers and churchgoers are willing to get in touch with the radical message of the ruff rap prophets. Yes, rappers are prophets for our time, in touch with the pulse of dissatisfaction, disillusionment, and rage that typifies Black existence in the U.S.A. They are not prophets in the biblical mode, calling us to return to the ways of our faith-filled ancestors, because that is *our* job! They do not have a message of rebuilding and uplift as the prophets of Scripture had, because that is *our* calling. They do not have a spiritually empowering vision of divine glory sweeping away all wrong, because that is what we, a revived Xodus ruff church, ought to be about the business of proclaiming on every streetcorner. It is time to get hard-core, defiant, and ruff, in the name of Jesus, and for the sake of a threatened community.

Notes

1. Cornel West, *Prophetic Fragments* (Grand Rapids, Mich.: Eerdmans, 1988), 185–87. This type of understanding was also expressed by Henry Louis Gates, Jr., in his defense of the pornographic lyrics of rap group 2-Live Crew in their public indecency trial of 1991. Gates explained his ideas in the *Boston Review*, December 1991; cited by Houston A. Baker, Jr., *Black Studies Rap and the Academy* (Chicago: University of Chicago Press, 1993), 64–65.
2. Michael Eric Dyson, *Reflecting Black: African-American Cultural Criticism* (Minneapolis: University of Minnesota Press, 1993), 21.
3. Tricia Rose, *Black Noise: Rap Music and Black Culture in Contemporary America* (Hanover and London: Wesleyan University Press, 1994), 10–12.
4. David Tracy, *Blessed Rage for Order: The New Pluralism in Theology* (New York: Seabury Press, 1978), 32.
5. David Tracy, *Plurality and Ambiguity: Hermeneutics, Religion, Hope* (San Francisco: Harper & Row, 1987).
6. Ibid., 18–19.
7. Cornel West, "Cultural Politics of Difference," in *Keeping Faith: Philosophy and Race in America* (New York: Routledge, 1993), 16.
8. Ibid., 20.
9. "Ghetto Girlz," Cheo Coker's interview with Conscious Daughters in *The Source: The Magazine of Hip Hop Music, Culture & Politics* (July 1994), 42.
10. Jawanza Kunjufu traces the term "hip hop" to "an early New York rapper named Lovebug Starski, who "coined it in a phrase 'chap hippity hop don't stop keep on body rock.'" *Hip Hop vs. M'aat: A Psycho Analysis of Values* (Chicago: African American Images, 1993), 11.
11. Carter Harris's interview, "Eazy Street," *The Source* (July 1994), 76.
12. The Huichol Indians of the North American Southwest have a yearly festival at which peyote is smoked at the climax of the ceremonies.
13. Yo Yo, "Mackstress" and "Can You Handle It?" on the album *You Better Ask Somebody* (New York: EastWest Records America, Division of Atlantic Recording Corporations for the United States of America, 1993, 7 92252–4).
14. Salt-n-Pepa, "Somebody's Gettin' on My Nerves," from *Very Necessary* (London: Next Records, 1993, 828392–4).
15. Queen Latifah, "U.N.I.T.Y.," from *Black Reign* (Los Angeles: Motown, 1993, 374636370–4).
16. This criticism of sexist Black church practices was offered by C. Dale Gadsden, an M.Div. candidate at Harvard Divinity School, when I read an early version of this chapter at the 1994 American Academy of Religion annual meeting in Chicago.
17. Salt-n-Pepa, "Whatta Man," from *Very Necessary*.
18. "Shoop," from *Very Necessary*.
19. Rose, *Black Noise*, 166–67.
20. Wreckz-N-Effect, refrain from "Rumpshaker" on *Hard or Smooth* (Universal City, Calif.: MCA Records, 1992, MCAC-10566).
21. This interpretation comes from D. Nosakhere Thomas, as discussed by a group of female teenagers at his church in Riverside, Calif., spring 1994.

22. Sister Souljah, "Brainteasers and Doubtbusters," *360 Degrees of Power* (New York: Epic Div. of Sony Music Entertainment, 1992; ET48713).
23. *Guerilla Funk.*
24. Ibid.
25. Arrested Development, "Children Play with Earth," from *3 Years, 5 Months, and 2 Days in the Life of.* . . (New York: Chrysalis Records, 1992; FA-21929).
26. Idem, from "Fishin' for Religion," in *3 Years, 5 Months.* . . .
27. Ibid.
28. Queen Latifah, "Rough," from *Black Reign.*

Rage, Privilege, and Perseverance: The Middle Class

Being Black in America is not a monolithic experience. There are many ways to be "Black" and still be "down" (in solidarity) with the community and to be for the liberation of all Afrikans. Ellis Cose has written a controversial book entitled *The Rage of a Privileged Class*, which brings to light the complex business of being Black and middle class in the late-twentieth-century, high-tech, postindustrial, corporate down-sizing United States of America. Despite having attained a high degree of education, professional competence, and job experience, Black middle-class women and men are haunted by lowered peer expectations, limited by a "glass ceiling," and filled with a growing sense of rage at the invisible yet tangible racism that still prevails in corporate America.

Nathan McCall's autobiographical *Makes Me Wanna Holler: A Young Black Man in America* reveals, in a more intimate fashion, the tensions of criminalizing expectations of growing up Black and male in America — even if one hails from a hard-working family. While such problems do not appear to have the intensity and immediacy of the various crises facing young and poor Afrikans in the city, they are part of the dilemma that faces African Americans in the United States. How important is it to "make it" in America? What price to my self, my pride, and my sense of us-ness will being middle class exact? Being Afrikan in the middle class is still regarded as a problem rather than as a solution. Questions of integrity arise from within and without. The burning question for the Afrikan middle class is: Is the Xodus for middle-class, highly educated, and affluent Afrikans too?

While it is not productive to recap all of Cose's findings, I would like to use his research as a basis for Xodus reflections. With the attention of a qualitative sociologist, Ellis Cose has gathered poll upon poll, survey upon survey to drive home his thesis — namely, (1) that there is a perceptual gap between African Americans and European Americans about the grip of racism; (2) that Euro-Americans tend to deny the Black sense of outrage, frustration (the *disillragedeterminassion* I spoke of in chapter 1); and (3) that African Americans are tired of struggling for acceptance and confused about the extent to which factors of race should be passed on as important social skills to the next generation. Cose cites a 1986 survey of 107 (out of 305 questionnaires sent) Black professionals by Edward Jones, published in *The Harvard Business Review*. Its findings reveal a staggering level of discontent:

> Nearly all respondents claimed that black managers did not enjoy equal opportunity at their firms. Ninety-eight percent said that subtle prejudice pervaded their companies. Ninety percent reported a "climate of support" worse than that for their white peers. Eighty-four percent said that race had worked to their disadvantage when it came to ratings, pay, assignments, recognition, performance appraisals, and promotion. Fewer than 10 percent reported a work atmosphere that encouraged open discussion of racial issues.[1]

Yet Cose's most telling points come not from such polls but from the accumulation of many personal interviews with professional women and men. In the accumulated weight of their stories of slights, insults, insinuations, and outright rejections, Cose brings to light the reality of racial prejudice in the halls of "objective" Euro-American corporations and workplaces.

One of the most powerful of those interviews was conducted with a man whom Cose described as "a senior partner in one of the nation's premier law firms . . . a bona fide rainmaker, one of the biggest generators of billings for the partnership." Cose described him as having a tremendous sense of rage, a rage that he could not safely express to anyone in his workplace. This senior partner (whose name was not mentioned, for obvious reasons) stated that despite the "tens of millions" he brought to the firm, he believed that his partners wanted him to do well, "but not *that* well." His partners, uneasy about how to reward him for all of his successes, were "fumbling with my compensation." But the real "rub," the center of his rage, was this recent encounter with a junior associate of his firm:

> One source of resentment was an encounter of a few days previous, when he had arrived at the office an hour or so earlier than usual and entered the elevator along with a young white man. They got off at the same floor. No secretaries or receptionists were yet in place. As my friend fished in a pocket for his

key card while turning toward the locked outer office doors, his elevator mate blocked his way and asked, "May I help you?" My friend shook his head and attempted to circle around his would-be helper, but the young man stepped in front of him and demanded in a loud and decidedly colder tone, "May I help you?" At this, the older man fixed him with a stare, spat out his name, and identified himself as a partner, whereupon his inquisitor quickly stepped aside.[2]

His initial impulse was to laugh off the incident, but instead it burned and burned inside of him. He remembered that "he had been dressed much better than the associate," that "*his* clients paid the younger man's salary," and that the only reason he could have been interrogated in such a fashion was his race. As the senior partner put it, "Because of his color, he felt he had the right to check me out." The partner went on to express his exasperation at the fact that despite doing "all the things I was supposed to do," going to Harvard, laboring for years to "make his mark in an elite law firm," marrying "a highly motivated woman who herself had an advanced degree and lucrative career," raising three "exemplary children," surmounting all obstacles, he still was exposed to the "crap" of such encounters.[3] The senior partner's self-evaluation is telling for all Xodus travelers because it reminds us of the obstacles we face and the reality of race factors, however denied by the Euro-dominators who practice and enforce those factors:

> "Blacks who have made it up the ladder have had to put up with a whole lot more crap" than have those who had given up along the way. But these successful people, he mused, were the very ones likely to be especially sensitive to the "crap" they encountered. For if they were not hypersensitive to the unspoken racial messages, they would never have been able to avoid the society's traps, they would never have gotten as far as they had. He was convinced, however, that the disaffection he felt was not merely a reflection of heightened sensitivity. The world, from his vantage point, was in fact very unfair. "You do have to work harder, every step of the way, and you have got more obstacles than a white person." White people, he added, did not have to put up with such affronts as he had experienced at the hands of the young white associate. He was not at all sure what whites who didn't know him personally saw when they encountered him, he said. "I think they see a dark blur, and to them that is inferiority."[4]

I have quoted from this senior partner's narrative extensively because it reminds me of several personal encounters I have had as a faculty member with colleagues and students. It was always irritating to me that despite my impeccably tailored dark suits, bow ties, wing-tip shoes, and precise English, I was addressed by white students and some white staff members in the coarsest (and most inaccurate) imitation of what they thought was Black

English ("What's goin' ON?"). The irritation came from the fact that these were students and staff who knew me, had read my résumé, knew that I held advanced degrees from Harvard and had penned several articles. None of those things made any difference to them. They saw a "soul brother" and were trying to relate to him in "his own" language. They saw, I believed, an "uppity nigger" who needed to be brought down a few pegs, and they were glad to do it. At first I laughed off this manner of address. Sometimes I simply ignored the greetings. They still occurred, day after day, until I had my Africentric awakening. Dressed from head to toe in African clothes, placing a distinctive scowl on my face for persons such as my "vanilla soul family," I began to stride down the halls as if I was taking possession of the land in a Joshua-like manner. The pseudo-familiar greetings abruptly ended. Was I was now considered a militant, a troublemaker, one who was unapproachable because I had taken this turn? I do not know even to this day. I do know that I was glad when the coarse greetings stopped.

My Africentric awakening was not the first step in my Xodus Journey, but it was the most dramatic because I stopped trying to "make it" on the terms, values, and norms assigned by Euro-domination. I read the enraged anguish of an Elder who has "made it" and wonder whether he now believes that he has given up too much of his self. I wonder whether he has regrets, or whether he is just plain mad and "won't take it anymore." The fundamental transformation of Africentric awakening is giving oneself permission to enjoy one's Afrikanity, to revel in the beauty and uniqueness of one's Afrikan self, and to develop that self with a fierceness and pride. Such a step of consciousness is transformative because it frees one from trying to dress "right," act "right," look "right," and talk "right." "Rightness" has always been whiteness in the United States, the West, and most of the Euro-dominated world. I would rather be wrong Africentrically than "right"/white. I would encourage lawyers, doctors, corporate climbers, and movers-and-shakers to take the leap of faith and become Africentric while they are young rather than wait until they become embittered Elders still "out of the loop" of Euro-acceptability.

After experiencing Africentric awakening, I have come to realize that Afrikans cannot wait for Europeans or any other people to accept us, because it is likely that they never will. The weight of history is against any dramatic shifts in European-American attitudes, friendliness, and inclusion of Afrikans into the inner loop of Euro-domination. After all, by definition such a form of domination is not open to all comers. We must acquire the best education we can to become doctors, academics, engineers, and anything else we want to be — because we want to do so, because Afrikans ought to do so, and not to gain access to the upper echelons of Euro-domination.

Africentric awakening of the sort that I have just described is especially difficult for middle-class African Americans, many of whom have been raised in the integration consciousness of the post-civil rights era. We were all raised to be conversant with the etiquette, manners, speech patterns, and material values of our white counterparts. We were raised to believe that we could join the mainstream of Euro-dominated America and be "acceptable." We have fought our way through the stares of disbelief, the scorn of peers in school who accused us of being "affirmative-action incompetents," and the dismay of elder colleagues who marveled that we could be competent in areas of expertise not specifically labeled "Black." We have not really been accepted. With all of the middle-class accoutrements of success — the cars, the clothes, the houses in the "right" neighborhoods — we are left with a sense of isolation, alienation, and frustration. Cose captures all of this very well, and his book ought to be read by anyone who is interested in understanding what it means to be African American and middle class. Yet Cose does not offer an Africentric awakening as an answer. He never questions the underlying value assumptions that cause the *isoalienatedresentment* (a newword combining the isolation, alienation, and resentment that he describes). Cose's last chapter spends a good deal of time outlining strategies for sublimating rage into productive energies, and calling Euro-Americans out of their denial of racism, but does not offer a radical critique of African American middle-class values.

I believe that we are subverting ourselves because the African American middle class has not sufficiently distanced itself from Euro-dominating values of success. We buy into the idea that we ought to be invited to the local private clubs. Why? We feel the need to have the latest gadgets, the best clothes, and the finest automobiles that money can buy. Why? We believe that our children should get the best in education without looking at who defines "the best" in classist, imperialist, sexist, and racist Amerikkka, and then wonder why our children are not being accepted in those "best" schools. Why? We are subverting ourselves, undermining our future hopes by uncritically accepting Euro-dominating middle-class values. It is not important for African Americans to live in the same types of houses as Euro-Americans, nor drive the same cars, nor go to the same schools. Having the material resources to be comfortable is an important value, and in capitalist America it is a necessity, but "making it" is not important. Part of "making it" is "acceptance," an ever-elusive carrot dangled in front of the faces of many unsuspecting Sepia masses. Being familiar with advanced technology is liberating because it will aid in Afrikan independence from Euro-domination and Afrikan interdependence with the rest of the world, but "making it" as an engineer is a self-defeating goal because we shall not be included in the inner circle as confidantes most of the time.

Black men do not "make it" in America, because Amerikkka uses Black males as the ultimate signifier of evil. For those of us who think we have "made it" and disagree with my analysis, remember Clarence Thomas, the ultimate "made it" Black lawyer who wound up being sexually exposed as a "harrasser" for the prime-time entertainment of millions. Remember O. J. Simpson, formerly signified as football star and all-around "good guy," now uplifted and re-signified as the convenient example of the abusive man. Remember the boy-from-the-'hood Mike Tyson, who "made it" as celebrated and wealthy boxing champion only to become a convicted rapist. Even sweet and "innocent" Michael Jackson, former signifier of one who loves children, is now re-signified as suspected child molester. I do not excuse these particular men from their illegal or wrongful acts, I am simply noting the pattern. The pattern of Amerikkka, sometimes even for its White heroes and heroines, is to build up image and destroy it. Most North Americans buy into this pattern unconsciously, keeping all of us off-balance. Eventually the pattern may destroy our capacity to believe that anyone is trustworthy at all. For Black males it is an evil pattern because it destroys our hopes. "Making it" in America, if you are African American and particularly if you are also male, is a highly dangerous business because you are never ever really accepted. The sooner the Black middle class deals with that reality, the sooner we can find good reason to turn our energies toward aiding Xodus liberation.

We are one community, even though we are divided along the materialistic lines of class and status; we are Afrikans. Xodus Space affirms the value of being Afrikan and making decisions that are pro-Afrikan because we all suffer from the ambiguous weight of an educational and cultural system that privileges individual responsibility more than group responsibility. The best of Black resistance has always struggled mightily against these individualistic urges in the United States and the West, and organized all sectors of Afrikans to become active in liberation struggle. As Afrikans share Common Ground with all people and the earth, we ought to remember that we share Common Ground with each other. We come from the motherland of all humanity — Africa. No matter how many other nations and lands are represented in our genetic pool, we are Afrikans first and foremost. To believe that one is "American" first and foremost is to remain a mental slave, because that is precisely the way that Afrikans are "duped" into believing in individualistic "differences." Such an affirmation of Americanness has never aided other Afrikans, nor enabled us to throw off the shackles of poverty, discrimination, and racial preferences. Xodus Space boldly declares that Afrikans ought to aid Afrikans. That is what it means to be Africenric and awake!

Give Back for the Common Good

Down through the history of Africans in America, an ethical mode of survival has helped Black folks to "keep on keepin' on." That ethical mode was a prevailing ethos named "give back." To give back meant that no matter how high one rose in social rank, education, refinement, and the "favor" of whites, one ought to always "remember where you came from, remember whose you are." Middle-class African Americans who live in tidy suburban homes, worship in Anglo-dominated churches, and whose social life is entirely Euro-American have often been accused of "forgetting who they are." So the give-back ethic is predicated on a strong notion of racial solidarity. It suggests that because one is Black, one ought to be loyal to one's race first and foremost. It is not explicitly exclusionary, but its primary focus is on aiding and uplifting the downtrodden of Sepia persuasion.

Is a give-back ethic anachronistic in a time where the current energies of progressive-minded peoples have turned toward multiculturalism? No. The give-back ethic is one of solidarity that envisions justice as actions that contribute to the uplift of the common good. A give-back ethic ought to be understood in both universalizing, global terms, and in particular terms that stress the interests of small local communities. In global and universal terms, the common good of the world can only be realized when those who have "give back" to those who have not. The common good of the world cannot be realized until those who take resources from the earth "give back" in time, ecological awareness of sustainability, and patient stewardship of nature's finite capacity to sustain life. The common good cannot be achieved without the haves of the world remembering "who they are" in relationship to the have nots, and then finding just ways to live in Common Ground solidarity.

Global common good cannot be attained while nations understand themselves to be self-sufficient, sovereign units having no responsibility to each other or to the whole of nations. Sovereignty has merits as an Enlightenment political project, but it has failed us miserably in its lack of concern for a global common good. With the ethic of sovereignty nations believe that it is necessary to act in such a way that the interests of one's own nation are upheld. Such a notion undercuts and precludes envisioning ways to come together to save the environment of the earth, and warps alliance projects such as the feeding "adventure" sponsored by the U.S.A. and the United Nations in Somalia (1992–93), which wound up as a military operation.

Military divisions cannot feed the hungry; other organizations ought to have done so, but in a world controlled by the political ethos of sovereignty, the military is the institution most organized and best capable of all major works. Xodus thinking relates the give-back ethic to the global milieu as a principle of political criticism necessary in creating an ethic of solidarity among various peoples, tribes, and nations in order for the capabilities of the strong to be utilized to aid the weak, and all may learn to contribute their cultural gifts to each other. Such a view of give-back might be termed a contributive rather than distributive notion of justice — as a contributive ethic.[5] Such an ethic resonates with womanist understandings of individual and social contribution to the health and survival of the entire community as found in the writings of Karen Baker-Fletcher, Delores Williams, Marcia Riggs, and others.[6] Give-back is contributive, emphasizing what all parties have to give to each other in order for the common good to be realized. For example, although many nations in Africa lack the technological and medical capacity of the West, they possess powerful wellsprings of spiritual wisdom, treasures of community-oriented values systems, and gifts of spirit that many in the West have already recognized — because they "stole" them!

The contributive concept of justice embedded in give-back can also do a great deal for local African American and pan-African communities. It grows out of the soil of struggle in African American communities, but its roots go all the way back to the village ethos of many West African cultures. The Ibo, Ashanti, and Yoruba believe in the proverb, "It takes an entire village to raise one child." Nathan McCall speaks about the surrogate parents who formed a network of adults that "raised" him. While McCall admits that "the kids hated the surrogate system," after he became aware of his self-destructive tendencies and witnessed the destruction of traditional Black communities, he now realizes its value:

> It was only years later, when black communities as we knew them started falling apart, that I came to understand the system [of surrogate parents] for the hidden blessings it contained: It had built-in mechanisms for reinforcing values and trying to prevent us from becoming the hellions some of us turned out to be.[7]

The power of surrogate parents — of every parent taking personal responsibility for the care, nurturing, and discipline of all the neighborhood children — is the power of contribution. Such community concern for the raising of children is a custom that demonstrates the fundamental praxis of *Ujamaa* — the principle of family and cooperative economics that is celebrated in the seven-day holiday Kwanzaa. The practice of contribution, of working together and building together for a common good, is embedded in the celebration of Kwanzaa. While many celebrate the Seven Principles *(Nguza Saba)* of Kwanzaa, this distinctively African American holiday — based on the first-fruits festivals of several West African cultures — has not been widely embraced. Many African Americans do not celebrate the ritual of Kwanzaa because they are disturbed that it was "created" by an African American, Ron Maulana Karenga, in the 1960s. In Xodus Space such creativity is rewarded, admired, and encouraged. We ought to find ways to create an entire set of rituals celebrating the ways in which we practice a contributive, give-back ethic. But I am getting ahead of myself . . .

The so-called affluent Black middle class has a stake in developing a self-consciousness of the contributive ethic because we are the beneficiaries of the positive contributions of the civil rights movement as well as the front-line soldiers in the corporate battle that reveals the underbelly of "civil rights." As beneficiaries we were the ones who, thanks to the parents, grandparents, and supportive community around us, went on to become the "Children of the Dream." We are the generation of "the first" Blacks, "the only" Blacks, who "integrated" classrooms, workplaces, and offices, taking titles that had never been associated with Black folks in the history of the United States. We "integrated" such places alone, in isolation, often at great cost to our psyches and self-confidence. Today we have almost achieved economic parity with our middle-class Euro-peers, although we lack the inherited family wealth to rely on in hard times. We are the beneficiaries of all those marches, all those water-hose-doused protesters, all that dangerous rebellion that took place on the streets during the '50s and '60s. We are the beneficiaries of boycotts, sit-ins, pray-ins, and Freedom Riders. Our affluence, however tenuous and frustrating, is the result of the "blood of the martyrs," those who died for us. As beneficiaries we remember those mothers, fathers, grandfathers, and grandmothers who worked two and sometimes three jobs so that we could go to "good" schools and "get ahead" in life. We cannot repay those who have gone before us, but we can give back to those who were not able to join us as beneficiaries. When we give back, we remember who we are and whose we are.

The Children of the Dream were front-line soldiers as well as beneficiaries. We know better than most the stinging whip of insults and the bitter taste of swallowing one's pride in order to "get along." As front-line soldiers we sometimes had to fight for another Black person even when we didn't like that person, simply because he or she was another front-line soldier. We studied, ate, and worked next to "the Man," sometimes dated the children of "the Man." Some of us have even married and had children with "the Man's" children. We are front-line soldiers, trained and disciplined for battle in the corporate, academic, medical, legal, and other professional fields.

We have emerged in the '90s as a significant quartile of the African American population, but not without serious battle scars. Some of us have retreated from the battle, investing our time and energies in domestic and local affairs where we do not have to meet on the field of battle with Euro-dominators every day. Others have learned to wear the invisible shield of professionalism, a shield that is easy to put on in the morning and to take off at the end of the day. Others, a pitiable few, have become what folks in the 'hood call "sellouts," completely assimilating and accommodating themselves to the realities and values of Euro-dominators, and proudly "succeeding" at that game. Some of us move among these three alternatives with skill and ease — Afrikan embodiments of the protean personality that Cornel West writes about in *Prophesy Deliverance!* (1982).

Nevertheless, whether in retreat, bearing an invisible shield, selling out to the dominators, or masterfully moving in protean fashion, we are all battle-scarred. Sometimes in my dreams I am haunted by remembrances of disgusting racial encounters — with teachers, police, and even "friends." Those are nightmares that I cannot shake. Many other front-line soldiers experience similar memories. We are like soldiers who have suffered battle shock and relive traumatic experiences in our dreams over and over again. Unfortunately, there is really no place where we can avoid engaging this enemy, because the enemy of race domination often hides in an unspoken attitude of an otherwise "friendly" Euro-American peer.

Middle-class Afrikans move in a shielded mode, lest we be taken unawares. Such a stance is similar to the "tip-toe stance" Martin Luther King, Jr., described so eloquently in his "Letter from a Birmingham Jail" in 1963.[8] On "tip-toes," with our invisible shields in place, we "wear the mask that grins and lies,"[9] and like our forebears, we keep on keepin' on. The wisdom gathered in the midst of such pain must not be forgotten or neglected, but it ought to be contributed to the entire Afrikan community, for our common good. Those battle scars and psychic wounds are part of what makes middle-class African Americans a persevering people.

The Virtue of Perseverance

Rage is the word used most frequently to describe the general state of mind of African Americans. Rage is a limiting concept not large enough to handle the complex mixture of feelings Afrikans experience here in the United States. In the first chapter I created a word — *disillragedeterminassion* — to describe that complexity of Afrikan lived experience. In this chapter I coined yet another word — *isoalienatedresentment* — as partially expressive of the peculiar psychic twist felt by middle-class Blacks.

Both words are long, awkward, and difficult to speak. Such awkwardness is intentional, a way of reminding English-speaking people of the mis-fit between the English language and Afrikan experience. As a young middle-class African American, I witnessed in my parents, aunts, uncles, grandparents, and "surrogate parents" in our church the presence of another, more comprehensive, word describing African American life: perseverance.

Perseverance is a character issue, the inculcation of a long-term psychic readiness to stay "on the battlefield" and not give up, give in, or retreat, except for periods of necessary rest and recuperation. Perseverance is a virtue, an inner power or excellence. It is something that African American parents of all personality and character traits attempt to pass on to their children. Its practice arises from the need for African Americans to learn to withstand the continual onslaught of humiliation and degradation of our humanity.

I learned about perseverance from any number of parental sources. I grew up hearing stories about my mother as a brilliant woman (some even said genius) whose progress toward becoming a principal or public school administrator had been blocked for some twenty years because of her race and gender. I remember hearing my mother bitterly complain about having to support co-workers and principals who had half her experience, a quarter of her wisdom, and not a whit of brilliance! But she stayed on course, struggling to maintain her sense of dignity, integrity, and dared to believe that someday her hard work would pay off. During the last several years of her career she was promoted to head guidance counselor of a newly "integrated" junior high school, a position she cherished.

From my father I learned about perseverance by observing his capacity to work overtime for weeks at a stretch. He got up at five A.M. to begin work at six, and he might not return home until seven and sometimes eight P.M. These long hours working on a factory line took their toll on my father's health, and at the age of sixty-two, just three years from retirement, he collapsed from complications of cancer. He died about a month later in a hospital bed. From his childhood in Jamaica he had always been considered a "special child" — a "seventh son born with a veil," able to "see spirit's them" as my Uncle Roy used to say. This special spiritual charism was borne in a frail body that needed special rest and care in order to function. That he was able to work for more than thirty-five years in the harshness of a General Motors factory line amazes me. It remains for me a remarkable example of perseverance — an excellence of character demonstrated regularly and faithfully.

My parents' stories could be endlessly repeated by many African Americans of my age who grew up as "Children of the Dream." Our parents were energized by the utopian hope that their children would "have it better" than they had and live in a less racially biased environment. Several of my friends watched their parents work themselves to death, or die at work from the violence of the streets. Such parents persevered despite aches, pains, and the ongoing litany of slights and insults because they were filled with a spiritual hope that could not diminished.

Criminal Expectations

Nathan McCall's *Makes Me Wanna Holler* reminds us that the African American "middle class" is usually much closer to the Euro-American "working class" in educational status and employment configuration than to the professional and managerial class of the people Ellis Cose has chosen to write about. The "Black middle-class" neighborhood of Cavalier Manor in Portsmouth, Virginia, where McCall grew up had many families in which the father and mother put their "pennies together" from two menial jobs. His neighborhood consisted of many military retirees, shipyard workers, and domestics. Not all African American "middle-class" persons have an Ivy League pedigree or are all upwardly mobile with expectations of running corporations. Many of us watched our fathers work for the government while our mothers stayed home while we were young or took jobs as saleswomen and in various cottage industries to help "make ends meet."

The most disturbing thing about McCall's autobiographical volume, however, is the way he demonstrates how the unjust legal and power dynamics in Amerikkka affect the maturation of young Black boys. McCall and all of the males that he "hung" with grew up watching their fathers working hard for "white folks" during the day and getting drunk when they were not working, eating, or sleeping. These were not lazy men unmotivated to work or too broken in spirit to even look for employment. Rather, they were hardworking men, many of whom had grown up as impoverished sharecroppers in the South and learned how to be competent at many jobs. McCall remembers how his stepfather had converted the garage into a den and paneled its walls, installed a brick walkway around the house, did all the repairs and maintenance of his autos and household, as well as doing part-time lawn-maintenance jobs besides his full-time shipyard position.[10] Such a highly motivated man, like most men of his pre-civil-rights generation, had disciplined himself to take whatever abuse Euro-Americans dished out in order to survive and support his family.

Nathan's generation, influenced by the militant dynamics of the Black Power movement, restlessly pushed for equality *now,* and resented the insults and slights that his father's generation had taken in stride. Neither

Nathan nor his friends remember wanting to be anything like their dads; rather, they wanted to be the opposite of the tired, drunken, downtrodden men who came home after long hours sweating "for the Man." Filled with a raging sense of the injustice of racial matters, Nathan recalls that the wealthy whites of Sterling Point for whom his father gardened appeared tan, rested, and living well, while his father stayed so bone-tired from his labors that most of the time he was home he slept.[11] Nathan's rage grew as he realized that Euro-domination was pervasive, affecting his aspirations, education, and potential. He and his street buddies dreamed of finding ways to make it on their own without resigning themselves to the "white man's system."

Unfortunately, the way that Nathan's buddies found to "make it" outside of the system was by idolizing the drug-dealing life typified in the "Blaxploitation" film *Superfly*. The "Superfly" life seemed to hold the promise of financial independence, wealth, and an integrity not based on mere survival. Nevertheless, such a life required hustling illegal substances that drew the attention of police to Nathan's street life. Not wanting to deal in drugs, Nathan succumbed to a life of robbing stores at gunpoint. Eventually he was caught, arrested, sentenced to prison, and then began the process of self-rehabilitation that led him out of the penal system and into the journalism mainstream. McCall now works for the *Washington Post*. He had already completed a year at Norfolk State University with a 3.0 gradepoint average before he was arrested and imprisoned. After prison he went on to become the first in his family to receive a college degree. In prison he met many much poorer African Americans who had never finished high school, let alone gone to college, and had no prospects of doing either. Much as it did for Malcolm X, prison became a place where Nathan McCall was awakened, found his Afrikan self, and (like Malcolm) eventually turned to Islam.

Theologically I was interested in how McCall's Africentric awakening led him through Christianity to the orthodox Islamic faith of the American Muslim Mission. It is to the shame of Christians, particularly Afrikan Christians, that prisoners and those who have suffered the most under the boot of Euro-oppression find in Islam a more sturdy, "ruff" faith that fits with their experiences on the streets. McCall writes about how a friend named Jim opened his eyes to the ways in which Europeans used Christianity as a tool for mollifying peoples — teaching them to "turn the cheek" just before conquering their territories with military machinery. Such a Christianity is a heinous abomination of the religion of the followers of Jesus. If Afrikans have any self-respect, and any real compassion for how such "Christianity" has become the tool of Euro-oppression, we ought to rename ourselves followers of Jesus, right on the spot!

Being a follower of Jesus in Xodus Space is challenging because we share this Space with those who are truly unwilling to forgive Europeans. There is too much rage, too much hurt, too much historical harm for the soothing promises of "forgiveness" to roll off the lips of many Afrikans. What do the followers of Jesus do with this attitude as we Journey together with such brothers and sisters? For someone like Nathan McCall there is no place for the hypocrisy of forgiveness for a people who are still virtually unrepentant and unwilling to look at what the destructive legacy of racism has left in its historical path.

Perhaps one of the best things the followers of Jesus can do on Xodus is to clarify the difference between the religion of Jesus and the pitiful tool of exploitation and manipulation called "Christianity." Perhaps we can allow our brothers like McCall the Holy Space for ventilating and healing their rage, knowing that such ventilation is healing in and of itself when exercised within the safety of Xodus Space. In fact, Xodus followers of Jesus must always demand genuine change from so-called Christians who demand such automatic forgiveness from angry Blacks. We ought to be the first ones to defiantly ask, Why? Why should any Afrikan people decide to "forgive" when the social, economic, and power relations put in place during slavery and the colonial period are still intact and operative? We must allow space for the rage in order to make room for any possibility of genuine forgiveness.

McCall's life reveals how intensely strong the ideological lure of street life is for young African American males. Even when one's neighborhood, family, and church community are active and supportive, the lure of the criminal element is present, whether we are conscious of it or not. More disturbing, however, is the way in which Black males are criminalized — perceived as criminals. All Black males are seen as guilty first until proven innocent, according to Amos Wilson.[12] Such a viewpoint adversely affects our self-respect and self-affirmation. To a policeman we are not highly educated, upstanding citizens, or hard-working self-motivators, but are suspects for whatever crime has recently taken place. Like every Sepia-colored man, I have a catalog of police stories that could fill another book, and someday I will have to write *that* one! Suffice it to say that there is nothing more terrifying than having a white policeman two inches from your face, yelling at you, egging you on, trying to make you "do something" so that he can "use all necessary means" to "regain order." It is a horrific moment that Black parents train their sons to face with a cool demeanor, a rational voice, and slow, controlled bodily movements. I have not been physically assaulted . . . yet. I will teach my son the same things my mother and father taught me, and pray.

McCall's book reminds me of another fact that I have not fully shared. Besides being an African American, I am "born Jamerican," child of a Jamaican immigrant father. I grew up with the smells of curry, akki, and the sounds of calypso. My earliest memories are of a visit to my father's ancestral home in the lush vegetation of Mocha Jamaica. Jamaica is an independent island country whose mixed peoples epitomize the pan-African ideal. There African, English, German, Chinese, and Indian have come together to form the Jamaican people. Jamaican immigrants are famous for their work ethic. It has been satirized in a caustic fashion by the outrageous comic antics of "In Living Color." My father and his family were also hard working and often exhausted by the sheer volume of their labors. Many of my uncles have struggled mightily with alcoholism, as has Nathan McCall's community. I believe that there is a profound connection between the experiences of my father's family and McCall's. Yet these same uncles believed in both a contributive ethic and perseverance as a highly valued character trait.

Everybody helps everybody in the Fletcher family. Those with an extra bed shared that bed with a newly arrived cousin, niece, or nephew until they could "get out on their own." My uncles and aunts shared their townhouses, so that often two or three generations of a family would be living under the same roof on different floors. This kind of sharing embodies the contributive ethic, and provided a way for the Fletcher family to become active members of "middle-class America" within a generation of arriving in the United States. Xodus Space must encourage the kind of active embodiment of shared space that I witnessed as a child, because the liberation of our communities begins with a contributive family. As a Jamerican, I am grateful that I carry within myself a pan-African embodiment of how resourceful and creative Afrikan people can be when we apply a contributive ethic to our lives.

Xodus Church as Body of Christ

The embodiment of the virtue of perseverance and the contributive ethic make tangible the Pauline "body of Christ" metaphor as a valuable way for the church to operate. The body of Christ as described by Paul in 1 Corinthians 12–14 is a place where all the gifts of the spirit are necessary, no one gift is more important or valuable than any other, and all gifts are granted by the Holy Spirit for the building up of the church. The body of Christ is the holy Space of love — a love that perseveres, trusts, believes in the best, is just, is truthful, does not boast or act in an irritated fashion. The body of Christ, according to these Pauline verses, is a Space where prophecy is uplifted. Black churches, at their best, are institutions where the gifts of the spirit are exercised in a contributive way in order to "build up the church" — a favorite phrase in 1 Corinthians 14. The Xodus church arises from this tradition of Black churches, the tradition of resistance, prophecy, and the gifts of the Holy Spirit. Xodus church ought to carry forward the contributive agenda of Black churches that have resisted, been prophetic, and exercised the gifts of the spirit. To build Xodus church on such a foundation is to deeply root it in the history and mission of Black churches.

A contributive Xodus church will incarnate the practice of contribution as a better way of revealing the love of Jesus Christ. Contribution to the needs of all the "saints" — those who are members of one's local ecclesia — is what creates a supportive community for Xodus men and women. An ecclesia is a community of persons who are "called out" by the Spirit of Jesus Christ to be God's people. Xodus ecclesiology is based on this notion of a spiritual calling, an inner summons by the divine power, to form contributive community. Xodus church, as an embodiment of the contributive ethic, is a place where the powers of African middle-class perseverance can readily join forces with the street-smart skills of the hip-hop rapper generation.

African American scholars have defined African American churches as being primarily of two types: class churches, carryovers of the more ancient form, which divide along class, color, and educational lines; and mass churches, which combine all the class, status, color, and educational levels. The Xodus church is necessarily a mass church, because it self-consciously debunks the formerly valued "differences," such as having a lighter complexion (signifying that one has "white blood"), more education (signifying that one has access to better jobs), and "dignified worship" (signifying that the order and decorum of the service have been borrowed from Eurocentric practices). Such class church values will not be helpful in creating an Xodus church; they will be harmful because such praxis reveals the ways in which assumptions of dominance are divisive within the group being dominated.

Xodus church is a Space in which practices of dominance are exorcised as demonic manifestations that possess our wills, hearts, and minds. One of the special charisms of Xodus is that after one has been awakened, one realizes the need for immediate exorcism. Therefore those who have the gift of exorcism are highly valued members of the Xodus church because it is their gift and contribution to clear the "atmosphere" of demonic presences — those inner voices that compel Afrikans to judge each other by the standards, principles, and norms of Euro-dominance rather than from a place of Christian love or liberating solidarity.

In Xodus church the practices of contribution move Xodus people beyond redistributive measures that are highly vaunted as "just" by Eurocentric moral philosophers. Contribution, as I have stated before, arises from the concrete needs of the oppressed. In academic terms, this means that a contributive ethic practices a norm of liberation, basing its contributory praxis on the principle that it is fundamentally good and right to liberate those who are suffering by combining the gifts, powers, skills, and abilities of the many for the uplift of the many. Xodus church incarnates the contributive praxis by preaching that the love of Jesus must be *shown*. As the gospel group "Commissioned" sings:

We need a life that shows
You need a life that glows
Show everyone the love of Christ.[13]

The love of Jesus Christ manifests itself in actions that build up the common good of the community. It is a love that seeks to aid and not dominate, to make more complete and not to simply make choices and decisions for those who have never been given such choices before. As such it is enabling, spending itself on works that reveal a deep and abiding faith. In the true spirit of the Letter of James, Xodus contributory praxis believes in the verse that states, "For just as the body without the spirit is dead, so faith without works is also dead" (James 2:26). The "works" Xodus church folk perform are contributory, working together for the glory of God and the uplift of the community.

The gift of perseverance is a charism of the spirit that the African American middle class ought to offer cheerfully and freely as its spiritual contribution to the formation of Xodus. Such a gift has the potential of re-forming and reshaping lost and hopeless lives, the lives of those who have given up hope of finding any way out of poverty, discrimination, and injustice. There may not be any "justice" for Afrikans in the United States or in the West, but there ought to be contributive justice in the Xodus church. In such a Space the instructional experience of teachers, the academic rigor of scholars, the mathematical precision of engineers, and the creative scientific imagination of physicists should be combined into an energy of liberation that cannot be overwhelmed even by the most unyielding oppressive policies practiced outside Xodus walls. The gift of perseverance combines the active love of Jesus Christ with the energy of liberation found in Xodus Space.

Such a view of contributive justice is admittedly inspirational, and even utopian. It is necessary to have an inspirational utopian view of the world in order to provide a vision large enough, inviting enough, and nurturing enough to hold us as we Journey in Xodus. All of us require something beyond ourselves that can lift us, especially when cold analysis cannot do anything but provide a clearer picture of impending doom. Afrikans are bombarded with "bad news" about ourselves from the pervasive media. We ought to go out of our way to imagine ourselves into a better Space and praxis. I choose to do so as my contribution, as a humble offering of one who has been given the gift of vision. If the proverb is true that "where there is no vision, the people perish" (Prov. 29:18, KJV), then the task of the last chapter is contributing to such a vision.

Notes

1. Ellis Cose, *The Rage of a Privileged Class* (New York: HarperCollins, 1993), 44.
2. Ibid., 48.
3. Ibid., 49.
4. Ibid.
5. This term resonates with the "pebble ethics" of Katie Cannon and the "stone soup ethics" Karen Baker-Fletcher describes in *A Singing Something: Anna Julia Cooper and the Foundations of Womanist Theology* (New York: Crossroad, 1994), 176–78.
6. Karen Baker–Fletcher, *A Singing Something,* 141–50, 175–82; Delores Williams, *Sisters in the Wilderness* (Maryknoll, N.Y.: Orbis, 1993), 108–9; Marcia Riggs, "A Clarion Call to Awake! Arise! Act!" in *A Troubling in My Soul,* edited by Emilie Townes (Maryknoll, N.Y.: Orbis, 1993), 67–75.
7. Nathan McCall, *Makes Me Wanna Holler: A Young Black Man in America* (New York: Random House, 1994), 9.
8. Martin Luther King, Jr., "Letter from a Birmingham Jail," in *Why We Can't Wait* (New York: New American Library, 1963), 81.
9. The famous first line of Paul Laurence Dunbar's poem, "We Wear the Masks."
10. McCall, *Makes Me Wanna Holler,* 81–82.
11. Ibid., 82.
12. Amos Wilson, *Black-on-Black Violence: The Psychodramatics of Black Self-Annihilation in Service of White Domination* (New York: Afrikan World Infosystems, 1990).
13. Commissioned, "A Life That Shows," *Ordinary Just Won't Do* (Polygram CGI Records, 1989; Poly–1021).

CHAPTER 10

Souljahs
in Partnership

Forget the former things; do not dwell on the past. See, I am doing

a new thing! Now it springs up; do you not perceive it?

(Isa. 43:18-19)

A s the twentieth century nears its end, there is a new eruption of
Afrikan consciousness in the North American continent. The African
American, once so willing to smile and be cooperative with employ-
ers, teachers, and colleagues, is ready for a "new thing." The African
American, once so hopeful that change could come through the peaceful
means of the boycott and ballot, is ready for a "new thing." This new thing
is a resurrection of African-centered consciousness — Africentricity. It has
not been fashioned, systematized, and intellectualized by academics but is
arising creatively out of the twisted remains of urban uprisings, the shattered
bodies of drive-by shooting victims, and the angry voices shouting
"No Justice, No Peace!" A kind of revolution is happening, described by
rappers with a back-burner beat of hip-hop rhythm, moving the minds,
bodies, and feet of the masses away from the control of the system toward
a new place.

This book has reflected on the nascent Africentric social and spiritual
revolution with the intent of providing a theological ethic appropriate to

our times. In particular, it has elaborated on the development of Sepia ("dark reddish-brown," according to Webster's) or Xodus maleness as an essential part of Africentric revolution — the construction of a Black male self (in a society that systematically erases and devalues the Black male) in such a way that he can empower himself, join in partnership with Afrikan women, and love the children and the folk. In this last chapter we must plumb the ecclesial dimensions of that partnership model of manhood. Indeed, in honor of those artists/activists or "raptivists" in the cause of race consciousness and freedom (borrowing "Souljah" from Sister Souljah's name), we are called to rise and become creative and powerful Souljahs for the downtrodden, left-out, and mistreated of our people. Souljahs are men and women called out into loving and liberating partnership into the creative holy Space — the Xodus church.

Somehow Xodus males must learn to respond beyond personal intellect, in activist communal praxis to the ethical demands for justice in womanism. The historical situation that has shaped Black women has also shaped Black men. We have taken leadership roles in politics, inspiring the faithful with rousing oratory (as Jesse Jackson continues to do for the Democratic Party), as well as becoming highly paid sports idols. Yet the Sepia male, particularly the young Black male between fourteen and twenty years of age, finds himself criminalized, brutalized, and dehumanized by a new virulent form of racism. The call to activism is a demand for African American males to be transformed into active Souljahs on the battlefield of injustice. Such a cry is not alarmist, exaggerated, or extreme. In order for the Sepia peoples of America to continue to exist, all African American men and women are called to the prophetic task of resurrecting Black manhood as well as Black womanhood. Indeed, if we are participants in any kind of faith, from Christian to Muslim, from pragmatist to idealist, from the most educated to the least, from the middle class to the so-called underclass, we should be compelled by the startling facts of erasure to join together and cry out, "Xodus men and women, awake, arise, act!"[1]

As was stated in chapter 5, the "X" in Malcolm X's name symbolized for him the unknown yet powerful identity that resided in him simply by virtue of the fact that he was a Black man. "X" reminded him that he was ancestor to kings, queens, and an immensely rich civilization that the white race had destroyed and then lied to us and said never existed! "X" is a powerfully positive and constructive way of renaming oneself in opposition to one's "slave name" or name of European derivation. So in the consciousness-awakening moment of joining the followers of Elijah Muhammad, Malcolm Little became Malcolm X. To take on the name "X" is to symbolically and spiritually move out of European "space" into a Space of one's own.

The biblical story of Exodus as well as the theological symbol of liberation are suggested in the name Xodus. The significance of Exodus (Exod. 12:31-40) comes not so much from the releasing of slaves from Pharaoh as from the powerful theological meaning of understanding that God's intention for liberation will move God's "hand" to intervene on behalf of the oppressed. The intervention of God compelled Pharaoh's will to liberate the slaves. The Xodus in our time is a divine intervention within one's own life causing one to liberate oneself from bondage. Without awaiting "pharaoh's orders," without "permission," Africentric Blacks have arisen and awakened, coming out of the "Egypt" named "America . . . land of the free, home of the brave." The Xodus suggests a more massive, groupwide self-deliverance than has been experienced for more than a generation since the freedom struggle of the mid-twentieth century. Instead of individuals becoming aware of the need to "come out" of white American-controlled space, the Xodus implies the need for the entire race to awaken, arise, and be resurrected!

The "X" represents the sacred crossing of lines of ancient ritual custom by many indigenous peoples. It is at the point where the lines intersect, the place where the spiritual aspirations of humanity and the sacred flow of divinity cross, that a holy Space is re-created, recognized, and celebrated.[2] Xodus churches are sacred Spaces wherein the flow of the divine intersects with the potent aspirations of Xodus people. The "X" is a re-signification of the ancient consecratory gesture by which an *axis mundi* or meeting point of the cosmos is incorporated into Xodus spirituality. If an *axis mundi* is the place where heaven, earth, and hell meet,[3] then Black churches have functioned as "X"-odus Spaces since they came into existence. Creatively responding to the hell of racism, Black churches have functioned as places of an "eternal return"[4] to the "homeland of my soul."[5] Black churches have served as the place where the sacred power of heaven's divine Spirit flowed into the hearts of earthbound, oppressed Afrikan humanity. So Xodus churches are places where believers are self-conscious about being places of eternal return, recognized as the sacred center of the cosmos where holy powers flow.

African American Christians must not allow the theological implications of Xodus for our churches to be lost. Xodus is as applicable to Black Christians as to Black Muslims, because the Xodus relates to our existential bonds as children of Africa living in a space controlled by the children of Europe. We share the same oppression, albeit in differing degrees in accordance with our "class," a term that implies the depth of our participation in the punish-reward economic system devised by Europeans. The existential bonds of commonality between Afrikan Christians and Muslims are deepened theologically by the fact that we share with Muslims belief in one almighty God. The deep differences in our beliefs about salvation, the role of Jesus, and the parameters of application of doctrine still point back to a common belief in God, from whom all things have been created and die, and toward which all creation is moving toward a final apocalyptic end. Our shared monotheism as well as our shared existential oppression at the hands of European-controlled space suggest that we can share a common Xodus.

What does sharing the Xodus imply for African American Christians and Black churches? It does not mean that we must change our names as do our sisters and brothers in Islam, although creative reflection on that idea is long overdue for Black Christians. If anything, the tradition within Christian history of taking a confirmation name has radical implications for Africentric Christians. At my confirmation I took the name of the great African doctor of the Church Universal, Augustine. It was a profound experience for me to be anointed by a bishop and called by my new name. Perhaps after verbal recognition and invitation of Jesus Christ into our lives, we need to take on a new name.

In order to initiate a concrete conversation about this topic, one suggestion might be for African American churches to begin encouraging their members to take on a Swahili title of communal relationship and a chosen Christian name (preferably of a historic African Christian). Choosing a Swahili name symbolizes one's self-ownership of pan-African ties. The Xodus is a pan-African movement of spiritual commitment. For instance, as a father ("Baba"), my new name might be Baba Augustine. Another relationship I have to the community is as brother ("Ndugu," pronounced "in-*doo*-goo"). So I might also be addressed as Ndugu Augustine. Such a name is a far cry from Garth Anthony! The Swahili words for mother ("Mama") and sister ("Dada") could be chosen in a similar fashion by women in our communities. The relationships of son and daughter are also profoundly important and could be added variously. Or, as is true in many circles of Christianity (as well as in Moslem naming practices), some aspect of God's character could be chosen as a name, such as Love ("Upendo") or Justice ("Sheria"). Again, the importance of taking a Swahili name as a symbol of one's Africentricity is in its Xodus appeal, virtually breaking away from a European-sounding sense of self.

I have chosen to be renamed in accordance with my most likely African tribal ancestry, that of the Yoruba and Ibo. My mother's features were distinctively Yoruba, and the Ibo tribe dominated the area from which my Jamaican father came. In keeping with the ecological assumptions of one who is an "enclosed garden" (a "Garth"), the name "Kasimu" (keeper of the forest) seemed to come to me and give itself to me as my African name. Out of the X-ness mystery of my Afrikan background, seemingly erased forever, this name has revealed itself to me as *my name*. I use it in this book as my Xodus name.

Changes in clothing are also symbolic of a deeper spiritual reorientation. In the Moslem community the traditional garb worn by all Moslems is made and sold by members of the mosque. Afrikan Christians should not be ashamed to take this example and run with it. Imagine what kind of clothing industry we could develop if the millions of African American Christians all produced, bought, and wore distinctively Afrikan clothing! If African Americans comprise the seventh-largest economic "nation," consuming some six billion dollars per year, then surely we ought to consider the multimillion-dollar productive possibilities,[6] not to mention the political "fashion statement" some Euro-Americans would make by joining us. So, while clothing symbolizes outwardly the inward change of spiritual orientation, Black Christians should consciously recognize a profound economic implication as well. Not only could we develop an abidingly different way of symbolizing ourselves as followers of Jesus, but gain economic self-determination at the same time.

Changes in eating patterns begin to step on some cherished ideals of what "soul food" should be. The emphasis of our developing conversations, however, should be on reorienting ourselves from dependency on the European system to self-determination. For Afrikan Xodus Christians it might involve developing direct distributive relations with Black farmers so that we "Produce Black and Buy Black." With the problems of poor nutrition and overeating rampant in our churches, incorporating a new diet into our plan of salvation surely would be a welcome change.

From the above paragraphs it is clear that Xodus must be: (1) communal and not merely individual, (2) interfaith, (3) economic, and (4) cultural. In order for the Xodus to become concrete, embedded in our habits of eating, buying and selling, and naming, we need to go beyond abstract ideas to spiritual empowerment.

Empowerment

Empowerment is the spiritual force that both underlies all movement in Xodus and is the end of Xodus. In order for Afrikan men to be full participants in the Xodus, we must claim God's Spirit as the guide leading us on a Journey. Empowerment is intimately personal. It involves each individual African American man and woman opening up to the power of God's Spirit. As a Christian, I understand that Spirit to be inseparably linked to the saving acts of Jesus of Nazareth who lived and ministered to heal the sick, comfort the brokenhearted, and uplift the downtrodden. The Spirit, for me, is the very same divine power moving and breathing in me that worked through Jesus to drive demons out, and would not allow him to remain dead. It is that same resurrecting power that came "on the third day" that I believe will come into the hearts and lives of erased and devalued Afrikan men. We cannot "arise!" until its summoning powers fill our empty spaces and lift our vision to new heights. We must arise when its summoning powers call us back into our selves and out into Souljah partnership with Afrikan women. So the symbol of empowerment is not the last in value, but first, because without it Xodus is a mere idea.

As Baba Augustine Ndugu Watu ("Father Augustine Brother of the People"), I once believed that the Journey of male maturation was toward Baba-hood or fatherhood. This took place during 1984 as an act of mourning my own father's death. Since my Africentric awakening — becoming Kasimu — I self-consciously experience maleness as a Journey. More than Baba-hood, or the thrill of courtship, being a male has taken me through times of pain and suffering and grave disappointments in my ability to transform and eliminate my own sexism, slowly opening me up to trusting that the empowering Spirit could take me through all things. Trusting the empowering Holy Spirit to lead my life has not resulted in my being able to celebrate having now "arrived" at what it means to be an archetypal "Xodus male." Rather, trusting in the Holy Spirit to guide my life, the Journey has plunged me into the Abyss of self-criticism/self-knowledge. I offer that plunge as an example of what might be prototypical of Xodus Journeying.

The Abyss

In the Abyss I have learned that Baba-hood could not be the goal or new vision of masculinity but might reinforce an older and more established symbol of maleness, already filled with hard expectations, behaviors, and attitudes not conducive to being a partner with women on the Xodus. The Abyss (in contrast with Paul Tillich's positive notion of "abyss") is a Space of continual self-emptying where there are no predetermined selves or defined symbols to cling to. One comes to self in the Abyss only through a continuing emptying process, or what in Greek is called *kenosis*. In the Abyss one learns that Xodus male-self is that kenotic process of emptying oneself of inherited, prefabricated-but-false "selves." While the Journey of Black women celebrates what may be considered as positive and constructive (albeit devalued by traditional patriarchy) in women, the Xodus of Sepia men begins in the Abyss that strips away and deconstructs traditional assumptions of what it means to be a man.

Trusting the Holy Spirit to act as guide helps one to recognize that the experience of the Abyss is similar to the initiates' reliance on a spirit guide during traditional African rites-of-passage ceremonies. The Holy Spirit is a consummate spirit guide. Relying on the Spirit, however, does not mean that the individual/personal "I" has nothing to do. The Abyss is not a space of nonagency, but of kenotic-transforming agency. It is in the jarring experience of self-emptying that the "I" is continually encountering the Holy Spirit. Through the empowering Holy Spirit operating in the Abyss, "I" am able to go on despite the frustrations and uncertainties of the Journey. The Spirit grants perseverance to go on, despite failures of my "I" to live up to the highest and best ideals of what it means to be an egalitarian "partner" of my closest of sisters — my wife — and to reengage in the struggle.

Perseverance also recognizes that as my "I" is fundamentally interconnected with all of my brothers and sisters, the psychic pain and despair of those living in prisons is my pain too. Perseverance is a virtue whose importance goes far beyond its value as something passed on by Afrikan middle-class people. Perseverance is the most important spiritual gift offered to an Xodus male journeying in the Abyss, because without it one can fall into self-doubts, self-pity, and endless self-recrimination for one's failures. Focusing on one's failures does not allow one to "do justice, love kindness, and to walk humbly with your God" as Micah 6:8 requires. Self-recrimination stops one's journeying and takes attention off the goal of being a transformed male in the end — one who is able to follow the ethical imperatives of Micah 6:8 in both public and private spheres.

In the Abyss I came to understand more fully the implications of the Souljah imperative in regard to its personal application. For Xodus men to make "War!" against the system of erasure and degradation of European derivation, we must begin with an emptying of our unconsciously sexist assumptions and actions. Our sexism is the private-sphere war that threatens the liberation of our community as deeply as does the racism of the public sphere. Until the Xodus male is willing to engage the inner battle on all three fronts — race (public), sex (private), and class (an elusive mixture of both spheres) — womanist ethicist Katie Cannon suggests he is not really willing to be a Souljah. Souljahs are partners with women, the poor, and all the oppressed.

Womanism suggests that women, suffering from the ill effects of the "triple jeopardy" of race/gender/class oppression, have no choice but to become Souljahs engaged on all three fronts. Our response, if we really are to become "new" men who are willing Souljahs, ought to be to join them.

We ought to do so not because we want to protect our sisters or direct their energies — both traditional ways to rally men behind a "woman thing." Such attitudes deliberately buy into patriarchal attitudes and ways of dealing with women. Our becoming Souljahs, rather, is part of our Journeying in and through the Abyss. It is part of the way that we discover our deeper humanity, and thereby emphasize the liberation of "US" (men, women, and children), and not just "us" (men).

Becoming a Souljah means finding ways to reaffirm our community's humanity, or what the Swahili call *Kibinadamu*. If our vision of *Kibinadamu* is to genuinely liberate, it should follow three criteria: (1) it ought to be Africentric; (2) it must intentionally include a nonsexist Xodus Journey away from traditional race/sex/class notions; and (3) it must be constructed mutually by all members of the community. The embrace of all three criteria will open us up to the future possibilities for a new masculinity not as a separate enterprise deserving the entire energies of the Black community, but as a necessary integral part of the community's liberation.

Male Souljahs are the prophets of a new masculinity in solidarity with female Souljahs of a new womanhood. We are constantly reminding ourselves of the necessity of moving away from any static image of what it means to be a man, boy, father, son, or brother, since none of these can be transformed outside a communal-centered quest that includes the Journey of sisters, daughters, girls, and mothers. *Kibinadamu* for the Xodus male will mean breaking out of the "old wineskins" of patriarchy, and searching for ways to become the wine itself. Wine, a flowing, pouring symbol, rather than anything fixed and static, ought to be what male Souljahs are about the business of discovering.

Partnership in Liberating Community

Black churches have a responsibility to participate in Xodus by becoming holy Spaces of Xodus liberation. It is in keeping with the ongoing *missio dei* (the "mission of God") that the Church Universal has always understood itself to be undertaking. That same *missio dei* has expressed itself in Afrikan churches throughout the world by nurturing both the spiritual life of individuals and communities, as well as the physical welfare of individuals and communities. The Great Commission of Matthew 28:18–20 is not merely a sending forth to ritually baptize persons in the trinitarian "name" of God, it also adjures the believers to teach everything that Jesus had commanded.

To teach all that Jesus commanded might be summed up by examining the Sermon on the Mount (Matthew 5–7) and the Sermon on the Plain (Luke 7:17–49); any number of different "parables of the Kingdom";

the encounters with Nicodemus (John 3) and the rich young man (Matt. 19:16–29); and that unforgettable prophetic passage about the sheep and the goats (Matt. 25:31–46). Jesus commanded a holistic gospel centered in intimate adoration and trust in God and expressed by loving actions of service to the spiritual and bodily needs of human beings. If Black churches are to become the holy Spaces of Xodus that God is calling us to become, we must minister to the whole of humanity. Theologically we must minister to the *Kibinadamu* of the entire human race, and in particular to those hurting local communities of women, men, and children who require renewal, awakening, and resurrection.

As male and female Souljahs join their collective energies toward the fulfillment of each other's mutual concerns, our justifiable rage at the injustices we have suffered can be transmuted into the more productive ethos of self-reliance. A liberating partnership model of the Xodus church is not merely intellectual, but rests on a blessed assurance of the guiding Holy Spirit that our faith teaches us to believe. As criminalization, drug-related crimes, and AIDS threaten to bring the series of crises to an overwhelming pitch, the role of African American churches becomes critical . . . yet where are the churches? When will Black churches join the Xodus, or are they already functioning as the frontline offensive forces? The last turn in the Journey of Xodus will deal with this troubling question of how outspoken, potent, and relevant Black churches are in African American communities.

THREE OPPOSING VIEWS

Three prevailing tendencies inform the many studies of Black churches: celebration, dialectical tension, or cynicism. Celebratory ones, such as Andrew Billingsley's *Climbing Jacob's Ladder,* cite surveys and statistics to bolster the compelling argument that Black churches are actively involved in community-outreach ministries. Billingsley celebrates the comprehensive community ministries of ten "exemplary" churches throughout the United States, noting that dealing with issues of education, healthcare, AIDS, food and clothing, housing, senior citizens's concerns, youth programs, and even prison ministry are typical of Black churches. Citing figures that 70 percent of Black churches are involved in community outreach programs, Billingsley believes that the church has a central, strategic, and pivotal role in the future strengthening and revitalizing of Black families.[7]

The acclaimed volume *The Black Church in the African American Experience,* by C. Eric Lincoln and Lawrence Mamiya, is a strong representative of the dialectical-tension view, which sees Black churches as ambiguously involved in six pairs of opposing concepts. The pairs include: priestly vs. prophetic, other-worldly vs. this-worldly, universal vs. particular, communal vs. privatistic, charismatic vs. bureaucratic, and resistant vs. accomodating (or liberation vs. survival).[8] Lincoln and Mamiya's research indicated that 91.6 percent of clergy respondents believed that the churches should express their political views "on day-to-day social and political questions."[9] At the same time Lincoln and Mamiya were careful to note that 8 percent of the clergy and 31 percent of the laity "supported non-involvement in politics or rejected any influences of the recent black consciousness movement."[10] Citing the influence of a "strong evangelical tradition" as the cause of political reticence, nevertheless Lincoln and Mamiya believed that Black churches stand within a historically verified tradition that had valorized strong commitment to the social-political life of the community.

Xodus ecclesiology sees wisdom in both celebrating the Black churches' accomplishments, and clarifying those areas of ambiguity, tension, and disunity in the churches' involvement in political issues, social justice, and community outreach.

However, as Lincoln and Mamiya note in their research, only tiny percentages of the churches were involved in coperating with: employment agencies (2.3 percent), day-care centers (1 percent), drug and alcohol abuse agencies (2.3 percent), tutoring and educational programs (2.1 percent), food programs (2.7 percent), or health-related agencies (3.3 percent).[11] Of some 1,459 respondents, a full 588 (29.5 percent) stated that they were not cooperating with any agencies. Since the model of partnership is one that needs to be applied to all church life, and Black churches do not have the resources to create all the necessary community-support structures, then part of the Xodus Journey needs to be helping Black churches to form partnerships with other established community agencies.

What of the third response, that of cynicism? Negative criticism of Black churches will never empower or reveal ways to positively impact the community. Still the cynic asks: *How can African American churches stand at practically every corner of the African American community and be so silent, impotent, and irrelevant in the face of our community's destruction?*

This question cannot be ignored. Questions of silence, impotence, and irrelevance are particularly urgent for young Black males who suffer from the silence of Black churches when they are brutalized by police, the impotence of Black churches in effecting economic empowerment to answer their joblessness, and irrelevant to their concrete socioeconomic and spiritual state of disaffection.

Within a two-mile stretch from Florence Avenue to Imperial Avenue in Los Angeles stand eighty-seven churches. On every corner with a church, stands a liquor store across the street or next door. Numerous pawn shops are the sites of gun availability and actual distribution, not to mention underground gun-running operations. Churches become the silent partner of the drug culture, present but not addressing the problems.[12]

The presence of a fundamentalist, charismatic, Heaven-oriented interpretation of the gospel can actually provide religious justification for drug culture. Its otherworldliness is, in effect, the spiritual mirror of the drug culture. It reflects escapism and contributes to resignation and political apathy. The other side of white fundamentalist, charismatic teaching, however, is its crass materialist thrust. This vulgar aspect of "the gospel" sets material gain as an ultimate goal (after all, there are more preachers who drive high-priced, status cars than any other "professional" in the community). The value of material gain is individualist: It is not important for one's church or one's block to become wealthy. God "blesses" only those who "Name It and Claim It." Great cathedral-like structures situated in inner-cities often proclaim this "gospel" while displaying an appalling lack of community solidarity. This is Black flight. Is Black flight an example of the colonization of white desire within Black minds? Is this hate crime against our own? Is this the result of accepting as our own the Kenneth Hagin "Name It, Claim It" white charismatic-fundamentalist doctrine? For Xodus travelers Black flight may best be understood as a parable of "Reverse Exodus." Reverse Exodus turns the biblical account on its head into a demonic tale of woe.

REVERSE XODUS

Here, some of the most talented and crafty freed slaves cross back over the Red Sea into the arms of Pharaoh's soldiers. They are expecting to be welcomed, but the "welcome back" mat is a demand to drink the poisonous drought of complete accommodation, or die. So they drink complete accommodation, and live — if such could be called "living." Their lifeless life feels no pain of responsibility, accountability, or solidarity with those who are struggling on the other side of the Red Sea. The completely accommodated North American Black, transformed by imbibing such a drink, preaching the Gospel of Otherworldliness and Material Success, is utterly indistinguishable from his or her white counterparts. A freed slave who does not desire to build his own country or shape her own destiny, prefers instead to enter into the house of Pharaoh and spread Pharaoh's ways. In fact, such a Black really believes that Pharaoh was right all along! The ancient Hebrew prophets would call such acts whoredom and prostitution, spiritually speaking.

Having imbibed the Gospel of complete accommodation, being spiritually prostituted, these former slaves now recross the Red Sea to spread the gospel. Across the Red Sea, wandering in the wilderness of cutbacks, nonopportunity, and self-destructive acts, the liberated slaves are trying to build their own system. It is hard because Pharaoh's soldiers and chariots prevent access to resources, acceptance, and confidence. But as the liberated slaves struggle to affirm their dignity, the reality of their brothers preying on each other for survival becomes clear. The power of God's pillar of fire seems a distant memory, a sweet opiate in times of despair. Here comes the completely accommodated preacher with all the answers. Instead of preaching self-liberation, love of community, and the sacred responsibility of raising our children likewise, the completely accommodated preacher preaches a prostituted Gospel that allows the liberated wandering former slaves to continue in their course of self-destruction. What an abomination! What curses we are drawing down upon ourselves not to speak directly to this situation. Reverse Exodus is a contemporary functional reality of many African American churches, to our shame.[13]

XODUS CHURCH ALTERNATIVES

An Xodus church must create positive alternatives, remembering that the genuine gospel of Jesus Christ is wholistic, addressing both spiritual needs and physical requirements. The gospel is not something that can be subverted into crass Amerikkkanized materialism. Rather, it awakens those Afrikan minds lulled into the perverse sleep of accommodationism and calls awakened lives into communities of resistance. Moving through the abyss of self-emptying toward a love of self and community exemplified in the life and teachings of Jesus Christ, the Gospel cannot be distorted into personal "fulfillment," but fulfills itself by spreading itself as a message of hope, liberation, and Xodus Journey.

Five Souljah Imperatives

RADICAL ECONOMIC RECOVERY

Black churches need to aid young drug dealers in their desire to escape the insecurities and dangers of the drug culture. By developing a sanctuary program for drug dealers, churches would be give youth the opportunity to transform and use their enormous organizational leadership skills in developing legitimate businesses for African Americans. Some preachers have already started to do this, according to various preachers in the Los Angeles area. Many young drug dealers genuinely desire escape from the insecurities and dangers of the drug culture but do not know how.

If Black churches provide a way out, a disturbing but legitimate question could be raised: "If we help drug dealers to become legitimate, are we not legitimating their activity, cash-flow, and way of life? It needs careful consideration. Maybe the powers of no single church should be used but only those empowered by a grassroots organization of churches, community activists, and concerned citizens. Together they can serve as economic development organizations and "elders councils." First A.M.E. Renaissance program in Los Angeles and the West Los Angeles Economic Development Corporation serve as a positive models of providing professional church-related economic aid to all kinds of people. In post-rebellion Los Angeles, organizations such as Rebuild L.A., F.A.M.E. Renaissance, SACC (Southern Area Clergy Council), and Operation Hope provide concrete examples of how the ideal of an economic development organization can work with a council of elders (like SACC) functioning as a bridge between the chamber of commerce and the chamber of "the streetz." They can fulfill this Xodus Imperative.

RADICAL PAN-AFRICAN EMPHASIS

African American churches cannot become Xodus churches if they are enervated by the pressing demands of a predominantly local vision. The demands of "the streetz" and the despair of the folk require a vision that stretches beyond the geographical, cultural, and political boundaries of Amerikkka. Possibilities for spiritual growth and political empowerment cannot be fully explored without an understanding of the struggles for self-determination, economic interdependence, and cultural affirmation that are occurring throughout the Afrikan Diaspora. Afrikanity — pan-African consciousness — is not the demonization of all Europeans or whites. It is a spiritual focus on the possibilities of a global vision of Afrikan selfhood before God.

Is Afrikanity an exclusionary ideology of dark skin colorism? Some African American churches pride themselves as adhering to so-called "colorblind" interpretations of various Scriptures. They look, for example, to 1 Pet. 2:1-10. It describes the church as that body of Christians who understand themselves to be a "chosen race, a royal priesthood, a holy nation, God's own people, in order that you might proclaim the mighty acts of him who called you out of darkness into his marvelous light" (NRSV). To many African American Christians this Scripture clearly negates giving nationality, skin color, and culture any place of significance when describing the self-understanding of the church. Primacy, in this view, is given to a new identity as God's people, chosen and called out of former bonds of loyalty in this "world" — such as to race, class, and color — into a new and powerful relationship. This new identity reinforces itself in love, forgiveness, and the continual proclamation of the "mighty acts" of God. I agree that we ought to interpret this Scripture in such a way that being a Christian means having our fundamental loyalties realigned toward God-based community rather than toward the divisive and conflicting cultural loyalties of "the world." Yet such a view of this Scripture does not disagree with the promotion of Afrikanity. For African Americans, and other Afrikans throughout the Diaspora, the struggle to affirm our Black skins is internally related to our spiritual joy in being Christian. That is to say, if God grants us a new identity, then part of that new identity is the affirmation that our Blackness, our "difference" from other peoples, is beautiful, acceptable, and made righteous in the universally inclusive embrace of God. To emphasize that God is "colorblind" is completely inappropriate, because the whole concept of "colorblind" arises from a *legal* doctrine of justice, a concept that has proven effective for African Americans in demanding and achieving a measure of social equality.

God is not "colorblind," God is color-full. Afrikanity is not a sinful slide down the slippery slope of colorism and racism, but rather a joyful affirmation of God's color-fullness. God created all peoples, the Earth, and all of the creatures living on the Earth. Every creature, human or otherwise, has a unique shading, texture, and tone. What a strangely reactionary vision of God to say that God is "colorblind" when all of the evidence suggests the contrary! God is the consummate Artist, the color Genius.

To affirm our Afrikanity is theologically based on an Xodus doctrine of Atonement, which affirms God's color-fullness as an aspect of spiritual joy. Christ's death and resurrection were not to display the redemptive power of unmerited suffering, but to open up the possibilities for human beings to become "God's new creation" (2 Cor. 5:17), for peace to be made between formerly warring peoples (Eph. 2:11-22), and for genuine reconciliation to occur. Christians ought to be joyful about *these things*, not the suffering, pain, torture, and death of Jesus on a cross! The spiritual and social implications of the resurrection must become the focus of Afrikan churches as they move in Xodus.

When we affirm the social and ethical implications of the resurrection, we cannot help but be filled with joy. As we rejoice in our Black skin we affirm God's choice to create us Black, as a gift and not a curse, a blessing and not a burden. It is upon this theological foundation that we can proclaim to others the necessity of being joyful about who and what God has created all the peoples of the world to be. We cannot wait for a "colorblind" justice to treat us "right"; we must begin to affirm our Afrikan color-fullness as the basis upon which we also affirm our cultural, historical, political, artistic, economic, personal, and communal achievements. Thus the theological affirmation of God's color-fullness draws us into a deeper spirit of rejoicing and thanksgiving for all God has brought us through.

African American churches have a public voice in the United States. That voice has been established through long and dangerous years of protest, bombed churches, eloquent oratory, and the long list of slain martyrs.

An Xodus church takes a global perspective on ways in which all the various members of the Diaspora can aid and support each other. We saw this kind of global perspective in regard to the torture and injustice rampant in South Africa; now we must continue to expand our vision, outreach, and compassion to the many other African nations on the brink of disaster.

The pan-African imperative helps the Xodus church also to struggle with being a church within a pluralist religious environment. Xodus churches cannot afford a parochial vision of Christianity but must find ways of following Jesus in the midst of a vibrant ecology of beliefs. Following Jesus can be done while becoming acquainted with Islam, traditional African religions, Buddhism (the newest religious "visitor" to pan-African peoples), and Hinduism (the faith of many of our Brown sisters and brothers, particularly in Jamaica and India). As amazing as it might seem, learning to respect the ways of another person's religion can open one's mind to the specific wonder of following Jesus. Xodus churches are not afraid of proclaiming Jesus as the Way (rather than the imperialist "*the* Way"). We love Jesus because Jesus first loved us, and because of that love relationship we cannot help but proclaim Jesus as the Way. But affirming Jesus as the Way is our affirmation of our singular adoration, analogous to the way in which human beings speak about their beloved as "the only one for me."[14] As we walk down the broken "streetz" and allow the pain and despair to touch us deeply, Xodus churches are moved to find ways to work with all peoples and all faiths for the common good of Afrikan community liberation. Therefore a pan-African emphasis is really the partnership model writ large. We are Partners-in-God with all Afrikans, even those who do not believe in Jesus Christ, because that is what God has called us to be.

RADICAL ETHIC OF HEALTH

In "the beginning" (of the modern Diaspora) there was slavery, and slavery begat brokenness, and the offspring of brokenness were wounded bodies pushed beyond their natural capacities to work as tools of an unmerciful system of injustice.

In the beginning of Black churches there was a recognized need to uplift the God who comforted the wounded, consoled the broken-hearted, and healed "the sin-sick soul." As a new millenium beckons, Black churches must recover the emphasis on health — spiritual and physical.

Overlapping crises threaten the future of our life on the planet Earth, crises that might be characterized as plagues. This entire book has examined the plague of psychospiritual brokenness. Another plague is that of violence. The post-Cold War world has not been de-nuclearized. It is threatened by dozens of interethnic armed conflicts. From the two-week genocidal rampage by Hutus of Tutsis in Rwanda to the "ethnic cleansing" campaigns in Bosnia, the world is being assaulted by a plague of violence. In African American communities the psychophysical aspects of the plague are promoted in every newspaper headline, every daily media news report that choses to broadcast images of Black males as dangerous criminals while ignoring and erasing Black females as having any significance at all. Violence is glamourized in Hollywood films in which Black bodies are always the first to die gory deaths. The glorification of assault weapons, guns, and martial arts on film provides a steady unwholesome diet of brutality and death. Imitators of Hollywood gangsters and violent heroes are spreading a red stain of death within Black communities. These are everyday facts, not a victimization plea.

Black churches have a unique role to play in remedying the plague of violence as it sweeps through our communities. If we actually believe in the love of Jesus Christ, then it is time for us to demonstrate how God's Agapic love can produce a spirit of antiviolence. In the midcentury Freedom Struggle advocates of nonviolence helped Black people overcome social barriers. Now we face a plague that corrodes self-love as it destroys Afrikan bodies, wounds self-esteem, and threatens our future. As Martin Luther King, Jr., developed a program of nonviolence that combined the teachings of Jesus' Sermon on the Mount with the satyagraha-strategy of Mohatma Gandhi, so we must encourage antiviolence. Antiviolence insists that violence must be overcome with a self-love rooted in God's love. Self-love cannot be established politically or culturally because such a version of self-love easily falls prey to prejudiced tyrannical views that lead to hating "others." This is what is missing in Afrocentric agendas that waste time blaming Jews, "Ice People,"[15] and Europeans.

African American churches can move toward becoming Xodus churches by displacing the lure of violence and rerouting Black Rage into the powerful praxis which can flow from a God-based self-love. Antiviolence reroutes rage by encouraging self-affirmation and self-reliance. Antiviolence insists that a people preoccupied with doing constructive things has no time for participating in anything that can harm its future. It moves beyond finger-pointing toward planning, refocusing energies and time on producing rather than destroying. More an attitude than a philosophy, antiviolence is an ethos and praxis. It is imperative to proclaim that the gospel of Jesus Christ is antiviolent, and that following Jesus confronts the plague of violence with this powerful medicine.

Afrikan communities throughout the world are dying from the plague of HIV/AIDS. Out of fear of this deadly disease, people looked for scapegoats. Haitians were blamed for creating and spreading the disease before its origins were better known. While North Americans were busy pointing fingers at promiscuous homosexuals in the 1980s, African nations such as Uganda were being decimated by this plague. Now many African nations are facing the AIDS pandemic as *the* major crisis looming in their future. Here in Amerikkka Black women (and Latinas) are being eliminated in record numbers by HIV/AIDS. While attention has been rightfully placed on saving Black males from prisons and criminalization, the fate of Black women with AIDS has been neglected by Black churches. As recently as November 1994 77 percent of the newly reported cases of HIV/AIDS were Black and Latina women.[16] While attention has been readily given to naming Black-on-Black male violence as "genocide," concrete facts suggest that poor Black women are being decimated by AIDS.

AIDS is not a homosexual disease. The sooner African American churches disabuse our members of that notion, the healthier. Our future depends on helping to save physical as well as spiritual life. AIDS is a merciless killer, behaving toward the human body as if following a CIA covert operations manual—invading, disguising itself within the DNA of the host body, breaking down the defenses of the body from within, and taking over that body until death ensues. The astronomical healthcare costs, as well as the emotional effects of accompanying someone through the declining slope of an AIDS death, must be addressed. African American churches must respond as Xodus churches to this plague in very practical ways by:

1. *Holding workshops where health issues are discussed, and AIDS is given prominence.* The expertise of health professionals in our congregations can be tapped and noted doctors invited to address the congregation. Such workshops can become an annual part of Black History Month celebrations, Juneteenth, Malcolm X Day, or any other celebrations throughout the church year.

2. *Creating health ministries in our churches.* Having grown up in a large urban church in Cleveland, Ohio, I learned that often the best ministers to the sick and dying were not necessarily the pastor, dea-

cons, or officers of the church. Often it was a certain woman or man who had the "gift," could sit with a sick person, could comfort the family, and had the knack for "being there" just when one needed them. Such a person at Antioch Baptist Church is "Mother" Margaret Potter. Her skills, developed over many years of comforting the afflicted and consoling the dying, are an invaluable asset to that church's overall ministry. Mother Potter accompanied me through the death of both my parents with grace. poise, warmth, and wisdom when I had was at one of the lowest points in my own life. Her health ministry "gift" is deeply appreciated by the pastor, deacons, officers, and members of Antioch. There are "Mother Potters" scattered throughout the churches. All we need to do is affirm them in their work, and support their endeavors with prayer, financial support as necessary, and a great deal of love.

3. *Promoting the physical aspects of the gospel.* Pastors can remind congregations that Jesus' entire life was a minsitry of healing. Jesus of Nazareth was concerned about the physical and spiritual well-being of the people he met. He touched their infirmities, healed their weaknesses, and drove out the inner demons that oppressed and controlled their psyches as well. His was a wholistic healing—bodily, psychic, and spiritual. If we are genuinely to represent the gospel he preached, we ought to focus our preaching and teaching on the healing power of Jesus.

Another plague demands a radical ethic of health, although it is overlooked by African American churches. Environmental pollution threatens to destroy clean air, fresh water, and safe foods. This plague was created by profligate policies of a consumer-obsessed Northern Hemisphere in which many Afrikans are residing. Therefore Black people are required to lift our voices in the growing cry for planetary health and healing. Is environmentalism "our" concern? Most certainly. Black people tend to live in the poorest neighborhoods, and such neighborhoods tend to lack the political clout to ward off business interests who have no regard for the community's health. They build power plants and incinerators that fill the air with stinking smoke and dump deadly toxic waste in the communities or just outside of them. The health of the Earth is ghettocentric because the Earth is also polluted in the ghetto. Xodus churches can help Afrikans unite with each other by seeking national and international partnerships with those struggling to cleanse the Earth. I hope to build on this health ethic more specifically in future writing.

RADICAL THEO-RITUAL TRANSFORMATION

Black churches need to bring the cultural art/music forms of rap, hip-hop, and funk off the streets into the church. Those churches which are successfully attracting and converting gang members have already ventured in this direction. Combining the "streetz" sounds of hip-hop with traditional "church" gospel music has also been bringing back dis-affected middle-class, and college-educated women and men. Such contemporary gospel music turns the hardcore rage and disillusionment of the streets into meaningful messages of God's grace. A good example of this kind of music is that of new gospel "King," John P. Kee. His ministry, which includes a great deal of call and response, and dancing from both the choir members and the congregation, has brought an entirely new generation back to church. While there can be no set formula for such transformation, each city and region of the country needs prayerfully to seek to find ways to both hold on to cherished traditions and build new ones.

XODUS FAMILY

Xodus ecclesiology culminates in the imperative that the starting place for reenvisioning our communities is the family. As Souljahs in partnership we must believe that God can provide us with a vision bigger than patriarchal reimpositions of "male headship." Embracing so-called biblical patriarchal models of family has been proclaimed as the answer to all of our woes. But those providing that "answer" often have no idea of how God has blessed African Americans with egalitarian traditions built on the bedrock of our own understandings of God. Rebuilding the African American family will not be achieved by imitating Charles Dobson's vision of family, even if he is a popular Christian family counselor. Brother Dobson's history and culture are not that of African Americans. His grandparents were not slaves here in America, nor is he stigmatized for his color. African American pastors must be bold enough to create our own models of family, ones that value egalitarian practices in our history, and celebrate the shared roles of males and females.

An Xodus ecclesiology offers a revised view of rebuilding power in the family by reenvisioning partnership as the human event precipitated by God's grace. Just as God has provided all human being the grace to become sons and daughters of God, so God has provided Afrikans living in North America the resources to rebuild ourselves, our communities, and our lives — whether the Euro-dominated world likes it or not.

Now is the time for African American Christians to "take back the streets" because God's Spirit of power, love, and a sound mind is with us. Xodus liberation must be boldly proclaimed from pulpits and lived in the pews. Our children's future depends on the capacity of Afrikans to awaken, arise, and be resurrected. As our ancestors cried out to God and moaned until they found the spiritual help to make a way out of no way, for the *Kibinadamu* of our families, for our communities, and for the flourishing of the earth, we cry "XODUS!"

Notes

1. The phrase "Awake, Arise, Act!" is borrowed from the prophetic cry of Ida B. Wells-Barnett and is the title of an excellent womanist ethics text by Marcia Riggs, *Awake Arise Act!* (Cleveland: Pilgrim Press, 1994).
2. Much in this paragraph is owed to a powerful conversation with Al Wilson, a charismatic Christian who is well read on the spirituality of Black Elk.
3. Mircea Eliade, *The Myth of the Eternal Return* (New York: Princeton University Press, 1954), 12.
4. An allusion to the title of Mircea Eliade's book.
5. A phrase in the famous gospel song "How I Got Over," by the Clara Ward Singers.
6. The six-billion-dollar consumer figure was widely circulated in 1990 at various conferences by the Congress of Black Churches. The figure may have risen since.
7. Andrew Billingsley, *Climbing Jacob's Ladder: The Enduring Legacy of African-American Families* (New York: Simon & Schuster, 1992), 361–71, 374, 379.
8. C. Eric Lincoln and Lawrence H. Mamiya, *The Black Church in the African American Experience* (Durham: Duke University Press, 1990), 12–16.
9. Ibid., 225.
10. Ibid., 229.
11. Ibid., 220.
12. Rev. Sylvester Warsaw, graduate of the School of Theology at Claremont and associate pastor of First New Christian Fellowship Missionary Baptist in South Los Angeles.
13. The story of Reverse Exodus was created in a series of lively conversations with Rev. Sylvester Warsaw.
14. The ideas presented above owe a great deal to the teaching of Krister Stendahl, who understands the exclusivist language of John 14, "I am the way and the truth and the life," as a powerful rhetorical expression of early Christian "love language."
15. The controversial characterization by Leonard Jeffries of New York City College of whites as "Ice People" and Afrikans as "Sun People" is an excellent example of this kind of agenda.
16. This information came from a presentation on HIV/AIDS by Professor Emilie Townes, at the Annual Meeting of the American Academy of Religion, Chicago, November 19, 1994, as obtained from updated census data on Internet.

INDEX

Conscious Daughters, 138
Conversion, 85–88
Coon, Zip, 54
Cose, Ellis, xix, 3, 157–59, 161
Creation accounts, 113–18
Criminality, 168–70, 190
Crossover rap, 137
Crow, Jim, 54
Cultural critique, 35, 47–48

Daly, Mary, 106
Davis, Angela, 30
Davis, Miles, 136
Declaration of Independence, 95
disillragedeterminassion, 4, 22, 158, 166
Dobson, Charles, 193
Dr. Dre, 8, 139
Dream of Martin Luther King, Jr., 94–98
D.R.S., 144, 148
Drugs, 139–42
DuBois, W. E. B., 149
Dyson, Michael Eric, 33, 131

Eannes de Azurara, Gomes, 48
Easy-E, 139
Ecclesiology, 132, 171–73, 178–94
Ecology, 7, 111, 117–18, 122, 124–26, 192
Economics, 24, 186–87
Egypt. *See* Kemet
Elders, 19, 70, 93. *See also* Ancestors
Eliade, Mircea, 11
El-Shabazz, El Hajj Malik. *See* Malcolm X
Empowerment, 179–80
Enlightenment, 5, 7
Environment. *See* Ecology
Ethics, 7, 94, 151–54, 163–65, 178–79, 189–90
Eugene, Toinette, 30, 109
Euro-American domination, 4, 6, 12, 13, 82, 86, 159, 160
Eurocentrism, 48–49, 68

Family, 39–40, 193
Farrakhan, Louis, 3
Fatherhood, 39–40
Felder, Cain Hope, 38, 68

Finegan, Jack, 80
Fletcher, Superia, 24
Foucault, Michel, 10, 69, 86
Freud, Sigmund, 55
Fundamentalism, 185

Gandhi, Mohandas K., 190
Gangsta rap, 137, 138–44
Generation X, 8, 131
George, Nelson, 132
Ghana, 100–103
Gillette, Douglas, 18, 22
Give-back ethic, 163–65
God, 37, 79, 85, 88–89, 107, 125, 145, 188
Government programs, x
Grant, Jacquelyn, 28, 32

Hagin, Kenneth, 185
Haley, Alex, 75
Health, ethic of, 189–92
Henry, John, xv, 57–60, 68
High John de Conquer, xv, 60–63, 68–69
Hill, Renee, xv, 35
History, 11–12
Homosexuality, 35–36
Hopi myth, 114–17
Hopkins, Dwight, 28, 34
House of Pain, 135
Hoyt, Thomas, 38
Human rights, 78
Humor, 56–57, 68–69
Hurston, Zora Neale, xv, 28, 60, 61
H.W.A., 143, 148

Ice Cube, 136, 142
Ice-T, 136, 139, 151–53
Inspirational rap, 138
Intimacy, 23
Islam, Nation of. *See* Muslim faith

Jackson, Bo, 59
Jackson, Jesse, 176
Jackson, Michael, 162
Jamaica, 4, 39–40, 171
Jesus. *See* Christ, Jesus.
Jeter, Ruanne, 29
Jews, 13